BUSINESS TENANCIES

Other Legislation Guides from Law Society Publishing

Criminal Justice Act 2003

A Guide to the New Law
Andrew Keogh
1 85328 877 2

Enterprise Act 2002

The New Law of Mergers, Monopolies and Cartels
Tim Frazer, Susan Hinchliffe and Kyla George
1 85328 896 9

Sexual Offences Act 2003

A Guide to the New Law
Paul Lewis
1 85328 965 5

The New Law of Insolvency

Insolvency Act 1986 to Enterprise Act 2002
Vernon Dennis and Alexander Fox
1 85328 812 8

All books from Law Society Publishing can be ordered through good bookshops or direct from our distributors, Marston Book Services (telephone 01235 465656 or e-mail **law.society@marston.co.uk**). Please confirm the price before ordering.

r further information or a catalogue e-mail our editorial and marketing office **blishing@lawsociety.org.uk**.

BUSINESS TENANCIES

A Guide to the New Law

Jason Hunter

The Law Society

ISBN 1 85328 956 6

Published by the Law Society in 2004
113 Chancery Lane, London WC2A 1PL

Typeset by J&L Composition, Filey, North Yorkshire
Printed by Antony Rowe Ltd, Chippenham, Wilts

CONTENTS

Preface vii
Abbreviations ix
Table of cases x
Table of statutes xi
Table of secondary legislation xiii
Introduction xv

1 Notices 1

1.1 Contractual expiry, the effect of the tenant vacating and section 27 notices 1
1.2 Section 25 notices 3
1.3 Tenant's counternotice to a section 25 notice 6
1.4 Section 26 requests 8
1.5 Landlord's counternotice to a section 26 request 8
1.6 Section 40 notices seeking information 9

2 Applications to court and time limits 13

2.1 Introduction 13
2.2 Pre-RRO 2003 13
2.3 Tenancy renewal proceedings 14
2.4 Landlord's tenancy termination proceedings 17

3 Interim rent 20

3.1 Introduction 20
3.2 Pre-RRO 2003 20
3.3 The new right to interim rent 21
3.4 The date from which interim rent will be payable 21

3.5 Approaches to valuation of interim rent 22

4 Contracting out of the protection of the Act 26

4.1 Debate over contracting-out provisions 26
4.2 Pre-RRO 2003 27
4.3 Post-RRO 2003 27
4.4 New tenancies and contracting out 28
4.5 Other considerations 34
4.6 Transition 38
4.7 Agreements to surrender and contracting out 39

5 Miscellaneous matters 41

5.1 The terms of the new tenancy 41
5.2 Companies 41
5.3 Severed reversions 43
5.4 Consequential amendments 44

6 Compensation 46

6.1 Statutory compensation 46
6.2 Compensation for misrepresentation 48

7 Changes to the Civil Procedure Rules 1998 50

7.1 Introduction 50
7.2 Pre-RRO 2003 51
7.3 Outline of post-RRO 2003 53
7.4 Priority of claims 53
7.5 Type of procedural claim 54
7.6 Commencing the claim 55
7.7 Responding to the claim 58
7.8 The management of the claim 62
7.9 Interim rent 63

Appendices

A. Regulatory Reform (Business Tenancies) (England and Wales) Order 2003, SI 2003/3096 65
B. Landlord and Tenant Act 1954 (Keeling Schedule) 92
C. Landlord and Tenant Act 1954, Part 2 (Notices) Regulations 2004, SI 2004/1005 125

Index 181

PREFACE

That Part II of the Landlord and Tenant Act 1954 ('the Act') was to be amended has been flagged for some years and I review, in outline, the process that has led to those changes in the opening chapter.

My objective in writing this short guide is to provide what I hope is a ready, practical, tool to the practitioner who wants, almost at a glance, to see how the Act has changed and what impact those changes will or could have.

I aim to do so by comparing the existing law and procedures under the Act with the law and procedures after the implementation of the amending legislation in what is hoped will be considered a convenient and user-friendly format.

It is not the intention that this work should attempt a wider, in-depth assessment and consideration of the Act; for that, there are other well-known texts to which the reader should refer.

In this book, I have assumed a certain minimum level of knowledge on the part of the reader of the workings of the Act. Thus, I have done no more than provide a reminder of why a step is required, e.g. the service of a notice under section 25 of the Act.

For the avoidance of doubt, I state what I consider to be the law up to 1 March 2004.

I should add a note about my approach to the text and the order in which the subject-matter is addressed. I have attempted to deal with the reforms in an order that has regard to the scheme of the Act and the order in which it would affect the practitioner.

I should also add a word of warning. In some cases, matters under discussion concern new procedures and processes. While I have expressed an opinion about various issues that I consider might arise, it is stating the obvious to say that there is an alternative view, but it is of course always possible. Only time will tell whether the issues concerned do in fact raise problems that require answers.

Finally, I must express my sincere gratitude to my colleague, Paul Greatholder, who on rather short notice agreed to give up a large amount of his own time to review an advanced draft of this text, offer criticism of the proposed approach, its contents, and suggest additional matters that he thought the practitioner would find helpful to see considered. His assistance was invaluable. I must also acknowledge the Property Litigation Association; membership of the Government's sounding board on the reforms as the Association's representative has put me in a better position to be able to write this text.

Jason Hunter
Russell-Cooke
5 May 2004

ABBREVIATIONS

RRO 2003	Regulatory Reform (Business Tenancies) (England and Wales) Order 2003, SI 2003/3096
CPR	Civil Procedure Rules 1998
ODPM	Office for the Deputy Prime Minister

TABLE OF CASES

CA Webber (Transport) Ltd v. Railtrack plc [2003] PLSCS 179 4
Egg Stores (Stamford Hill) Ltd v. Beanby Estates Ltd (2003) 21 EG 190 (CS) 4, 6
Esselte AB v. Pearl Assurance plc [1997] 2 All ER 41, CA 2–3
Kammins Ballrooms Co Ltd v. Zenith Investments (Torquay) Ltd (No. 1) [1971] AC 850 14–16
Mannai Investment Co Ltd v. Eagle Star Life Assurance Co Ltd [1997] AC 749 29
Receiver for the Metropolitan police District v. Palacegate Properties Ltd [2001] Ch 131 37
Shaws (EAL) Ltd v. W Pennycook (2004) 08 EG 135 (CS) 7
Surrey CC v. Single Horse Property Co Ltd [2002] EWCA Civ 367 2–3

TABLE OF STATUTES

Housing Act 1988
s.20 . . . . 28, 32
Landlord and Tenant Act 1927
s.23 . . . . 4, 34, 36
Landlord and Tenant Act 1954 . . xii, 26, 50
Pt II . . . . vii, xi, 1, 55
s.23 1
(1A) 42, 56, 59, 62
(1B) 42
ss.24–28 27
s.24 . . . . 1, 2, 15, 21, 25
(1) . . 13, 18–19, 47, 53–4, 56–7
(b) 16
(2A), (2B) 17
(2C) 16
s.24A 20, 51
(1) 21–2, 25, 63
(2) 21
s.24B 51
(1) 21
(2), (3) 21–22
s.24C 22, 25, 51, 63
(1) 24
(a), (b) 23
(2) 23–4, 64
(3) 23–4, 64
(4)–(6) 23–5
(7) 23, 25
s.24D 25, 51
(1)–(3) 25, 63
s.25 . . . . vii, xiii, 2–11, 13–16, 18, 20–4, 29, 32, 35–6, 47, 51–2, 55–6, 64
(5) 6–7, 13
(8) 5
s.26 . . . . xiii, 4–5, 7–11, 13–16, 20–4, 35–6, 47, 51–2, 55–6, 64
(5) 13
(6) 8, 15, 18, 22, 24
s.27 . . . . 1, 3
(1) 2
(1A) 2
(2) 2–3
s.29 7
(2) 6–7, 13, 18–19, 47, 53–4, 58, 61
(3) 13, 18, 54
(4) 18
(5) 17
(6) 18–19
s.29A 14
(2) 14
(3) 15
s.29B 14–16
(2), (4) 15
s.30 40
(1) 3, 6, 8, 18–19, 24, 46–7, 54, 56–8, 61
(e) 46–7
(f) 42–3, 46–8, 56, 62
(g) 3, 42, 46–8
s.31 45
s.31A 45, 56, 62
s.32 41
(2) 57, 59, 61
s.33 41
s.34 . . . . 23–5, 41–2, 45
(1), (2) 20
s.35 41
(1) 44
s.36(2) 25, 63
s.37 46
(1) 46
(1A)–(1C) 46–7
(2) 47
(3) 46, 48
(3A) 47
(3B) 48
s.37A 49

s.38(4) 27–8, 34, 39
s.38A. 27–8, 34, 39
(3) 28, 35
(a) 31
(b) 30
(4) 39
s.40 9–12
(1) 10
(2) 10, 12
(3) 10, 12
(4) 11
(5)(a) 10
(b) 10–11
(7) 11
(8) 10
s.40A 9, 11
s.40B. 12
s.41. . . . . 42, 56, 59, 62
s.41A 43
s.42. . . . . 42, 56, 59, 62
(1) 42
s.43. 1, 28
s.44. 43
(1) 44
(1A) 43
s.46. 42
s.55. 48–9
s.64. 19, 21
(2) 2
s.66. 10, 34
(4) 4, 6, 34
s.69(2). 15
Landlord and Tenant Act 1969. 20
Leasehold Reform Act 1967 6
Leasehold Reform, Housing and Urban Development Act 1993
ss.13, 42 5
Regulatory Reform Act 2001 xi
Statutory Declarations Act 1835. 33

TABLE OF SECONDARY LEGISLATION

Civil Procedure Rules 1998, SI 1998/3132 . . . . . 14, 19, 50, 59–60
Pt 7 . . . . . 54–6, 58, 60, 63
r.7.7 54
Pt 8 . . . . . 51, 54–6, 58, 60, 63
Pt 15 60–1
Pt 23 63
Pt 56 . . . . . 47, 51–7, 60–2, 63
r. 56.3 . . . . . 54, 63
(2) 57
(c)(i) 57
(3)(c) 62
Pt 56 PD 51, 55–6, 60–2, 63
para.3.1(3) 58
para.3.12 60
para.3.13 61
para.3.14 62
para.3.15 62
para.3.16 63
para.3.17 60
Landlord and Tenant Act 1954, Part II (Notices) (Amendment) Regulations 1989, SI 1989/1548
Sch., Form 1 4
Landlord and Tenant Act 1954, Part II (Notices) (England and Wales) Regulations 2004, SI 2004/1005 6–7
Sch.2, Form 1 . . . . . 4, 6
Form 2 . . . . . 5, 6
Form 3 8
Forms 4, 5 12
Regulatory Reform (Business Tenancies) (England and Wales) Order 2003, SI 2003/3096 . . . . . xii, xiii, 1–9, 11–13, 15–17, 19–20, 22–3, 26–7, 33, 37, 41–54, 56, 62
art.4 5
art.22(1) 39
art.29(1) 8, 51
(2)(a)(i) 40
(ii) 38
(b) 3
(3) 39
(4) 51
(5) 49

Regulatory Reform (Business Tenancies) (England and Wales) Order 2003, SI 2003/3096 (*cont.*)
Sch.1 . . . . 27–36, 38
Sch.2 . . . . 27–28, 30, 33–6, 38–9
para.3 31
para.4 33
para.5 34
para.7 30–2
para.8 33
Sch.3 . . . . 28, 35, 39
Sch.4 . . . . 28, 35, 39
Schs.5, 6 45

INTRODUCTION

In March 2001, the Government issued a consultation paper on its proposed reforms to Part II of the Landlord and Tenant Act 1954 ('the Act'). As is well known, the Act provides a form of security of tenure to tenants under business tenancies. Among other things, the Act sets out procedures for the termination of such tenancies. It also provides a scheme for the exclusion of its protection.

The introduction to the consultation paper said:

> [The Government] considers the current legislative framework to be philosophically sound: the legislation aims to be fair to both landlord and tenant, while underpinning the free operation of the property market. But there is some scope for modernising the detailed operation of the law. In particular, the Government proposes to remove certain anomalies that have come to light, especially those resulting in unequal treatment for the parties; to ensure that the Act's procedures are consistent with the new civil justice system; to reduce the amount of litigation; and generally to promote a less adversarial relationship between suppliers and occupiers of commercial property.

The consultation proposals flowed substantially from the Law Commission's recommendations in their 1992 report *Business Tenancies: A Periodic Review of the Landlord and Tenant Act 1954, Part II*, but took account of the outcome of a consultation exercise by the then Government in 1996.

The Government proposed making use of the procedure under the Regulatory Reform Act 2001. The Regulatory Reform Act 2001 provides what might be described as an abbreviated means of amending legislation in a manner designed primarily to remove or alleviate burdens on those affected by it. It can lead to the imposition of burdens provided that, taken as a whole, a balance is struck between the removal or reduction of burdens and the imposition of new ones. Such a process eventually leads to the creation of a statutory instrument in the form of a regulatory reform order.

Interested parties and organisations were consulted. In addition, the Government set up a sounding board of representatives of the principal organisations whose members would be affected by the intended reforms.

Following the March 2001 consultation, the Government issued a paper reviewing the responses it had received and the subsequent discussions with the sounding board. It concluded that:

> Overwhelmingly, respondents welcomed proposals to streamline the workings of the Landlord and Tenant Act 1954. Some respondents made it clear, however, that their comments were subject to wider reservations about the continuation of security of tenure, which was outside the scope of this exercise. There were a number of detailed comments on the proposals, especially on agreements to exclude security of tenure and for the surrender of leases; the tenant's counternotice; termination of fixed term tenancies; and interim rent.

The Government was satisfied that it was appropriate to proceed, making use of a regulatory reform order.

The proposals were first laid before Parliament on 22 July 2002, and in December 2002 the relevant committees of the House of Commons and the House of Lords reported. The committees were largely supportive of the intended reforms. However, the House of Lords committee in particular expressed concerns about the changes proposed, in relation to the provisions for the intended landlord and tenant to agree the removal of security of tenure.

The result was that the Government was obliged to address the expressed concerns. It commissioned some research on the existing procedure for the exclusion of security of tenure (often referred to as 'contracting out'). It is not the purpose of this text to consider that research in any detail; suffice it to say that following receipt of the results of the research, the Government's conclusion was that the reforms for contracting out could proceed albeit in modified form.

On 17 September 2003 the Government therefore lodged a revised draft regulatory reform order with Parliament with additional material explaining what steps had been taken since the committees' reports of December 2002.

Those steps were deemed to have satisfactorily resolved the perceived problems and, on 1 December 2003, the Minister signed off the regulatory reform order with the effect that it would come into force on 1 June 2004. The full title of the amending legislation is the Regulatory Reform (Business Tenancies) (England and Wales) Order 2003, SI 2003/3096. For convenience it is referred to in this text as RRO 2003.

This work is intended to consider RRO 2003 and its effect.

For convenience, the distinctions will be described as 'Pre-RRO 2003' and 'Post-RRO 2003'.

To assist in meeting the principal objective of this text, Appendix B of this work is a 'Keeling schedule', which sets out the relevant sections of the Act highlighting the amendments that have been made.

Since the Keeling schedule of the Act forms part of this text, I have not repeated, in the body of the text, the legislation to which I have referred. I consider that it would be more convenient to the reader to see the text of the legislation in context and, therefore, where a section is referred to, one should turn to the Keeling schedule.

On a review of the Keeling schedule, one will note that there are large sections of the Act that remain unchanged. This is important. Steps and procedures that were relevant prior to RRO 2003 will remain relevant. For example, the approach to be adopted by a landlord or tenant where the landlord intends to oppose a claim by the tenant to a new tenancy will still need to be applied.

Given the remit of this text, save in a limited number of exceptional cases, it is not intended to consider areas of the Act that have not been altered by RRO 2003, but it is important to remember that the changes only operate from 1 June 2003. Where, say, a section 25 notice or section 26 request has been given before that date, the 'old' law will apply.

1 NOTICES

1.1 CONTRACTUAL EXPIRY, THE EFFECT OF THE TENANT VACATING AND SECTION 27 NOTICES

Tenancies to which the Act applies are described in section 23. These are tenancies of property where the tenant occupies the property for the purposes of a business (although there does not need to be exclusive business use) and are not excluded by section 43.

The effect of section 24 of the Act is that a tenancy protected by the Act will not come to an end other than in accordance with the provisions of Part II. Rather, it will continue, effectively subject to the terms of the expired tenancy. The continuation of the tenancy is often known as 'holding over'.

Conversely, where the tenant is not in occupation at all at the contractual expiry date, or not in occupation for the purposes of a business carried on there by it, the Act should not apply. There have been a number of cases that have considered what might amount to occupation, and the circumstances in which occupation might have ceased, but it is not for this work to consider them.

There has, to some extent, been confusion about whether the Act will apply to the tenancy of a tenant who vacates a property before the expiry of a fixed-term tenancy, which will be looked at in the following paragraphs.

1.1.1 Pre-RRO 2003

The original wording of section 27 of the Act provides a procedure by which the tenant can notify the landlord, before the expiry of the tenancy, that it does not want the tenancy to continue under section 24 or, after the expiry of the tenancy, that it wants to bring the continuing, holding-over tenancy to an end.

If there were not less than three months before the tenancy was to expire, then under section 27(1) of the Act, the tenant could give to the landlord not less than three months' notice that it did not want the tenancy to continue, and thereafter section 24 would not apply.

At one time it was thought that if the tenant wanted to bring the tenancy to an end on the contractual expiry date, such a notice would always have to be given, whether or not the tenant had actually vacated the property by the end of the tenancy.

This was addressed by the Court of Appeal in *Esselte AB* v. *Pearl Assurance plc* [1997] 2 All ER 41, the effect of which was that, provided the tenant was not in occupation beyond the expiry of the tenancy, the tenancy could not continue under section 24 of the Act, occupation being an essential ingredient of the protection of the Act.

The question as to whether the Act would or would not apply to a tenancy where the tenant was not in occupation at its expiry was further considered and confirmed in *Surrey County Council* v. *Single Horse Property Company Limited* [2002] EWCA Civ 367. Even though the tenant had issued its application for a new tenancy, since it had vacated the property before the expiry of the contractual tenancy and had told the landlord that was what it had done, the tenancy came to an end at that date. It had previously been thought that, in such a situation, the tenancy would be subject to the provision of section 64 of the Act. Section 64(2) states that where a tenant has made an application to court for a new tenancy under the Act, the effect of the discontinuance of the proceedings resulting from that application is that the continuation tenancy will come to an end three months later. The court held in the *Single Horse* case that section 64 in fact had the effect of extending the section 25 notice. If the tenant was not in occupation on the expiry of the lease then the tenancy was not one to which the Act applied. The effectiveness of a section 25 notice is therefore to be judged not when it is given but at the contractual term date. (This conclusion will have an impact on the landlord's consideration of whether or not to serve a section 25 notice at a point in time when the tenant is apparently not in occupation for the purposes of the Act. In the circumstances, it would seem that the landlord might still serve a section 25 notice to guard against the tenant resuming occupation, but perhaps doing so without prejudice to the contention that the Act does not apply by virtue of the tenant's non-occupation.)

In comparison, under section 27(2) of the Act, if the contractual tenancy had come to an end and, by virtue of section 24, the tenant was holding over, then unless the tenant had issued a court application seeking a new tenancy, it could bring the tenancy to an end by giving notice under section 27(2) of not less than three months' duration, the notice then to expire on a quarter day.

1.1.2 Post-RRO 2003

The government confirmed the *Esselte* case by introducing section 27(1A), even though the landlord could have little or no warning the tenant was vacating and the property would revert to the landlord. This makes it clear that a tenant vacating the property by the expiry of the contractual term of the tenancy would bring the tenancy to an end without the need for the service of a section 27(1) notice. It did not repeal section 27(1), leaving it open to the tenant to put the issue beyond doubt by serving such a notice. In confirming *Esselte*, the Government recognised that it may be imposing a burden on the landlord, but the Government felt that such burden would not be unduly onerous.

Some commentators have contended that the logic of the *Single Horse* case could be applied to a continuation tenancy, i.e. a continuation tenancy would come to an end on the tenant vacating, which will inevitably be after the expiry of the contractual term. Section 27(2) has, however, been amended. It is now clear that merely the act of the tenant vacating will not be enough to bring a continuation tenancy to an end – notice will be required. The required notice, however, need only be of at least three months' duration; it no longer has to expire on a quarter day. Any rent paid by a tenant which relates to a period falling after the termination so effected shall be recoverable by the tenant on an apportioned basis.

Under new section 27(3), where notice is given under section 27(2), provision is made for the apportionment of rent, including rent which may contractually have to be paid in advance.

By virtue of article 29(2)(b) of RRO 2003, any notice served under section 27(2) prior to 1 June 2004 will be unaffected by the changes.

1.2 SECTION 25 NOTICES

Where the landlord wishes to bring a protected tenancy to an end, either at or after the expiry of the tenancy, and the tenant has not vacated the property or otherwise complied with section 27 of the Act, then it must do so in accordance with section 25 of the Act. Section 25 requires the service of a notice by the landlord. There are a variety of section 25 notices, all prescribed. Only the type of section 25 notice used in the vast majority of cases will be considered here.

Even though the landlord may terminate the tenancy by the service of a section 25 notice (and any other notice required by the lease, e.g. a break clause notice), a tenant whose tenancy is protected by the Act will (subject to the following paragraph) be entitled to have a new tenancy of the premises it occupies, provided it takes certain steps prescribed by the Act. If the tenant does this, the terms and duration of that new tenancy will be determined by the court, if they are not agreed between the landlord and tenant.

The tenant can only be prevented from having a new tenancy under the Act if the landlord can satisfy one or more of the seven grounds of 'possession' set out in section 30(1) of the Act. These grounds are largely unaffected by RRO 2003, save one of them (own occupation – ground (g) of section 30(1)) which is affected by the changes concerning companies and shareholders, etc. (see below).

1.2.1 Pre-RRO 2003

The section 25 notice most used is to be found as Form 1 in the Schedule to the Landlord and Tenant Act 1954, Part II (Notices) (Amendment) Regulations 1989, SI 1989/1548.

The notice carries what might be described as the usual warning, directed to the recipient, of its importance.

In order to be valid, the notice must:

- be addressed to the tenant by name;
- explain that it is a notice given under section 25 of the Act;
- describe the property to which it relates;
- specify the date on which the tenancy is to terminate;
- explain what the tenant must do in response.

In the notice, the landlord must state whether or not it will object to the tenant having a new tenancy and, if it does object, on what basis. The notice must include a correspondence address for the landlord and state the name and address of the landlord. It must be signed by or on behalf of the landlord. Form 1 also carries prescribed notes, which describe the tenant's rights and procedural obligations if it wants to protect its position.

Section 66(4) of the Act explains that section 23 of the Landlord and Tenant Act 1927 applies to notices under the Act. Section 23 of the 1927 Act sets out methods of serving notices, and the circumstances in which service will be deemed to have taken place. They are not the only permissible method of service, but unless there is some contractual provision in the lease that addresses the issue, they are the only way of being able to achieve 'deemed' service.

Thus, as was emphasised in the recent cases of *Egg Stores (Stamford Hill) Limited* v. *Beanby Estates Limited* (2003) 21 EG 190 (CS) and *CA Webber (Transport) Limited* v. *Railtrack plc* [2003] PLSCS 179, a notice sent by recorded delivery (or registered post) is deemed to have been served at the time it is posted regardless of whether its intended recipient ever actually received it.

1.2.2 Post-RRO 2003

The RRO 2003 introduces new, but still prescribed, section 25 notices.

The new section 25 notices (and a series of other notices relevant to business tenancies under the Act) are prescribed by the Landlord and Tenant Act 1954, Part II (Notices) (England and Wales) Regulations 2004, SI 2004/1005.

A significant difference is that, under the pre-RRO 2003 regime, there was one main prescribed form of section 25 notice which the landlord modified to explain to the tenant whether or not it would object to the tenant having a new tenancy. Under the new section 25 there will be two alternative notices: one to be used where the landlord will not object to the tenant having a new tenancy (Form 1 of schedule 2 to the Landlord and Tenant Act 1954, Part 2 (Notices) Regulations 2004, SI 2004/1005), and another where the landlord will so object (Form 2).

The new section 25 notice, where the landlord does not oppose the tenant having a new tenancy, requires information largely similar to the pre-RRO 2003 section 25 notice. An important difference is that the landlord must set out its proposals as to the property to be comprised in the new tenancy (being either the whole or part of the property comprised in the current tenancy), the rent payable under the new tenancy, and the other terms of the new tenancy (see section 25(8) of the Act introduced by article 4 of RRO 2003). A section 25 notice will therefore require a landlord to include proposals which are the same as those required from a tenant when it serves on the landlord a request for a new tenancy under section 26 of the Act.

It is not clear whether it would be sufficient to seek a 'market rent' or whether a figure should be specified. One suspects that the latter is correct because otherwise no practical information would be given to the tenant in respect of the new rent.

A failure to include such information in the section 25 notice will invalidate it, or in the words of RRO 2003, it 'will not have effect'.

Notwithstanding the requirement to include certain proposals, the prescribed form of notice makes it clear that the terms proposed are merely a basis for negotiation, and do not bind the landlord – in the same way that a tenant's proposals in a section 26 request do not bind it. This was made clear when the Government consulted on the then proposed reforms in 2001.

The 'health warning' on the notice reads:

> The landlord . . . has set out proposed terms in the schedule to this notice. You are not bound to accept these terms. They are merely suggestions as a basis for negotiation. In the event of disagreement, ultimately the court would settle the terms of the new tenancy.

Consequently, it must follow that were the landlord to cite an unreasonably high proposal for the rent to be payable under the new tenancy, the notice would not be invalidated. Contrast this with the position in relation to notices served under sections 13 or 42 of the Leasehold Reform, Housing and Urban Development Act 1993 (which respectively initiate a claim for the purchase of a freehold of a block of flats or for a new lease of a flat). Under the 1993 Act, the inclusion of an unreasonably low price would render a notice invalid.

In practice, those responsible for preparing and serving section 25 notices will need to ensure that slightly more by way of instructions is received from landlord clients to enable a valid notice to be served.

While the proposals may represent no more than a negotiating position, the time limits and procedure for applying to court under the Act have been somewhat extended (see Chapter 2). It may be that by setting out supportable proposals for the new tenancy, a landlord could accelerate a speedier compromise as to the terms of the new tenancy.

The new section 25 notice where the landlord does oppose the tenant having a new tenancy is Form 2 of Schedule 2 to Landlord and Tenant Act 1954, Part 2 (Notices) Regulations 2004, SI 2004/1005. The information it requires and gives is similar to Form 1, except that, obviously, it does not require the landlord to make proposals for a new tenancy and it does require the landlord to specify the ground(s) of objection it will rely upon under section 30(1) of the Act.

The new section 25 notices also note the possibility of there being an extension of the termination date specified in the section 25 notice. Again, this will be considered in Chapter 2.

It must not be forgotten that, while only the main types of section 25 notice have been considered, there are other variations that must be used where the appropriate circumstances arise, e.g. where the Leasehold Reform Act 1967 may apply (the legislation that allows a tenant of a 'house' to seek the freehold or an extended lease of it). Consequently, one must check carefully the provisions of the Landlord and Tenant Act 1954, Part II (Notices) (England and Wales) Regulations 2004, SI 2004/1005 to make sure that the correct prescribed form of notice is used.

Section 66(4) of the Act remains unchanged, so the issues concerning service of notices under the Act pre-RRO 2003 will still apply. For a useful discussion of those issues, see *Renewal of Business Tenancies* (Kirk Reynolds QC and Wayne Clark; Sweet and Maxwell, 2002), sections 3.3 and 3.4, although one should bear in mind subsequent case law, notably the *Egg Stores* case referred to above at section 1.2.1.

1.3 TENANT'S COUNTERNOTICE TO A SECTION 25 NOTICE

1.3.1 Pre-RRO 2003

Under the original wording of sections 25(5) and 29(2) of the Act, the court could not entertain a tenant's application for a new tenancy unless the tenant had, in response to a landlord's section 25 notice, notified the landlord within two months of the giving of that notice that it was not willing to give up possession of the property comprised in the tenancy at the date of termination.

Although some legal stationers had developed forms that could be used, there was no prescribed form or form of words for the tenant's counternotice. In many cases, the counternotice was given in a letter from the tenant (or more likely, its advisers) to the landlord.

1.3.2 Post-RRO 2003

The Government considered that the requirement on the part of a tenant to give such a counternotice to the landlord within two months was an unnecessary burden on the tenant, that could safely be dispensed with. It noted that this obligation represented a trap for unwary tenants and that, notwithstanding the number of years the legislation had been in place, rather too frequently tenants (or more likely, their advisers) failed to give the counternotice thereby losing the opportunity of having a new tenancy.

The potential for the 'trap' to be sprung in a rather different way was recently emphasised in *Shaws (EAL) Limited* v. *W Pennycook* (2004) 08 EG 135 (CS), where the tenant's adviser had served a counternotice erroneously confirming that the tenant would be willing to give up possession at the end of the tenancy. Although a 'corrected' counternotice indicating that the tenant was not so willing was served within the two-month period, the Court of Appeal held that it did not retrieve the position and the tenant had effectively lost the right to a new tenancy.

Therefore, sections 25(5) and 29(2) have been respectively omitted and amended. In fact, there has been a wholesale replacement of section 29. It must be remembered, however, that a counternotice will be required in response to a section 25 notice served before 1 June 2004.

Consequently, the landlord may find that it has a much longer wait before learning of a tenant's intentions. Having served a section 25 notice (particularly one that does not oppose the tenant having a new tenancy), a landlord might have no idea whether:

(a) the tenant wants to have a new tenancy or not, until the notice expires;
(b) the tenant (or the landlord) is to apply to court for a new tenancy (which could be up to 12 months later); or
(c) the landlord has to commence termination proceedings (see section 2.4 below).

This could adversely affect the landlord's ability to plan effectively for the future use of the property.

While it is appreciated that the landlord could bring matters to a head by making its own application to court for a new tenancy (see Chapter 2), in the view of the author such a procedure is likely to be rarely used by a landlord. Even when a landlord does not object to a tenant having a new tenancy, it is more likely than not that the landlord will wait to see whether or not the tenant protects its position by making the court application necessary to secure its entitlement to a new tenancy. This is because if the tenant does want a new tenancy, but fails to protect its position, the landlord could find that it is in an improved bargaining position, and might consequently propose that the tenant accept more onerous tenancy terms than the landlord could reasonably have expected to negotiate or secure by court order, by virtue of the renewal process under the Act.

Under article 29(1) of RRO 2003, where a landlord or tenant has served a section 25 notice before 1 June 2004, the RRO 2003 will not apply to that notice, 'or anything done in consequence of it'. While the purpose of article 29(1) is clear, one can imagine that there is scope for dispute as to what 'in consequence of' precisely means. Therefore, were the landlord to serve a section 25 notice just before 1 June 2004, a counternotice must still be given by or on behalf of the tenant within two months of service of the section 25 notice.

1.4 SECTION 26 REQUESTS

Although RRO 2003 does not amend the procedure for the tenant to serve a request for a new tenancy under section 26, the Landlord and Tenant Act 1954, Part II (Notices) (England and Wales) Regulations 2004, SI 2004/1005 provides for a new form of request (see Form 3 of Schedule 2, Appendix C).

As mentioned in para. 1.3.2 above in relation to section 25 notices, where a tenant has served a request under section 26 of the Act before 1 June 2004, RRO 2003 will not apply to that request, 'or anything done in consequence of it' (RRO 2003, article 29(1)). Again, while the purpose of this article is clear, there may be scope for dispute as to what 'in consequence of' precisely means.

1.5 LANDLORD'S COUNTERNOTICE TO A SECTION 26 REQUEST

1.5.1 Pre-RRO 2003

Under section 26(6) the Act requires that, where a tenant has served a request for a new tenancy, the landlord *may*, within two months, give notice to the tenant that it will oppose any application the tenant might make to the court seeking a new tenancy and, if so, state on which of the grounds in section 30(1) the landlord will object.

While a landlord was not obliged to give such a counternotice, a failure by it to do so would prevent it from relying on the grounds of opposition in section 30(1). It could, of course, oppose on other bases; for example, because it contended that the tenant did not have the protection of the Act at all.

There was no obligation on a landlord to give any counternotice if it did not wish to oppose the tenant's having a new tenancy. However, failure to give such a counternotice would not prevent a landlord subsequently opposing the terms of the tenancy requested by a tenant in its court application.

In similar manner to the tenant's counternotice to a landlord's section 25 notice, although some legal stationers have developed forms that could be used, there is no prescribed form or form of words for the landlord's counternotice. In most cases, the counternotice was given in a letter from the landlord (or more likely, its advisers) to the tenant.

1.5.2 Post-RRO 2003

The Government considered that, while it was appropriate to remove the requirement for the tenant's counternotice to a landlord's section 25 notice, there was still a need for the landlord's counternotice to a tenant's section 26 request.

Consequently, there is no change to this part of the Act.

The logic for this step was that, while a tenant might give counternotice, it did not mean that the tenant would in fact renew the tenancy. However, the landlord's counternotice (which only needs to be given where the landlord will oppose the tenant's request for a new tenancy) was felt to serve two purposes:

(a) it is a useful means of setting out the landlord's stance on renewal at an early stage; and
(b) it has an impact on the operation of the compensation provisions which become relevant if the landlord successfully opposes the renewal on certain grounds.

1.6 SECTION 40 NOTICES SEEKING INFORMATION

Under the Act there is a mechanism by which landlords and tenants can seek information about the other, its interest in the property, and interests held by third parties in the property that the other is aware of.

It was considered that while the principle of an information-gathering process should be retained, it could be extended, and more particularly, given more 'teeth'. While the original process was used relatively infrequently (given the number of business tenancies that exist), when it was used, there were no effective sanctions for a failure to provide information against the recipient of such a request. Section 40 of the Act pre-RRO 2003 made it clear that there was a duty on the recipient of a notice to respond; in effect, the only remedy as a result of default was a claim for damages for breach of statutory duty. In practice, such a remedy would rarely be helpful.

The need for information about the identity of the parties in occupation, for example, is key to the successful working of the procedures under the Act where notices need to be served correctly and timeously.

Given the difficulties encountered with the pre-RRO 2003 procedure, the whole of section 40 has been replaced by new sections 40, 40A and 40B.

In the circumstances, whereas in the case of the other changes brought about by RRO 2003, the pre-RRO position has been considered in order to put the post-RRO position into context, there seems little purpose in following that approach in this case since the old section 40 notices were largely disregarded (see Appendix B to review the pre-RRO 2003 legislation).

1.6.1 Section 40 notice served by landlord on tenant

Where a landlord serves a section 40 notice on the tenant, there is a duty on the tenant to respond with the information requested within one month of service of the notice (section 40(1) and (5)(a)). For the service of notices, upon which the calculation of the time to respond depends, see Chapter 4 and section 66 of the Act, or see para. 1.2 above.

The information required under subsection (2) is as follows:

- whether the tenant occupies the property or any part of it wholly or partly for the purposes of a business carried on by it;
- whether the tenancy is subject to a sub-tenancy;
- if the tenancy is subject to a sub-tenancy:
  - what premises are comprised therein;
  - its duration, or if appropriate, by what notice it can be terminated;
  - the rent payable;
  - the identity of the sub-tenant (as defined in subsection (8) – see Appendix B);
  - to the best of the tenant's knowledge and belief, whether the sub-tenant is in occupation of the sub-let premises or part of them and, if not, the sub-tenant's address;
  - whether the sub-tenancy is excluded from the protection of the Act;
  - whether a section 25 notice or section 26 request has been served in relation to the sub-tenancy and, if so, details of the notice or request; and
- to the best of the tenant's knowledge and belief, the name and address of anyone else who has an interest in reversion in any part of the property.

If, within six months of the service of the section 40 notice, the tenant becomes aware of any information given which is not or no longer correct, that person must give the correct information within one month of the date when he became so aware (section 40(5)(b)). This is an onerous requirement and one of which advisers should be particularly aware.

Section 40 does not apply to a notice served earlier than two years before the expiry of the fixed term of the tenancy or the date by which the tenancy could be brought to an end by notice to quit given by the landlord. The latter would include the date by which any break clauses could take effect.

1.6.2 Section 40 notice served by tenant on landlord

Where a tenant serves a section 40 notice on the landlord or other reversioner (as defined at subsection (8) – see Appendix B) or the reversioner's mortgagee in possession (also defined in subsection (8)), there is a duty on the recipient to respond with the information requested within one month of service of the notice (section 40(3) and (5)(a)). As discussed in para. 1.6.1, one must bear in mind the provisions as to the service of notices under the Act.

The information required to be given under subsection (4) is as follows:

- whether the recipient is the owner of the freehold of the property or any part thereof, or is the mortgagee in possession of such an owner;
- if the recipient is not the owner of the freehold, then to the best of his knowledge and belief:
  - the name and address of his or, if appropriate, his mortgagor's immediate landlord in respect of the property or part of the property;
  - the term for which his or his mortgagor's tenancy has effect and the earliest date (if any) that the tenancy is terminable by notice to quit served by the landlord;
  - whether a section 25 notice or section 26 request has been served in relation to the tenancy and, if so, details of the notice or request;
- to the best of the recipient's knowledge and belief, the name and address of any other person who owns or has an interest in reversion in any part of the property; and
- if the recipient is a reversioner, whether there is a mortgagee in possession of his interest in the property and, if so, to the best of his knowledge and belief, the name and address of the mortgagee.

If, within six months of the service of the section 40 notice, the recipient becomes aware of any information given which is not, or is no longer, correct, that person must give the correct information within one month of date when he became so aware (section 40(5)(b)). This is an onerous requirement and one of which advisers should be particularly aware.

Section 40 does not apply to a notice served earlier than two years before the expiry of the fixed term of the tenancy or the date by which the tenancy could be brought to an end by notice to quit given by the landlord. The latter would include the date by which any break clause could take effect.

1.6.3 Section 40 notices and transfers

Section 40A addresses the situation where there is a transfer by either the giver or recipient of a section 40 notice.

Where an interest in the property or part of it is transferred by a person on whom a section 40 notice has been served, provided he gives notice in writing to the 'appropriate person' (generally the server of a section 40 notice – see section 40(7)) of the transfer and the name and address of the person to whom the interest has been transferred, he then ceases to be under the duty imposed by section 40. Therefore, if he fails to give notice, then he remains liable to comply with the section 40 notice.

Conversely, where the transfer is by the person who has given the section 40 notice, then provided he or the transferee gives notice of the transfer and the name and address of the transferee to the person required to respond to the section 40 notice, the duty is to respond to the transferee in respect of the section 40 notice.

If notice of a transfer by the person who has given a section 40 notice as described above is not given to the recipient landlord or tenant, then the information may be given to either the transferor or the transferee.

Given the sanctions discussed in the next section, landlords, tenants and their advisers should be careful to ensure appropriate notice is given.

1.6.4 Sanctions for failure to comply with section 40 duties

As mentioned above, one of the significant problems with the pre-RRO 2003 procedure was the inability to enforce its provisions in a practical and effective manner.

Under section 40B, a person who has failed to meet any of the new section 40 duties can be made the subject of civil proceedings for breach of statutory duty and the court may require the person to comply with the duty and may also award damages.

1.6.5 Section 40 forms

Under Landlord and Tenant Act 1954, Part II (Notices) (England and Wales) Regulations 2004, SI 2004/1005, Schedule 2, there are prescribed notices under section 40(1) and (3) (Forms 4 and 5) – see Appendix C.

1.6.6 Transition

The new section 40 procedure does not apply to any notices served under the old section 40 before 1 June 2004, being the date on which RRO 2003 comes into force.

2 APPLICATIONS TO COURT AND TIME LIMITS

2.1 INTRODUCTION

As is well known, the scheme of the Act is that, where the tenant wishes to have a new tenancy, a court application must be made. As will be seen, although there are changes to elements of this process, the essential requirement of a court application remains, subject to the important addition that, post-RRO 2003, the landlord may also make the application. In addition, a new procedure is introduced where the landlord objects to the tenant having a new tenancy: in such cases, it can commence termination proceedings. Both situations will be considered in this chapter.

2.2 PRE-RRO 2003

The Act was intended to give the tenant the possibility of, as it were, the 'first refusal' of a new tenancy of the property on the termination of its tenancy and, pending the operation of the procedures in the Act, security of tenure. The Act therefore placed upon the tenant many of the burdens in terms of compliance with those procedures.

Thus, whether the landlord had served a section 25 notice or the tenant had served a section 26 request (subject to the counternotice provisions having been complied with either under section 25(5) and section 29(2) or, if appropriate, under section 26(5)), the tenant (alone) was required to issue an application in court seeking a new tenancy by virtue of section 24(1).

Section 29(3) required that the application had to be made not earlier than two months nor later than four months from either the giving of the landlord's section 25 notice or the making of the tenant's section 26 request for a new tenancy. An application made before the two-month limit would lead to the dismissal of the tenant's application, with the possibility that, by the time the question had been determined, it could not then make a valid application in time (i.e. not later than four months), and would thereby lose its protection under the Act. A failure to comply with the latter time limit would similarly lead to the loss, by the tenant, of its protection under the Act. The tenant would have to vacate the property by the date specified in the notice or request.

It is worth remembering that, while infrequently used, the effect of the principles in the case of *Kammins Ballrooms Co Ltd* v. *Zenith Investments (Torquay) Ltd (No. 1)* [1971] AC 850 was that it was within the gift of the landlord to agree with the tenant that the tenant could issue its application by a date after the four-month statutory deadline. However, if the tenant then failed to issue its application by the earlier of the date agreed with the landlord, or (if a 'general' extension was given by the landlord) the date specified in the section 25 notice or section 26 request, the tenant would lose the protection of the Act.

Of course, the tenant did not need to make such an application if it did not want a new tenancy, nor would it need to do so if the landlord had indicated that it would oppose any application by the tenant for a new tenancy and the tenant accepted that opposition.

Unfortunately, in a similar vein to the requirement to give counternotice, all too frequently the tenant (or its advisers) failed to comply with these time limits and the protection of the Act was lost. Thus, the Government considered that, to some extent, the burden of having to issue proceedings could be modified in a manner that might, it is hoped, reduce the incidence of the accidental (or negligent) loss of the Act's protection.

2.3 TENANCY RENEWAL PROCEEDINGS

Subject to the changes to the Civil Procedure Rules (CPR) (see Chapter 7), the basic approach to court applications will remain the same where the landlord does not object to the tenant being granted a new tenancy. There are, however, two important innovations: the introduction of the landlord's entitlement to commence lease renewal proceedings and the modification of the time limits for either the landlord or tenant to issue lease renewal proceedings.

2.3.1 The modified time limits

The amended Act adopts the *Kammins* principles and then extends them. The new requirement under section 29A is to issue the renewal proceedings by no later than the date specified in the landlord's section 25 notice or the day before the date specified in the tenant's section 26 request (under section 29A(2), the period up to this date is described as the 'statutory period').

However, under section 29B, the time limit for an application to court can be extended by agreement. Extension agreements will be considered further below.

The obligation not to issue renewal proceedings earlier than two months after the giving of the landlord's section 25 notice will now no longer apply (as a result of the abandoned requirement on the tenant to give counternotice within that two-month period). In such circumstances, an application can be made at any time after the giving of the section 25 notice. But, under section 29A(3), where the tenant has given a section 26 request, renewal proceedings cannot be commenced earlier than the expiry of the two-month period for the landlord to give counternotice under section 26(6) (which it only need do if it wishes to oppose the tenant having a new tenancy), unless the landlord has already given such a counternotice.

Extension agreements

The idea that a landlord and tenant can agree to the variation of the time for issuing renewal proceedings is quite radical in the context of the Act. As explained above in relation to the *Kammins* case, were the tenant (in that context) to issue the renewal proceedings after the date specified in the notice or request, the protection of the Act would already have been lost.

Under section 29B, at any time after the giving of a section 25 notice or section 26 request, but before the expiry of the statutory period, the landlord and tenant can agree that the time for issuing the renewal proceedings be extended to an agreed date after the end of the statutory period.

Indeed, under section 29B(2), the landlord and tenant can agree further extensions of the time by which renewal proceedings must be commenced. However, any such further agreements must be made before the end of the period specified in the then current extension agreement.

Under section 29B(4), the Act now makes it clear that, notwithstanding the passing of the date specified in the section 25 notice or section 26 request (i.e. the expiry of the statutory period), the tenancy will continue under section 24 until the expiry of the agreed period, or the latest of the periods agreed if there has been more than one agreement.

There are three important points to note:

(a) Any extension agreement must be in writing. Under section 69(2), save in some limited and specified circumstances, all agreements under the Act must be in writing to be valid. Therefore, bearing in mind that the protection of the Act is essentially for the tenant, the tenant or its advisers must ensure that, if an extension agreement is given orally, it is confirmed in writing. There has already been some debate about what would constitute a written extension agreement: for example, would an exchange of e-mails suffice? While it might, the cautious approach would be for one side to record the agreement in a letter and for the other to endorse the letter or a duplicate with its consent.
(b) If it is not in writing and either the statutory period or any valid (i.e. written) extension agreement period expires without the tenant (or the landlord – see para. 2.3.2 below) having issued renewal proceedings, the tenant will lose the Act's protection. While the date by which renewal proceedings must be

issued may have been put back by virtue of the replacement of the four-month period referred to above by the statutory period, whether or not augmented by an agreed extension in writing, nevertheless the point made in relation to the Kammins case above (that a failure to issue by the date specified in the notice or request being fatal to the tenant) will still apply, as 'amended' by RRO 2003.

(c) It is unlikely that one party or another could unilaterally withdraw agreement. If negotiations have stalled, then the remedy is to commence renewal or termination proceedings as appropriate.

2.3.2 Landlord's renewal proceedings

As explained in para. 2.2 above, prior to RRO 2003 only the tenant could commence renewal proceedings.

Section 24(1)(b) has now been amended to give the right to commence renewal proceedings to the landlord too. However, neither party can make such an application if the other has already issued and served its own application (section 24(2A)). In addition, the landlord cannot make a renewal application if it has commenced termination proceedings (see para. 2.4 below; section 24(2B) of the Act). (In fact, service by a landlord of termination proceedings also prevents a tenant's renewal application.) Although it might appear odd to do so and there appears to be an assumption within RRO 2003 that this is not the case, there seems to be no reason why a landlord could not commence renewal proceedings, even though it has served a section 25 notice or a counternotice to a tenant's section 26 request indicating that it will oppose renewal.

To guard against the danger for the tenant of a landlord making a renewal application (thereby preventing the tenant from doing so) and then abandoning it at a point in time when the tenant would have lost its protection under the Act, the landlord may not withdraw its renewal application without the tenant's consent (see section 24(2C)). It is submitted that because the word 'consent' connotes some form of agreement, the tenant's consent ought to be evidenced in writing in similar manner to extension agreements discussed in the preceding section.

The time limits for the landlord to make a renewal application are the same as those for the tenant (see section 2.3.1 above). The landlord can also take advantage of the new express entitlement to the right to agree to an extension of those time limits in section 29B. However, it will usually be the case that the landlord (for obvious reasons) will be much less concerned than the tenant with the validity of any such extension agreement.

If the landlord has made a renewal application and the tenant informs the court that it does not want a new tenancy, the court will dismiss the landlord's application (new section 29(5)). Oddly, there does not seem to be an obvious statutory bar to the tenant then making its own renewal application, but it is suggested that, firstly, there is likely to be an estoppel argument on the part of the landlord that the tenant should not be able to, as it were, change its mind, and secondly, on a strict reading of section 24(2A), the landlord's renewal application will have been made and 'served', and that alone might be construed to prevent the tenant from making its own application notwithstanding that the court may have dismissed the landlord's application under section 29(5).

At this stage, one can only wait to see whether the landlord's right to make a renewal application is one which will be exercised at all, and if so, to what extent.

The logic for introducing the right for the landlord to commence renewal proceedings is that it puts the parties on an equal footing in this respect. Additionally, since the landlord can initiate the process, it might encourage the tenant to negotiate because it would know that, were it to shy away from negotiations, the landlord could bring the matter to a head on its own.

However, as considered above (see para. 1.3), there may, in practice, be some doubt as to the extent to which it will be taken up. In theory the idea that the landlord is able to commence renewal proceedings might sound attractive. In practice, it is suggested that the pre-RRO 2003 approach of landlords will still apply. Therefore, as stated earlier, even when a landlord does not object to a tenant having a new tenancy, it is more likely than not that the landlord will wait to see whether or not the tenant protects its position by making the court application necessary to secure its entitlement to a new tenancy. If the tenant does want a new tenancy but fails to protect its position, the landlord could find that it is in an improved bargaining position and could require the tenant (assuming it has a strong need to stay in the property) to accept more onerous tenancy terms than might otherwise have been the case.

2.3.3 Tenant's renewal proceedings

Although the idea of the tenant's renewal proceedings remains largely unchanged, the effect of the new right for a landlord to make an application to court has an impact upon the tenant's rights.

As mentioned above under para. 2.3.2, if the landlord has in fact taken up its new right to commence renewal proceedings and has served them, the tenant cannot make a renewal application (section 24(2A)). In similar manner, if the landlord has commenced and served termination proceedings (as to which, see below), then the tenant is precluded from making a renewal application (section 24(2B)).

2.4 LANDLORD'S TENANCY TERMINATION PROCEEDINGS

As explained above, under the pre-RRO 2003 regime, only the tenant was entitled to apply to the court for the renewal of the tenancy.

Where the landlord did not object to the tenant having a new tenancy, the court proceedings would often be an irrelevance to the process of renewal with the parties frequently agreeing the terms of the new tenancy. If some or all of the terms were not agreed, then the court would direct the landlord and tenant as to what was required to be done, procedurally, before the outstanding items could be the subject of determination by it. The procedural steps might involve the narrowing of the areas of dispute on the terms of the new tenancy requiring, among other things, the production of statements of witnesses and experts. The expert evidence would frequently focus on the amount of rent that would have to be paid under the new tenancy.

Alternatively, the landlord might object to the tenant having a new tenancy on one of the seven statutory grounds in section 30(1) of the Act, on the basis that the tenant did not have the protection of the Act at all. In this situation the procedural steps would differ. Clearly there would be no practical purpose in requiring the parties to incur the time and costs of adducing evidence on matters such as the level of new rent if the tenant was not in fact going to have a new tenancy. Therefore, the court would frequently direct that the question as to whether the landlord could satisfy the ground(s) of objection in section 30(1) relied upon by it be determined as a preliminary issue. The court would then make appropriate directions for the conduct of that aspect of the proceedings down to its trial. Only if the court then found that the landlord had not satisfied the ground(s) of objection relied upon, would it proceed to deal with the determination of the terms of the new tenancy.

Reflecting what happened in practice and the reality that there is no purpose in having a determination of issues that will be irrelevant if the court decides the tenant is not to have a new tenancy, under new section 29(2)–(4) and (6), the landlord is entitled to commence its own application to terminate the tenancy.

The 'right' arises where the landlord has given either a section 25 notice opposing the grant of a new tenancy to the tenant or a counternotice under section 26(6) to a tenant's section 26 request for a new tenancy, in either case opposing on one or more of the grounds in section 30(1). Note that the 'right' only arises in those circumstances; there are other circumstances where a landlord might object to a tenant's claim for a new tenancy and these will be touched on below.

An application may not be made where either the tenant or the landlord has already made a renewal application under section 24(1) (see new section 29(3)). Note the distinction with renewal proceedings which cannot be commenced if other renewal or termination proceedings have been issued and served. In this case, a landlord is precluded from commencing termination proceedings if renewal proceedings have been commenced – the concept of 'service' is not carried over. One can only wonder how the landlord is to know whether the tenant has issued renewal proceedings. It may be that if the landlord's termination proceedings are dismissed because the tenant has commenced but not served renewal proceedings, the landlord may be able to recover its costs, particularly if it had previously asked the tenant to confirm whether or not it had commenced renewal proceedings.

Under section 29(6), once the landlord has made its application for the termination of a tenancy under section 29(2), it may not withdraw that application unless the tenant consents to that withdrawal. This is for the same reason that a landlord cannot withdraw its section 24(1) application without tenant's consent, i.e. an unscrupulous landlord could make an application to prevent the tenant from so doing, only to withdraw it once the tenant had lost its rights under the Act.

If the landlord satisfies the court that the ground(s) of objection are met, then the court will order the termination of the tenancy which will then expire in accordance with section 64, which has only been modified to reflect the introduction of the landlord's right to commence renewal or termination proceedings.

If the landlord does not so satisfy the court, then the court will make an order for the grant of the new tenancy and the termination of the 'current' tenancy immediately before the commencement of the new tenancy. While the court procedure will be considered below in greater detail, what in practice may happen in such circumstances is that the court will give directions for the further conduct of the proceedings as if they were renewal proceedings, i.e. with directions intended to result in the agreement or determination of the terms of the new tenancy. This would reflect current practice following the unsuccessful trial of a landlord's ground of opposition under section 30(1).

The time limits for the landlord to make its termination application are identical to those discussed in para. 2.3.1.

As mentioned above, the landlord's 'right' to commence termination proceedings only arises in the circumstances set out in section 29(2), i.e. where it objects to the tenant having a new tenancy under one or more of the grounds set out in section 30(1). The RRO 2003 does not make provision in relation to this new 'right' to address cases where the landlord objects to the tenant having a new tenancy because the landlord contends that the tenant is not so entitled. Such contentions are not infrequently made and will arise where the landlord considers that, for example, the tenant is or was not in occupation of the property when required or that occupation was not for the purposes of a business. In those circumstances, one would assume that there is no question of the landlord issuing termination proceedings (which assume that the tenant has the benefit of the protection of the Act) but that, if the tenant were to commence renewal proceedings, the landlord would seek to have them struck out as being an abuse of the process of the court and/or for summary judgment under the provisions of the CPR. Alternatively, as discussed in Chapter 7, the revisions to the CPR consequential on the RRO 2003 make provision for the trial of this issue.

3 INTERIM RENT

3.1 INTRODUCTION

The concept of interim rent was introduced by the Landlord and Tenant Act 1969 into the Act as section 24A, as a result of a perceived unfairness to landlords where the tenant had sought the renewal of the tenancy and there was a prolonged period of holding over, between the expiry of the original tenancy and the commencement of the new tenancy. The intention was to provide 'compensation' to the landlord who could otherwise suffer because of the delay before it would be entitled to receive the new rent under the renewal tenancy which, in many cases, was likely to be higher than the rent that was payable under the original tenancy.

Although not described in section 24A as such, it became known as 'interim rent' because it was intended to cover the interim period between the end of the old tenancy and the start of the new.

Following RRO 2003, the principle of interim rent remains but significant changes have been made.

3.2 PRE-RRO 2003

The entitlement to apply for an interim rent was the landlord's alone and arose only where the landlord had served a section 25 notice or the tenant had made a section 26 request. In a falling market, an interim rent could be lower than the passing rent under the current tenancy. Where market rents had gone down, the landlord would often deliberately not apply for an interim rent, so that the tenant would have to continue paying the higher rent payable under the old tenancy until the new tenancy came into effect.

The interim rent would only run from either the date the application was made, or the date specified in the landlord's notice or tenant's request, whichever was later.

The interim rent was valued by reference to the rent under the new tenancy (i.e. under section 34(1) and (2) of the Act), but having regard to the rent payable under the old tenancy and on the assumption that the new tenancy would be granted from year to year. The effect of this approach to valuation was, in many cases, to cushion the tenant for the interim period from the full impact of the new rent.

3.3 THE NEW RIGHT TO INTERIM RENT

That only the landlord could seek an interim rent was, perhaps understandably, considered to be very unfair to tenants. Consequently, whether the landlord has served a section 25 notice or the tenant has made a section 26 request, either the landlord or the tenant has the right to apply for an interim rent.

But there can only be one application, so that if one or the other has made an application for an interim rent and the application has not been withdrawn, then the other is precluded from doing so (new section 24A(2)).

To make sure that the possibility of a claim is not left outstanding for any undue length of time, no application can be made more than six months after the termination of the 'relevant tenancy'.

The 'relevant tenancy' is defined at section 24A(1) and is the tenancy being continued by virtue of section 24 of the Act. Where the parties agree the terms of and enter into a new lease, the termination date of the relevant tenancy will be clear, although for commercial reasons in this situation the parties will usually have negotiated an interim rent. However, bearing in mind the provisions of section 64, this means that the six-month period could be calculated from the date the new tenancy starts under the Act. This could be, for example, the expiry of three months and the appeal period (currently 14 days) after the conclusion of the renewal or termination proceedings, or three months after discontinuance.

3.4 THE DATE FROM WHICH INTERIM RENT WILL BE PAYABLE

The date from which the interim rent will be payable has been modified by section 24B.

By virtue of section 24B(1), it will be payable from the 'appropriate date'. This is then defined in section 24B(2) and (3) (which respectively concern the service of a section 25 notice and the making of a section 26 request). In either case, the 'appropriate date' is the 'earliest date . . . that could have been specified' in 'the landlord's notice' or 'the tenant's request'.

There is clearly scope for argument as to what 'could have been' means.

On one hand, in the case of a fixed-term tenancy (which is often the nature of the tenancy being renewed), the earliest date that could have been specified in the notice or request would have been the date the fixed term came to an end, on the assumption that the notice or request had been served at least six months beforehand.

On the other hand, the right may refer to the notice or request actually served.

In both section 24B(2) and (3) the date is calculated by reference to 'the' notice or request. Since the right only arises if a notice or request is actually *served* (section 24A(1)), then it may well be that the calculation of time flows from the particular notice or request in fact given. Thus, if the notice or request had in fact specified a date giving longer than the minimum period required, e.g. 12 months instead of, say, six, then, for the purposes of this new right to interim rent, the date from which it would be payable would be calculated from the expiry of the six months from the *giving* of the actual notice or request, because that would be the earliest date that 'could have been specified'.

One can only wait to see how the argument is eventually resolved, but in practice it is unlikely to be a issue of general concern because in most cases, section 25 notices and section 26 requests are frequently served as soon as possible and before the term of the old tenancy has come to an end.

In any case, the date from which new interim rent will be payable does not refer to the date the application for it is made, unlike the pre-RRO 2003 right (although an application must be made to trigger the entitlement to an interim rent).

3.5 APPROACHES TO VALUATION OF INTERIM RENT

The valuation of interim rent is considered in two ways. The first is where the new tenancy is of the whole of the property granted and the landlord did not oppose the grant of a new tenancy, and the second is 'in any other case'.

In theory, and perhaps in practice, in many cases the amount of interim rent to be paid is readily ascertainable.

Each approach will be considered separately.

3.5.1 New tenancy for the whole of the property granted and no opposition from landlord

What will probably be the most utilised approach to the calculation of interim rent is set out in section 24C. It applies:

(a) where 'the landlord gave a notice under section 25 . . . at *a time when the tenant was in occupation*' (emphasis added) of the whole of the property comprised in the 'relevant tenancy' (see above), and the landlord stated that it would not oppose the grant of a new tenancy, or
(b) where the tenant has made a section 26 request '*at a time when it was in occupation*' (emphasis added) of the whole of the property comprised in the relevant tenancy and the landlord did not give counternotice under section 26 (6) (see above), and

(c) in either case, a new tenancy of the whole of the property comprised in the relevant tenancy is granted to the tenant either by court order or otherwise (section 24C(1)(a) and (b)).

Subject to the matters set out in section 24C(3) to (7), in those cases the interim rent will be the rent payable under the new tenancy (section 24C(2)). The rent payable under the new tenancy will, unless agreed between the parties, be calculated in accordance with section 34 of the Act, the material parts of which, for this purpose, have not been amended.

In those circumstances, therefore, the position is relatively straightforward and the concept of the 'cushion' that arose in the valuation of the pre-RRO 2003 interim rent no longer applies.

It is not a prerequisite for the new tenancy of the whole of the property to arise from a court determination. A new tenancy could result from an agreement between the landlord and the tenant, even if the tenant had, perhaps inadvertently, otherwise lost the right to a new tenancy.

It should also be noted that since the interim rent will be linked to the new rent where section 24C applies, the interim rent cannot be 'determined' until the issue of the new tenancy has been resolved either by the court or by agreement.

'. . . at a time when the tenant was in occupation . . .'

It is not clear what objective is to be achieved by the use of the words 'at a time when [the tenant/he] was in occupation' in section 24C(1)(a) and (b). Where the fact of the tenant's occupation is relevant to the protection of the Act, it is generally an issue to be considered at the end of the term of the contractual tenancy and at the expiry of any section 25 notice or section 26 request.

The use of those words seems to create, as it were, a further need to establish whether or not the tenant was in occupation at the time of service of the notice or request.

That issue already causes problems for landlords in particular, because the protection of the Act depends on occupation and if the tenant is not in occupation at the time when, say, the landlord is considering serving a section 25 notice, there is often a concern as to whether a notice is appropriate at all. If the tenant is not in occupation, then, the argument goes, there is no need to serve a section 25 notice because the Act does not apply and, indeed, it could be of no effect. But such a position is not free from doubt in that, where the tenant is not in occupation at the time a section 25 notice is served before the expiry of the contractual term, but resumes occupation, it is possible that the protection of the Act will also resume.

Whether deliberate or not, the use of words 'at a time when [the tenant] was in occupation' may in fact help resolve the status of a section 25 notice served at a time when the tenant is not in occupation. That said, the fact that the tenant is not in occupation of the whole of the property comprised in the tenancy at the time of the service of the section 25 notice or section 26 request would not prevent an application for interim rent but merely means that the alternative approach to its assessment will apply.

'. . . the landlord stated that it would not oppose the grant of a new tenancy . . .' or '. . . the landlord did not give counternotice under section 26 (6) . . .'

What is also unclear is why the apparently straightforward approach to the quantification of interim rent under section 24C(2) should be excluded in all cases where the landlord has opposed the grant of a new tenancy under one or more of the grounds in section 30(1). Obviously, one can see that were the landlord to satisfy any of the grounds specified in the section 25 notice or counternotice given under section 26(6), there would not be a new tenancy with a new rent and some other process would be required. But, if the landlord were to fail, or withdraw or not pursue its ground(s) of opposition, and the tenant were to obtain a new tenancy of the whole of the property comprised in the 'relevant tenancy' either by agreement or court determination, there seems to be no reason why the interim rent should not be approached in the same way as if the landlord had not stated ground(s) of opposition. One possible argument for the approach adopted by section 24C(1) is that, if the landlord does specify grounds of objection, even though the landlord might eventually fail to substantiate the objection, there is a real prospect that by having taken that stance at the outset of the process, there will be a delay before the terms (including the rent) of the new tenancy are agreed or determined which could be prejudicial to the tenant.

What should be (but perhaps is not, given the points discussed above) a straightforward position achieved by subsection (2), is made less so by subsection (3).

The purpose of subsection (3) is to avoid what could otherwise be unfairness to the landlord or tenant if, respectively, market rents fell or rose significantly between the start date for interim rent and the new tenancy, or if the terms of the new tenancy had the effect of significantly decreasing or increasing the new rent.

Under subsection (3), the new rent will not be the interim rent if the landlord or the tenant satisfies the court:

(a) that the interim rent under subsection (2) differs substantially from the 'relevant rent' (see below); or
(b) that the terms of the new tenancy so differ from the terms of the relevant tenancy (i.e. the old tenancy) that the interim rent under subsection (2) is substantially different from the rent the court would have determined under section 34 for a tenancy that commenced on the same day as the new tenancy, the terms of which were the same as the relevant tenancy.

In case (a), the interim rent is contrasted with 'relevant rent' which will be the rent the court would have determined under section 34 (the section determining the rent under the new tenancy), as if the new tenancy had commenced on the 'appropriate date' (see para. 3.4 above and section 24C(4) of the Act). In other words, the valuation for the interim rent would not be calculated as at the date that the new rent is determined but as at the 'earliest date . . . that could have been specified in' the section 25 notice or section 26 request (section 24C(4) and (5)).

In case (b), or a combination of it and case (a), the interim rent will be the amount the court considers it reasonable for the tenant to pay while the relevant tenancy continues under section 24 (section 24C(6)).

In those circumstances, under section 24C(7), when considering the amount that it would be reasonable for the tenant to pay, the court will have regard to the rent payable under the terms of the relevant tenancy and the rent payable under any sub-tenancy of part of the property comprised in the relevant tenancy; but otherwise, section 34 will be applied (the section under which the rent under the new tenancy is determined) as if the new tenancy were granted for the whole of the property, and the duration of the new tenancy were the same as the duration of the tenancy actually granted to the tenant.

3.5.2 Determination of interim rent in any other case

Where section 24C does not apply, the interim rent is determined under section 24D.

In such cases, the interim rent will be the amount the court considers it reasonable for the tenant to pay while the relevant tenancy continues under section 24 of the Act (section 24D(1)). This is quite similar to the pre-RRO 2003 approach.

In considering the amount it would be reasonable for the tenant to pay, the court will have regard to the rent payable under the terms of the relevant tenancy and the rent payable under any sub-tenancy for part of the property comprised in the relevant tenancy; but otherwise, section 34 will be applied as if the new tenancy was a tenancy from year to year for the whole of the property comprised in the relevant tenancy (section 24D(2)).

The reference to 'the rent payable under any sub-tenancy' represents a departure from the pre-RRO 2003 position. The intention is to try and ensure that the intermediate tenant is protected from what could operate as an unfairness against it.

Under section 24D(3), where the court has ordered a new tenancy and an interim rent under section 24C, but either the new tenancy order is subsequently revoked under section 36(2) of the Act (see Appendix B) or the landlord and the tenant agree not to act on the order, the court, on the application of either the landlord or the tenant shall determine the interim rent in accordance with section 24D(1) and (2) without the need for any new application for interim rent having to be made under section 24A(1).

4 CONTRACTING OUT OF THE PROTECTION OF THE ACT

4.1 DEBATE OVER CONTRACTING-OUT PROVISIONS

The RRO 2003 was signed off on 1 December 2003 by the Minister of State at the Office of the Deputy Prime Minister. It was delayed by up to 12 months due to concerns that arose in Parliament on two intended modifications:

(a) to the procedure by which the proposed landlord and tenant could agree to exclude the protection of the Act from tenancies that were to be entered into, and
(b) to the procedure whereby they could agree to ensure that the Act was excluded from agreements to surrender tenancies which were within the protection of the Act.

Since they have been superseded, the proposals originally submitted by the Office of the Deputy Prime Minister to the Houses of Parliament on 22 July 2002 are not considered here.

The concern expressed by the House of Lords Delegated Powers and Regulatory Reform Committee was that the pre-RRO 2003 law offered a significant protection to tenants, and the then existing contracting-out procedure was not so burdensome that it deterred landlords from seeking to contract out of the Act. If the intended changes to the contracting-out regime were to lead to a reduction or removal of the Act's protection to tenants, then the reforms should proceed in the 'usual' way, i.e. by the introduction of and debate on a Bill which could lead to an amending Act.

The House of Commons Regulatory Reform Committee also expressed some views about the proposed contracting-out procedure and suggested some small amendments. That committee's recommendations were accepted by the Government.

As mentioned in the Introduction, the Government sought to address the concerns of the House of Lords committee by commissioning some research on the subject of contracting out. In particular, research was undertaken as to the extent to which the existing regime could be said to offer protection to tenants that would in fact be lost under the intended reforms. The Government also consulted organisations that primarily represented small business occupiers.

In summary, the conclusion of the research and further consultation did not undermine the Government's proposals. The court-based contracting-out procedure did not seem to offer any increased level of protection since it seemed that, in the vast majority of cases, the applications to exclude the Act were accepted with no difficulty. Where there was some reason for the initial rejection of the application, on resubmission the vast majority of the resubmitted applications were also accepted. Thus, only about 0.8–3.3 per cent of cases were unsuccessful. The overall conclusion was that the process was largely administrative with judges extremely unlikely to exercise any judicial role in the exercise.

Having modified the RRO slightly in relation to the contracting-out process (and in a few other limited respects) as explained above, it was resubmitted to Parliament on 17 September 2003. The revised RRO 2003 met with approval.

4.2 PRE-RRO 2003

Under the old section 38(4) of the Act, where a proposed landlord and tenant wanted to enter into a tenancy that would be excluded from its protection (derived from sections 24–28), or where an existing landlord and tenant who were party to a tenancy that was already protected by the Act wanted to enter into an agreement to surrender it, they were required to make a joint application to court for an order authorising the transaction. The agreement to exclude the protection of the Act had to be contained in or endorsed on the tenancy or the agreement to surrender.

4.3 POST-RRO 2003

Section 38(4) is repealed and section 38A is introduced.

Section 38A is relatively short and confirms that the Act can be excluded by the agreement of the landlord and tenant. One is then referred to the RRO 2003 and in particular schedules 1–4. Schedules 1 and 2 deal with contracting out in respect of tenancies to be entered into. Schedules 3 and 4 deal with contracting out of the protection of the Act when entering into an agreement to surrender a protected tenancy (see section 4.7 below).

In short, the new process requires the service of a notice by the landlord on the tenant, and the tenant (or someone duly authorised by him) has to make a declaration confirming, among other things, receipt of that notice.

While the full text of RRO 2003 and its schedules can be found at Appendix A, these procedures are considered in some detail here given their importance to day-to-day commercial landlord and tenant practice.

It is worth remembering that the new law only modifies the procedure for excluding the Act; it will not change the substantive law, and one is only concerned to comply with the procedure where the proposed tenancy would otherwise be protected and is not excluded by, say, section 43.

4.4 NEW TENANCIES AND CONTRACTING OUT

The new section 38A applies only to fixed-term tenancies, which was also the case under the old section 38(4). Unless the landlord has served on the intended tenant a notice in the form, or substantially the form, set out in schedule 1 to RRO 2003 (see Appendix A), any agreement to exclude the protection of the Act will be void (section 38A(3)).

In schedules 1 and 2 there is then a procedural distinction between cases where the notice is given more than 14 days before the transaction is entered into, and those where it is given less than 14 days before the transaction is entered into.

4.4.1 The notice

The form of notice is not particularly complex. The only information that the landlord or its adviser has to add is the name and address of, respectively, the landlord and the tenant. The rest of the notice is 'printed' information; there is not even a reference to the property for which the tenant is to take a tenancy, or to any of the intended terms of the tenancy.

The principal content of the notice is the prescribed information which, in effect, represents the 'health warning' the Government anticipated in its consultation paper issued in 2001.

Essentially, the notice informs the intended tenant that it is being offered a lease that will not be protected by the Act which, of course, means that when the tenancy comes to an end, unless the landlord agrees a new tenancy with the tenant, the tenant will have no choice but to leave the property. In addition, the tenant will not have the right to any statutory compensation otherwise payable if the tenancy were to be protected and if the landlord prevented the tenant from having a new tenancy on certain grounds of opposition (there are some changes to the compensation provisions of the Act which will be considered below).

The notice recommends that the tenant seek professional advice about what it is intending to do.

In many ways, the notice and the obligation to give it is analogous to the regime with which residential landlords and tenants were familiar when entering into assured shorthold tenancies between 15 January 1989 and 26 February 1997 ('old-style ASTs'), under section 20 of the Housing Act 1988.

In the case of old-style ASTs, it was thought that the procedure was relatively straightforward and not likely to be misapplied: but not so. In the event, there were many cases resulting from the failure to follow the section 20 Housing Act 1988 procedure. In some cases, the issue was the status of the tenancy enjoyed by the tenant where the notice given was incorrectly completed, or some information was not given at all. Other cases were concerned with the absence of the required notice or an inability to prove that it had been given. With time, and with a modified approach to such problems by the courts that flowed from cases such as *Mannai Investment Co Ltd* v. *Eagle Star Life Assurance Co Ltd* [1997] AC 749 to the consideration of problems arising where there were defects in the notice-based process, defects in the process did not automatically result in the tenancy being deemed to be assured rather than assured shorthold, i.e. having security of tenure which assured shorthold tenancies do not attract.

With such cases in mind, and remembering that only the names and addresses of the parties have to be inserted into the schedule 1 notice, it is difficult to conceive of difficulties arising from the drafting of the notice itself. Of course, there is always the possibility that those preparing and serving such notices will create their own notice, rather than use those that are likely to be printed by the legal stationers, and therein lies scope for the notice not to be 'in the form or substantially in the form' set out in schedule 1.

Problems have arisen in the past in relation to the service of, for example, section 25 notices that differed from the form prescribed at the time of the giving of the notice.

This issue was considered by the authors of *Renewal of Business Tenancies* (Kirk Reynolds QC and Wayne Clark; Sweet and Maxwell, 2002) at paragraphs 3.6.1.21 to 3.6.1.25. The view expressed was, in summary, that in considering the validity of a section 25 notice which differed from the prescribed form, any effect (or lack of effect) on the recipient would be immaterial. The question of validity would be a question of form and content. A notice that was not in the form or substantially in the form prescribed would be invalid. If the notice actually given provided information the effect of which was properly to address the matters that the prescribed form of notice addressed, then it may still be valid.

The schedule 1 notice is an innovation. One cannot, therefore, contend that it is inevitable that the principles relevant to, for example, defective section 25 notices, will be applied in similar manner, but it is submitted that the argument may well have a great deal of force.

However, it is stating the obvious that all such arguments should be avoided by making sure that the notice used is precisely in the prescribed form set out in schedule 1 to the RRO.

The requirement to give notice being vital to the validity of an agreement to exclude the protection of the Act, it might be prudent that a copy receipted by the tenant be kept with the tenancy and counterpart tenancy. This must be good practice and additional to the requirements concerning the declaration which are considered below.

As to service, etc., see section 4.5 below.

4.4.2 The declaration

As mentioned above, in addition to the requirement that the tenant be given a schedule 1 notice, there is also a requirement that the tenant make a declaration. Under schedule 2 there are two types of declaration, and the nature of the declaration required depends upon when the schedule 1 notice is given to the tenant. The date that is determinative is that which is 14 days before the tenant enters into the tenancy or becomes contractually bound to do so.

Whichever type of declaration is appropriate, it must be made before the tenant enters into the tenancy or becomes contractually bound to do so.

There has already been some discussion about the effect of the words 'becomes contractually bound to do so'.

Under the pre-RRO 2003 regime, it was often the case that the proposed landlord and tenant would enter into an agreement for lease conditional on, among other things, the parties complying with the court order-based contracting-out procedure.

The effect of the words 'becomes contractually bound to do so' may be such that conditional agreements for lease will be a thing of the past. The requirement is that before any agreement for lease is entered into, the schedule 2 requirements as to the notice and declaration must be met. It may be that a conveyancing solution will be contrived, but that remains to be seen.

The need for a declaration stems from the requirements set out in schedule 2 to RRO 2003.

By virtue of section 38A(3)(b), a failure to comply with schedule 2 to RRO 2003 will mean that any agreement to exclude the protection of the Act will be void.

The position 14 days or more before the tenancy or agreement for tenancy is entered into

Where the schedule 1 notice is given 14 days or more before the tenant enters into the tenancy or becomes contractually bound to do so, the requirement is that the tenant or someone duly authorised by it must, before the tenant enters into the tenancy or becomes contractually bound to do so, make a declaration in the form, or substantially in the form, set out in paragraph 7 of schedule 2 to the RRO (see Appendix A).

In summary, the declaration:

- identifies the parties to the intended tenancy;
- identifies the property which is to be the subject of the tenancy and the date its term is to commence;
- confirms that the parties intend to exclude the protection of the Act; and

- confirms that the landlord has served on the tenant notice in the form or substantially in the form of the schedule 1 notice, and that the notice has been read and its consequences accepted by the tenant.

The declaration then sets out verbatim the form of schedule 1 notice. The declaration also confirms that the date of service of the notice complies with the 14-day period described above. The declaration is then signed by the tenant or someone authorised to do so on its behalf.

While the declaration refers to the date the 'term' is to commence, it is not clear what that might be. It could be the date the instrument creating the tenancy is entered into or executed, or it could be the date, often earlier, when the term is stated within the lease to commence. Although the point cannot be said to be free from doubt, the latter is more likely to be correct, because after all, at the time the declaration is made, one might not know the date the instrument is to be entered into or executed.

The declaration does not annex a copy of the notice actually given to the tenant.

The question arises, therefore, as to what the position would be if, for example, the schedule 1 notice actually given by the landlord differs from the prescribed form of notice. It is suggested that, if the notice actually given can be said to be substantially in the form of the schedule 1 notice, no problem arises because the form of declaration set out in paragraph 7 of schedule 2 specifically caters for that. If the notice actually given is not in the form, or substantially in the form, of that set out in schedule 1, then the notice will not, of course, be valid; and with section 38A(3)(a) not then being satisfied, the problem of the status of the declaration becomes irrelevant – the agreement to exclude the protection of the Act will be void in any event. It is possible, however, that as a result of the contents of the declaration, the tenant would be estopped from challenging the schedule 1 notice in this way; but that would be an uncomfortable argument for a landlord to maintain if, in fact, the schedule 1 notice was so defective as to be invalid. The declaration by the tenant may not cure that.

What, then, is the position if the declaration is not in the form set out in paragraph 7? The requirement for the declaration is set out in paragraph 3 of schedule 2 to RRO 2003 and, like the schedule 1 notice, it too is valid if it is 'substantially in the form' set out in paragraph 7. It is difficult to see how the core elements (e.g. the names of the intended parties, etc.) of the required declaration might be omitted or altered to such an extent that the declaration would not be saved in this way.

But what if a required piece of information were not included in the declaration? It is quite likely that legal stationers will produce copies of the declaration which would then only require the addition of certain items of information, e.g. the names and addresses of the landlord and tenant. However, the document might omit the description of the property or misdescribe it, or it might omit the date the term of the excluded tenancy is to commence.

Since the procedure is new, one can only surmise what stance the court would take in such circumstances. There may be some help to be gleaned from the cases that have considered defects in section 25 notices and those that have considered defects in section 20 notices that related to old-style ASTs. However, even then the answer might be unclear, since, as is often the case, such examples will almost inevitably turn on their own facts. On the one hand, it might be said that a failure to include any property description might invalidate the declaration, but then it might be so obviously related to a particular property (by virtue of accompanying documents or letter, etc.) that it is 'saved'. However, the failure to include some required information must present a grave risk of invalidating the declaration. If there is a description of the property, but it is not accurate, then there is even more of an argument, again depending on the circumstances of the case, that the declaration might be invalid. The same could be true if the date is incomplete. These are probably issues that will only be resolved in due course, sadly, as inevitably such scenarios arise.

The declaration incorporates the form of the schedule 1 notice, including the 'health warning' information, but that could itself in some way be omitted, altered or incomplete. The potential problem of there being defects in the schedule 1 notice has been considered above. But what if the notice actually given is valid but, for some reason, the wording of the schedule 1 notice in the declaration (which only repeats the information that will, therefore, have been given to the tenant) is defective? Would the court approach the problem in a different way to situations where the notice actually given is defective? One can see that there is scope for the court to take, as it were, a slightly more lenient line in this instance but that cannot be beyond doubt. However, in practice the court will be required to adopt an approach equivalent to that required when considering the validity of the schedule 1 notice actually served (see above). Again, the arguments are best avoided by ensuring complete compliance with the requirements of schedule 2 and using the wording as set out in paragraph 7.

The further question arises, though, as to the purpose to be achieved by incorporating the form of schedule 1 notice in the declaration. Its presence is clearly no guarantee that the notice actually served was in the prescribed form, even though the two (the actual schedule 1 notice and the declaration notice) should be in identical terms. It may be intended to be some sort of reminder to the tenant of what it should have received to make sure that the tenant has every opportunity to make sure that the correct procedure has been followed. As discussed above, its inclusion may, however, undermine the ability of the tenant to contend, if it be the case, that the schedule 1 notice actually served was incorrect in some way (see the views expressed above about the effect of an incorrect schedule 1 notice) or was not in fact served.

In similar manner to the receipted notice, as the tenant's declaration is crucial to the validity of the agreement to exclude the protection of the Act, it (or a copy) should be kept with the tenancy and counterpart tenancy.

Less than 14 days before the tenancy or agreement for tenancy is entered into

The declaration process whereby the schedule 1 notice is given less than 14 days before the tenancy or agreement for tenancy is entered into is similar to, if a little more onerous than, the process described above where the notice is given not less than 14 days before that date.

In this case, the declaration requirements are set out in paragraphs 4 and 8 of schedule 2 to RRO 2003.

Paragraph 8 sets out the form of declaration. It is very similar to the declaration described above but it is in the form of a statutory declaration that must be made under the Statutory Declarations Act 1835.

Therefore, unlike the form of declaration described above, it will need to be made before someone empowered to administer oaths, i.e. generally a solicitor. A 'processing' fee will have to be paid to the solicitor, currently £5.00.

It is to be noted that the solicitor administering the statutory declaration must be 'independent' of those otherwise acting for the tenant, and will merely be making sure that the declaration is given in accordance with the 1835 Act. By its very nature that process does not involve the 'administering' solicitor in advising the tenant about the transaction it is about to enter into. One can only wonder, therefore, what benefit would be achieved by this additional procedural step, and how in fact the tenant is given greater protection.

Since the statutory declaration can still be made by someone other than the tenant (but who has been duly authorised by the tenant to make it), there is every possibility that, in practice, the tenant will not have much to do with the process other than to receive the schedule 1 notice (as to service, etc. see section 4.5 below). One can only assume that the Government, by requiring the making of a statutory declaration, is seeking to convey to the tenant a higher degree of seriousness, as it were, that will have the effect of causing the tenant to reflect even more carefully on what it is about to do.

The drafting of schedule 2 to RRO 2003 is such that there should be limited scope to depart from it and still retain the effect of excluding the protection of the Act. However, it could be argued that by creating this rather arbitrary distinction between declarations and procedures, there could in fact be a trap for landlords who find themselves using the wrong form of declaration.

If concerned about such a trap, one could argue that the use of the words 'substantially in the form of' in relation to the form of declaration required, might save the landlord. Equally, however, one could argue that the distinction between an 'ordinary' declaration and a statutory declaration is the principal difference between the two procedures. Consequently, the failure to use the appropriate procedure, as determined by the timing of the service of the schedule 1 notice, could result in the agreement to contract out of the Act being void. An obvious example of where this could arise is if there were to be some confusion about the date the schedule 1 notice was in fact served on the tenant (see section 4.5 below).

4.4.3 Other requirements for contracting out

In addition to the requirements for the service of the schedule 1 notice and the making of the appropriate declaration, in order to comply with schedule 2 (and therefore have a valid contracting-out agreement), one must ensure that a reference to the notice and the appropriate declaration is noted in or endorsed on the instrument creating the tenancy (paragraph 5 of schedule 2).

In practice, pre-RRO 2003 similar provisions were frequently included in contracted-out tenancies, referring to the court order that had been made authorising the exclusion of the Act's protection.

Further, the agreement to exclude the protection of the Act or a reference to it must be contained in or endorsed on the instrument creating the tenancy. Again the requirement is similar to the requirement in the former section 38(4) under the pre-RRO 2003 procedure.

It has been suggested by some that, to complete the process, a copy of the notice actually given should be annexed to the declaration and a copy of the declaration (with the copy notice actually given) be annexed to the instrument creating the tenancy. That is not a requirement of the RRO 2003 and one might suggest it is an over-complication that could cause problems.

4.5 OTHER CONSIDERATIONS

4.5.1 Service of schedule 1 notices

Clearly, RRO 2003 introduces new categories of notice. The enabling provision is section 38A which, obviously, is within the Act. Thus, schedule 1 notices must be notices to which the provisions of section 66 apply (the section setting out the provisions as to notices under the Act). Subsection (4) of section 66 applies section 23 of the Landlord and Tenant Act 1927 in relation to service of notices under the Act.

Section 23 has been discussed above briefly (see section 1.2.1). Since this section and the issues concerning service of notices remain unchanged by RRO 2003, it is not the intention to review it in detail here. Other works that provide a full discussion of them have already been referred to.

However, one should not lose sight of the fact that the service provisions apply to schedule 1 notices because, as is frequently the case in respect of the Act's procedures, the calculation of time depends on understanding when a notice has been served.

In the case of contracting out, it would not be safe for the landlord to enter into the instrument creating the tenancy (to use the language of schedules 2 and 4 to RRO 2003) unless it knew which form of declaration was required to be given by the tenant and that it was satisfied that the correct declaration had been made. This is for the obvious reason that an incorrect declaration might well render the agreement to exclude the protection of the Act void. Therefore, the landlord needs to be absolutely clear about when the schedule 1 notice was served in accordance with the Act,

Obviously, a note about the declaration needs to be included in the instrument creating the tenancy, but that does not mean that the landlord will necessarily have seen it. A landlord could seek to rely on confirmation from the tenant that the declaration has been made and on what date.

Since there is an argument that, as discussed above, were the tenant to make the wrong declaration, the agreement to exclude the protection of the Act could be void, the landlord should make sure that it has seen the declaration or a certified copy of the declaration to satisfy itself that the correct declaration has indeed been made.

This problem is, of course, primarily going to be of concern to the landlord who will want to ensure that the tenancy is indeed excluded from the Act. If it is not, the tenant will potentially be entitled to stay on at the property when the tenancy comes to an end. Also, since the issue of protection (or not) will usually have an impact on the rent that a tenant would be prepared to pay for property (often, but not always, being lower for an excluded tenancy), the landlord could find that it is receiving less rent than it could otherwise have negotiated.

4.5.2 Who may give and receive schedule 1 notices?

While schedule 2 allows the required declarations to be made by the tenant or 'someone duly authorised' to do so, there is no such provision in relation to the service of schedule 1 notices. In simple terms, therefore, under section 38A(3) the notice is to be served by the landlord on the tenant.

However, it is, of course, not as simple as that. For the reasons set out below, great care should probably be taken to consider both to whom the notice is properly addressed (i.e. the named recipient), and to whom or upon whom the notice is actually delivered.

The need to correctly identify the landlord and the tenant has often caused difficulties in relation to the pre-RRO 2003 service of section 25 notices and section 26 requests, and will probably continue so to do. The existing principles in relation to such notices and requests may well apply to schedule 1 notices as well (and certainly to schedule 3 notices concerning agreements to surrender – see below).

In practice, it appears likely that in most cases, the schedule 1 notice will be served by the landlord's surveyor or solicitor. There would seem to be no difficulty with that and indeed the service of section 25 notices and section 26 requests can be effected by someone duly authorised to do so on behalf of, respectively, the landlord or the tenant.

There appears to be no reason, in principle, why the landlord's agent or surveyor might not serve the schedule 1 notice with the heads of terms of the proposed transaction once it had been negotiated in outline. If the surveyor holds a stock of the forms (as will no doubt be printed by legal stationers) there should be no difficulty, at least in principle.

That said, while the giving of a schedule 1 notice is intended to be a simple procedure, the potential for problems has already been highlighted, and this course of action may not, therefore, be adopted in practice.

It is often the case that the precise identity of the tenant is not resolved until some time after the main terms of the transaction have been settled upon.

Since the notice must be served on the tenant by name (see the form of notice at schedule 1 to RRO 2003), if the exact identity of the tenant is not known and included on the notice there could be scope for argument that the notice has not in fact been served as required by schedule 2, with the result that the agreement to exclude the Act is or could be void.

Thus, even what should be a simple notice to fill in could be rendered defective if incorrect information is given. Indeed, the information could be right at the time it is given, but tenancy could then be granted to a different tenant. This is a frequent occurrence with groups of companies, where perhaps one company was originally intended to take the lease and then another in fact does so.

Consequently, best practice must be to ensure that:

(a) the notice identifies the correct landlord and tenant;
(b) it is served on that tenant (see below); and that
(c) if a notice has already been served but the identity of the landlord or tenant is to change, a new notice is served.

Assuming the notice is correctly completed with not only the landlord's name and address, but also that of the tenant, to whom can the notice actually be given?

Bearing in mind that one is inevitably concerned with property intended to be occupied for the purposes of a business, it is frequently the case that not only is the landlord represented by a surveyor (or agent) (in addition to a solicitor) but that the tenant is too. Can the schedule 1 notice be given to the tenant's surveyor or solicitor, whether or not at the same time as confirmation of the categories of the terms of the transaction that they have negotiated between them on behalf of their respective clients?

While section 23 of the Landlord and Tenant Act 1927 sets out methods by which service of notices is permitted, that does not prevent service by some other means, including, where appropriate, the agent of the tenant. If the surveyor or agent of the tenant (or its solicitor) has authority to accept service of such notices on behalf of his client, then service on him on behalf of the tenant would seem permissible, but that is not free from doubt.

To avoid any uncertainty about the position, however, it would be sensible to serve the notice by giving it to the tenant itself, copied to its representative. Indeed, if the notice were to be sent to the tenant by recorded delivery, it would be deemed to have been served on the date of posting even though the tenant might not actually have received it.

4.5.3 Alteration of the negotiated terms of the intended tenancy

Although the pre-RRO 2003 court-based exclusion order procedure did not technically require the parties to submit to the court a copy of the agreed lease that they intended to enter into, as it had become the practice, one cannot envisage a case where the court would have accepted the application without it.

Thus, before the exclusion order was obtained, in practice all of the terms of the intended tenancy would had been agreed.

The question would sometimes arise, therefore, as to the status of the tenancy if, following the making of the required court order, the parties negotiated revised terms or were required to make changes (slight or otherwise) to the agreed form of lease that the court had 'approved'. Indeed, the issue was considered in *Receiver for the Metropolitan Police District* v. *Palacegate Properties Limited* [2001] Ch 131 when it was held that, in effect, the parties could not make wholesale changes to the terms of the draft lease annexed to the application before the court when it made the exclusion order. Changes to terms of the proposed tenancy which were material to the exclusion of security of tenure would have the effect of undermining the need to seek the court order in the first place.

This issue (with specific reference to the *Palacegate* case) was raised in the consultation process undertaken by the Office of the Deputy Prime Minister (ODPM). However, having considered it, the ODPM concluded in its review of the consultation process, annexed to its explanatory note lodged when the proposals were first submitted to Parliament on 22 July 2002, that it was not an issue that caused concern. It concluded that the objective was 'simply to ensure that the tenant is aware of the implications of any proposal to exclude security of tenure'. It recommended that tenants would be well advised, however, to reappraise the proposed exclusion of security if there were subsequent changes to 'the overall package'.

Therefore, the post-RRO 2003 procedure does not require any of the terms of the intended tenancy to have been agreed, although one would have thought that it must be implicit that the tenancy was one to which the Act would otherwise give protection, e.g. because it was to be for a fixed term of more than six months, which would result in the assumption of an absolute minimum as far as the terms are concerned.

Therefore, a situation could arise under RRO 2003 whereby the tenant (or its agent) has negotiated the terms on which it would take a tenancy and at that point the landlord (or its agent) serves the tenant with a schedule 1 notice. The landlord's solicitor might then submit a draft tenancy agreement that, perhaps, seeks to impose terms more onerous than the tenant was willing to accept. While it may be stating the obvious, the tenant must make sure that it does not enter into the tenancy (having first made the appropriate declaration) unless it is satisfied that it wishes it to be excluded from the protection. It would not assist the tenant that the notice was served on it following the negotiation of different terms to those later proposed by the landlord – the (renegotiated) tenancy would still be excluded from the Act.

Alternatively, if the landlord seeks to renegotiate terms the tenant should ensure that the reference in the tenancy itself to the exclusion of the Act is removed, to avoid satisfying one of the schedule 2 requirements. One would hope that such a scenario would not arise, but it is quite possible, particularly in the case of unrepresented tenants.

Indeed, there is no mention in the schedule 1 notice of the property for which the tenancy is to be excluded from the protection of the Act: if the tenant had negotiated to take, say, one unit in a shopping centre but then took another one, provided schedule 2 was otherwise satisfied, the tenancy would still be excluded.

It has been postulated that if the negotiated terms of the proposed tenancy change significantly after the schedule 1 notice has been served, or there is a significant delay between the service of the notice and the tenant entering into the tenancy or becoming contractually bound to do so, a new notice might be served. While that might be a sensible precaution, it could be unnecessary and cause unwanted confusion.

4.5.4 Options to renew

Tenancies sometimes contain options in favour of the tenant to have a new tenancy. If the new tenancy is to be contracted out, how will the landlord know when to comply with the schedule 2 procedure until the tenant serves an option notice – by which time it is too late? Such situations may need to be catered for when drafting these clauses. However, it may be that schedule 2 will have to be complied with, in respect of the possible new tenancy, before the original tenancy is entered into or before the tenant becomes contractually bound to do so.

4.6 TRANSITION

Under article 29(2)(a)(ii) of RRO 2003, an agreement to exclude the Act entered into before 1 June 2004 will remain valid.

Where someone has entered into an agreement before 1 June 2004 by which there is agreement that the parties will obtain a court order under section 38(4), that agreement will remain effective after 1 June 2004 and the court will retain jurisdiction to make the sort of order required under the pre-RRO 2003 procedure.

Moreover, there are many thousands of existing tenancies requiring that, in the case of sub-tenancies, section 38(4) be satisfied. By virtue of article 29(3) of RRO 2003, such provisions are to be construed after 1 June 2004 as if the reference were to the procedure required by section 38A.

4.7 AGREEMENTS TO SURRENDER AND CONTRACTING OUT

The procedures, both pre- and post-RRO 2003, concerning agreements to surrender tenancies protected by the Act were, and are, very similar to those that apply to agreements for new tenancies to be excluded from the protection of the Act. Consequently, only some further minor matters that specifically apply to agreements to surrender post-RRO 2003 will be considered. It should be remembered, however, that many of the potential problems with the new procedure for excluded new tenancies are also of concern to the new procedure for contracted-out agreements to surrender a protected tenancy.

4.7.1 Post-RRO 2003

Article 22(1) of RRO 2003 introduces a new section 38A into the Act, and by virtue of the new section 38A(4) the relevant schedules relating to agreements to surrender are schedules 3 and 4 of RRO 2003. There is a prescribed notice (see schedule 3) and there are requirements for a valid agreement to surrender, including an appropriate declaration (schedule 4). The declaration, as for new tenancies, may be a simple declaration or a statutory declaration depending on the timing of the service of the schedule 3 notice.

The requirements under schedule 4 are largely similar to those under schedule 2. However, whereas in the case of an excluded tenancy, the agreement to exclude the protection of the Act (or a reference to it) must be contained in or endorsed on the instrument creating the tenancy, there is no similar requirement in the case of an agreement to surrender.

For the avoidance of doubt, it should be noted that RRO 2003 does not affect the existing rights of a landlord and tenant to agree to an immediate surrender of property which is protected by the Act.

The new procedure may create a problem with surrender-back clauses sometimes found in leases. On the face of it, since that might represent an agreement to surrender, one would assume that the schedule and procedure would have to be satisfied before the tenancy was entered into or the tenant became contractually bound to do so. That seems an odd result and one will have to wait to see how the issue is dealt with in practice.

4.7.2 Transition

Under article 29(2)(a)(i) of RRO 2003, an agreement to surrender a protected tenancy which is or was made before 1 June 2004 will remain valid.

5 MISCELLANEOUS MATTERS

5.1 THE TERMS OF THE NEW TENANCY

The RRO 2003 has made limited changes to the statutory approach to determining the terms of the new tenancy, i.e.

- the property to be comprised in the new tenancy (section 32);
- the duration of the new tenancy (section 33);
- the rent to be paid under the new tenancy (section 34); and
- the other terms of the new tenancy (section 35).

There are some small changes to sections 34 and 35 which arise from the amendments concerning companies (see section 5.2 below and Appendix B).

However, RRO 2003 has made one important change to section 33.

5.1.1 Pre-RRO 2003

Under section 33, the maximum duration of the new tenancy that the court could order was 14 years. The parties could, of course, agree a longer (or shorter) term.

5.1.2 Post-RRO 2003

Recognising that, in practice, tenancies were being granted with rent review patterns often of three or five years, and that their duration was sometimes quite short but sometimes for as much as 15 years, the Government concluded that section 33 should be amended to allow the court to order a new tenancy for a duration of up to 15 years.

As before, it is open to the parties to agree a longer (or shorter) period.

5.2 COMPANIES

Remembering that the Act gives protection to tenants who are in occupation of the property for the purposes of a business carried on at the property, problems can arise under the Act where there is a blurring of the distinction between the roles of an individual and a company. For example, this could be seen where the tenant is an individual but his company is carrying on the business; or where the landlord is an individual who wishes to object to the tenant having a new tenancy on the ground of redevelopment (ground (f) of section 30(1)), but his company will be carrying out the relevant works.

5.2.1 Pre-RRO 2003

Where the tenant was an individual and operated the business carried on at the property through a company controlled by him, then in practice the protection of the Act would not arise (although there might be scope for arguing that there was, in effect, a trust in operation by virtue of which section 41 would apply: see Appendix B).

Similarly, where the position is reversed and the tenant was a company, and the controlling shareholder was in occupation carrying on a business at the property, the Act might not apply.

The position was slightly different if the tenant was a company and the company in occupation carrying on a business was a subsidiary of it, or the opposite was the case, or if both of them were subsidiaries of a third company. In any of these cases, under section 42(1), the two were treated as the same, and the protection of the Act applied.

In addition, and as suggested above, there could be similar problems for landlords where there was a difference between the legal entity of the landlord and the person or company that was to carry out the works necessary to satisfy ground (f) or to occupy the property under ground (g), unless the 'subsidiary' point described above applied (it related to landlords too).

5.2.2 Post-RRO 2003

Some of these problems have, to a great extent, been resolved by RRO 2003.

To section 23 (which establishes the core protection of the Act) are added subsections (1A) and (1B). By virtue of these additions, the occupation or carrying on of a business at the property by a company in which the tenant has a controlling interest, or if the tenant is a company, by a person with a controlling interest in the company, will in either case amount to qualifying occupation for the purposes of the Act.

The purpose of the amendments is that the 'entities' of the company and the individual with a controlling interest are to be seen as synonymous. The concept of 'controlling interest' is carried through to section 30(1)(g) (the 'owner-occupier' ground of objection on which the landlord can rely), section 34 (under which the rent payable under the new tenancy is determined, at least in relation to the part that concerns licensed premises), section 42 (groups of companies) and section 46 (the interpretation section and the definition of 'company') – see Appendix B.

The amendments do not, however, change the position in relation to, say, the redevelopment ground of opposition (section 30(1)(f)) nor does it assist limited liability partnerships, although in the latter case section 41A may continue to apply.

5.3 SEVERED REVERSIONS

The Act does not readily cater for the situation where the tenant occupies a property under one tenancy but the reversionary interest in the tenancy is owned by two separate landlords. Such property interests are known as divided or severed reversions.

For example, a tenant of retail premises may have, perhaps through a sub-letting, taken on a tenancy of two adjoining shops from a landlord which itself had separate tenancies from each of the freehold owners of each of the shop units.

5.3.1 Pre-RRO 2003

The courts have in a number of cases considered this problem. It seems that unless the landlords of the different properties held by the tenant under one tenancy were to cooperate by giving a single notice in their joint names in respect of the whole of the property, there was every possibility that the tenancy could not be terminated under the Act until the reversionary interests fell into single ownership. It would not be possible for the separate landlords to give separate notices in respect of the part of the property that each owned, because that would not be sufficient to terminate the tenancy: such notices would each be purporting to terminate part of the tenancy, which is impossible under the Act.

While the courts, through the idea of landlord cooperation, had begun to a limited extent to develop a way of dealing with the problems of severed reversions, they did not resolve a number of related problems. For example, there is no guidance about the manner in which the required court application would be dealt with, nor is there any guidance about who will grant (by court order or otherwise) the new tenancy.

5.3.2 Post-RRO 2003

The problem concerning severed reversions arises from, among other things, the definition of 'landlord' under section 44 of the Act.

The Government considered that the issue was worth resolving, at least in part, and to that end section 44 has been amended with the introduction of subsection (1A).

Under section 44(1A), the Act now makes it clear that the separate landlords can, collectively, represent the 'landlord' under the Act, and therefore jointly give a single notice in respect of the entirety of the property comprised in the tenancy. In other words, the amendment confirms the position that has been developed by case law. But that is not necessarily a resolution to the problem. The idea that the landlords should act 'collectively' must still mean that there can only be one section 25 notice covering all the properties.

As mentioned below in para. 6.1, the Act has also been amended to deal with the claim for compensation in circumstances where there is a severed reversion.

Section 35(1) of the Act has been amended. Now, when a court considers the terms of a new tenancy (other than duration and the amount of rent), it can consider apportionment of rent under the new lease where there is a severed reversion.

Notwithstanding these changes, other problems that previously existed in relation to the workings of the Act and severed reversions have not been resolved by RRO 2003.

The changes do not allow the separate landlords under a single lease to serve individual notices, nor, therefore, for the tenant to serve separate notices on each of the landlords of the severed reversion. This seems odd because the ODPM explained in its explanatory note, lodged when the proposals were first submitted to Parliament on 22 July 2002, that:

> landlords in this position would need to take concerted action, but with separate notices relating to individual parts of the premises. Similarly, a tenant would need to serve separate notices on all the landlords, taking proceedings against all of them either separately or naming them all as parties in a single set of proceedings.

Notwithstanding the amendment to section 44(1), while the intention may have been reasonably clear, it is not apparent that the intended result has been achieved.

Moreover, there is no resolution of the problem as to by whom the new tenancy is to be granted. On the face of it there would have to be a single tenancy of the whole of the property comprised in the old tenancy with the separate landlords having to grant it together. The amendments to section 35(1), allowing the court to order apportionment of rent where there is a severed reversion, would seem to support this view. If so, that was the position pre-RRO 2003.

Nor is there any guidance about the conduct of court applications or the situation where one or more of the separate landlords wishes to object to the tenant having a new tenancy and the other does not.

5.4 CONSEQUENTIAL AMENDMENTS

There are a number of other relatively minor matters addressed by RRO 2003. They are mainly consequential on the more significant changes brought about by RRO 2003.

For example, RRO 2003 makes some consequential changes to sections 31 and 31A (which deals with the landlord's opposition to a new tenancy) and 34 (which deals with the rent to be paid under the new tenancy). Schedule 5 of the RRO also sets out some consequential amendments and schedule 6 sets out some consequential repeals. See Appendix B for the most convenient way of identifying them and the effect they have on the Act.

6 COMPENSATION

6.1 STATUTORY COMPENSATION

6.1.1 Pre-RRO 2003

The Act seeks to protect the position of the tenant to allow it to continue in occupation of the property until such time as its procedures are operated. Since, notwithstanding that protection, the Act allows the landlord to resist the tenant having a new tenancy under the seven grounds of opposition in section 30(1), it further allows, at section 37, for the payment to the tenant of compensation if some of those grounds (grounds (e), (f) and/or (g)) are made out.

That compensation, as will be well known, is calculated by reference to the rateable value of the property. There are mechanisms for dealing with problems such as establishing the rateable value, or the property to which it relates, or where the rateable value has to be apportioned.

In some cases, the compensation will be twice the rateable value and, in all others once, depending upon the tenant's length of occupation of the property (section 37(3)).

For the full provisions, see Appendix B.

6.1.2 Post-RRO 2003

Since the purpose of this work is primarily to consider the reforms, and since the majority of the pre-RRO 2003 section 37 remains unaltered, it is not intended to review the detail of the compensation provisions, merely those elements that have been changed or introduced.

6.1.3 When compensation will be payable

The old section 37(1) is substituted by a new one, with the addition of new subsections 37(1A), (1B) and (1C).

The purpose is to clarify the circumstances in which compensation will be payable, with particular reference to the landlord's new right to issue termination proceedings.

Compensation will thus be payable:

(a) where the tenant's renewal application is declined by the court because the landlord has made out one or more of grounds (e), (f) or (g) of section 30(1) (now referred to as the 'compensation grounds') (and not any of the other section 30(1) grounds); or
(b) where the landlord has commenced termination proceedings under section 29(2) and any of the compensation grounds is made out (but not any of the others); or
(c) where the landlord has indicated its opposition (on any of the compensation grounds only) to the tenant having a new tenancy in its section 25 notice or counternotice to the tenant's section 26 request, and either no application has been made under section 24(1) or 29(2), or, if it has been made, it has been withdrawn.

This would appear to have created a, perhaps theoretical, trap for tenants. As explained above (under para. 2.3.2), notwithstanding that the scheme of RRO 2003 seems to assume otherwise, there would appear to be a procedural possibility of the landlord commencing renewal proceedings even though it objects to the tenant having a new tenancy. This situation does not appear to be provided for by section 37(1A), (1B), or (1C) (which set out the three cases in which compensation would be payable, as summarised above), which could mean that the landlord could tactically contrive to somehow deprive the tenant of compensation. The first compensation case depends on the tenant having commenced renewal proceedings under section 24(1); case (b) depends on the landlord having commenced termination proceedings under section 29(2); and case (c) depends on the landlord objecting to renewal in the section 25 notice and counternotice to the tenant's section 26 request, where either no application has been made under section 24(1) or 29(2) – or if it has been made, it has been withdrawn. In the example, however, there would have been commencement of renewal proceedings under section 24(1) but they would have been commenced by the landlord. In practice, however, one can imagine that the court might decide that in fact the landlord had commenced termination proceedings. Indeed, given the procedural requirements of Part 56 CPR (see Chapter 7), it would be difficult for the landlord to commence renewal proceedings where it opposed a new tenancy (but see section 7.6.3 below).

6.1.4 Distinction between whole and part

Section 37(2) is amended and section 37(3A) is introduced to distinguish between the entitlement to compensation relating to the whole of the property comprised in the tenancy and that relating to part.

In the former case, the entitlement is unchanged and will amount to the rateable value or twice the rateable value if the relevant conditions (in subsection 37(3)) are satisfied.

In the latter case, the compensation will be the aggregate of the compensation sums calculated separately in respect of each part. This means that, for example, if the entitlement to the higher rate of compensation would be satisfied by the tenant in relation to one part of the property and not in relation to another part, one would work out the amounts separately for each part and then add them together to establish the total compensation.

6.1.5 Where a reversion is split

Section 37(3B) is introduced to address the situation where the reversion is split and to make it clear that, where the tenant is entitled to compensation, the 'claims' should be determined separately and made only against the relevant landlord of each separate part (see section 5.3 above).

6.2 COMPENSATION FOR MISREPRESENTATION

The scheme of the Act is such that, at a number of points, it depends on assertions, sometimes of intention, by the landlord. The landlord may assert that it would pursue a particular course of action (such as to redevelop the property), and then not pursue that action. In some of those cases, this could give rise to the possibility of the tenant seeking compensation for misrepresentation.

6.2.1 Pre-RRO 2003

Under old section 55 of the Act, where the court refused to make an order for a new tenancy, and it subsequently became apparent that it declined to do so or had been induced not to do so as a result of misrepresentation or concealment of material facts, the court could make an order for damages to compensate the tenant for the loss and damage suffered. Presumably the misrepresentation or concealment must have been by or on behalf of the landlord for this entitlement to arise.

Such a situation was most likely to arise where, for example, the landlord asserted that it wanted to carry out works under ground (f) of section 30(1) or wanted to occupy the property itself under ground (g) of section 30(1) and then subsequently failed to do so.

However, there would be no misrepresentation if the landlord failed to implement such proposals as a result of an honest change of mind. It is to guard against such an outcome that the landlord's proposals and intention are made the subject of such stringent scrutiny at the time the court considers whether or not to grant the tenant a new tenancy.

Nor would a right to compensation arise for a tenant where a landlord had asserted by way of misrepresentation or concealment an intended course of action, the result of which was that the tenant was persuaded to give up possession of the property without the need for a court hearing.

It should be noted that section 55 only applied where the court had refused to grant a new tenancy.

6.2.2 Post-RRO 2003

Section 55 is repealed.

The Government considered that while it should preserve the entitlement of the tenant (or by then, former tenant) to seek damages for misrepresentation, the pre-RRO 2003 rules were too limited. Thus, RRO 2003 introduces section 37A.

Under section 37A, the court may order damages against a landlord for misrepresentation (or concealment) in the following circumstances:

- where such misrepresentation induces the court to make an order for the termination of the tenancy but the court does not make an order for a new tenancy; or
- where such misrepresentation induces the court to refuse to order a new tenancy; or
- where such misrepresentation has induced the tenant to quit the property having made but withdrawn a renewal application; or
- where such misrepresentation has induced the tenant to quit the property without having made a renewal application at all.

Under the transitional arrangements in article 29(5) the amended right to compensation does not apply where the tenant quits the holding before 1 June 2004.

7 CHANGES TO THE CIVIL PROCEDURE RULES 1998

7.1 INTRODUCTION

While the purpose of this book is primarily to consider the changes to the substantive legislation and the procedures under the Act, it is appropriate to consider the impact of those changes on the Civil Procedure Rules 1998, SI 1998/3132 L17 (the CPR).

While RRO 2003 could mean that there are fewer non-opposed tenancy renewals that result in the commencement of court proceedings, nonetheless the procedure of the Act still requires, in the absence of agreement, the issue of renewal proceedings if the tenant is to preserve its entitlement to a new tenancy.

Although there are many reported cases concerning the Act, bearing in mind that there are many thousand sets of protective proceedings commenced each year, even with the introduction of the CPR in April 1999 the vast majority of them are still never actively pursued because, as should be expected, the parties negotiate and conclude the terms of the new tenancy.

Of course, there are exceptions. No survey of the nature of recently reported cases concerning the Act has been carried out, but the perception is that they mainly concern the entitlement of the tenant to a new tenancy, whether because the landlord is actively opposing renewal under one or more of the statutory grounds, or because the tenant is alleged not to have satisfied the conditions entitling it to a new tenancy, e.g. because it has failed to commence proceedings in time or it does not in fact occupy the property for the purposes of a business carried on there. Inevitably, there will still be such cases post-RRO 2003. Indeed, bearing in mind some of the points made above, there is potentially increased scope for dispute in a number of areas.

Therefore the CPR, being the rules by which civil litigation is conducted, will still be relevant to the workings of the Act.

7.2 PRE-RRO 2003

Although there may still be some live proceedings under the Act that were commenced prior to 15 October 2001, since that date renewal cases under the Act have been conducted under Part 56 CPR, and the majority of claims are subject to its provisions. Consequently, only the outline of the Part 56 procedure will be considered here.

They will remain relevant by virtue of the transitional provisions of RRO 2003. Under article 29(1), the old provisions of the Act will apply where the section 25 notice or section 26 request has been served before 1 June 2004. Moreover, although the court-based contracting-out provisions of the CPR will not be considered here, by virtue of article 29(4) of RRO 2003, the court will retain jurisdiction to deal with contracting-out orders after 1 June 2004, if the agreement under which there is provision to seek such an order was entered into before 1 June 2004.

Although there is an ability to commence such proceedings in the High Court, Part 56 CPR 'drives' tenants to use the County Court. The tenant is required to use the claim form required under Part 8 CPR, the Part 8 procedure being modified by Part 56 as summarised below.

The tenant's application has to contain information as required by the Practice Direction to Part 56 CPR, e.g. details about the tenancy, its termination, and the tenant's proposals for the new tenancy.

On the service of the application (which, unlike other types of claim under the CPR, must be within two months of issue), the landlord has a choice: it can either file and serve an acknowledgement of service form which must also contain certain specified information, or it can ask the court to suspended the proceedings for a period of three months. The court will automatically grant such a stay. Nevertheless, the CPR states that the purpose of the stay 'is to facilitate negotiation of a new lease'. Therefore, Part 56 also gives to either party the right to notify the court that the stay should be lifted, a right which, presumably, will be exercised where one party or the other considers negotiation is not or will not be productive.

Once the stay comes to an end (whether by the passing of time or because one of the parties has asked the court to lift it), the landlord must then file and serve a form of acknowledgement of service which, like the claim form issued by the tenant, must contain certain information.

The acknowledgement of service can include, if the landlord wishes to make it, an application for interim rent under the old section 24A of the Act (substituted in RRO 2003 by new sections 24A–24D: see above).

Under the pre-RRO 2003 regime (which will continue to apply where the notice or request was given before 1 June 2004), it is important to remember that the landlord should decide whether it wishes to make an application for interim rent when considering whether to ask for the automatic stay. If the stay is sought, then the landlord could not, in the tenant's renewal proceedings, apply for an interim rent without asking the court to lift it. This may not be in the interests of the parties because it could then result in an increase in litigation costs before it is clear that the parties are not otherwise going to be able to agree the terms for the new lease. If the landlord wishes to apply for interim rent without lifting the stay, it would have to commence its own proceedings for an interim rent and then, often, arrange for those proceedings to be stayed so that they 'tied in' with the tenant's claim.

The point is that the landlord's entitlement to an interim rent only arises on the making of the application, and would run from either the date specified in the section 25 notice or section 26 request, or the making of the landlord's application, whichever was later. This problem has been largely resolved by RRO 2003 (see section 3.4 above), although in practice it is, or was, only an issue where the date specified in the notice or request was the earliest possible, i.e. it was a six-months notice or request rather than a 12-months one.

On the acknowledgement of service, the tenant is then, within 14 days, required to file and serve its evidence in respect of the claim and, within 14 days after that, the landlord is required to do the same.

The requirement to produce evidence at that stage has resulted in some confusion, with parties not being clear as to what the court expected to see. This is because, notwithstanding one of the CPR objectives being to bring uniformity of procedure to all the courts in England and Wales, differences of application of Part 56 developed in different courts. Most practitioners contended that it is not appropriate or necessary at that early stage for expert evidence to be produced, but some courts require it. Indeed, while many consider that the evidence, should in practice it be given, would take the form of witness statements, there is nothing in Part 56, pre-RRO 2003, confirming that.

On the filing of the evidence (whatever it was), the court is then required to consider the case and decide how it should proceed. For example, if the landlord objected to the tenant having a new tenancy of the property, then the question as to whether the landlord satisfied the relevant ground(s) of objection would generally be tried as a preliminary issue. This is clearly so that the costs of preparing a case for a trial of the terms of the new lease would be avoided (since it would be unnecessary if the tenant was not in fact going to have a new tenancy). Alternatively, if the new tenancy were in dispute, the court might make an order directing the parties to take steps to reduce the issues in dispute (for example, by exchanging drafts and amended drafts of the proposed new lease), and to adduce the expert evidence of a rental valuation surveyor.

In an attempt to ensure that claims under the Act were conducted in, what is thought to be, an appropriate and consistent manner, the Property Litigation Association and the Central London County Court developed a Post-Action Protocol for Business Tenancy Renewal cases (post-action, because it was inevitable, given the Act's procedures, that litigation would have to be commenced). The protocol offers guidance as to the conduct of such cases and sets a series of directions for the conduct of both unopposed and opposed renewals. That guidance is likely still to be relevant to the post-RRO 2003 changes to the CPR and is available at **www.pla.org.uk**.

7.3 OUTLINE OF POST-RRO 2003

With the introduction of two new types of procedure (the landlord's renewal proceedings and the landlord's termination proceedings), it was inevitable that Part 56 CPR had to be modified.

Since changes were to be made in any event, it was also appropriate that there be a more general review of Part 56 CPR. But it must be remembered that the pre-RRO 2003 procedure (including as to the automatic stay and evidence) will remain applicable to pre-RRO 2003 cases.

The basic procedure will remain the same, but introduced into Part 56 are the information categories that need to be included in the different types of application and the acknowledgements of service or defence (see below). That information is largely a modified version of that already required.

Importantly, with the parties having potentially far more time to commence proceedings, it no is longer necessary for there to be an entitlement to an automatic three-month stay. It is, of course, the case that the court retains the power under the general provisions of the CPR to grant a stay if it considers it appropriate.

Also, as will be seen below, the requirement to file and serve evidence in the manner required by Part 56 CPR, pre-RRO 2003, has been modified, in some cases leaving the court (and the parties) a free hand to decide what evidence is required and by when it is to be served.

The requirements of the new elements of Part 56 now follow.

7.4 PRIORITY OF CLAIMS

As a result of both the tenant and the landlord being able to commence renewal proceedings and the landlord being able to commence termination proceedings, with the date of service of such claims being important to the procedural schemes created by RRO 2003, the revisions to Part 56 have to address the possible multiplicity of proceedings.

If more than one claim under section 24(1) or section 29(2) has been issued, then the procedure is as follows:

1. Once an application under section 24(1) has been served on a defendant, no further application under either section 24(1) or section 29(2) may be served by that defendant without the permission of the court.

2. If more than one application under section 24(1) is served on the same day, the landlord's application will be stayed until the court orders otherwise.
3. If an application under section 24(1) and an application under section 29(2) are both served on the same day, the tenant's application (which could only be the application made under section 24(1)) will be stayed until the court orders otherwise.
4. If a tenant is served with a section 29(2) application which was issued at a time when an application under section 24(1) had already been made, the service of the section 29(2) application will be deemed to be notice under Part 7.7 CPR requiring the service or discontinuance of the section 24(1) application within a period of 14 days from the service of the section 29(2) application. The effect of this is that the section 24(1) application will not be allowed to 'sit on the shelf', and because it will then have to be served or discontinued, it seems likely although not entirely clear (because it would inevitably not be served on the same day as the landlord's section 29(2) application) that, in default, the section 24(1) application would then have to be stayed by the court. There is a procedural possibility of this situation arising, even though under section 29(3), the landlord may not make an application under section 29(2) if either it or the tenant has already made an application under section 24(1). The procedure is required because RRO 2003 and the amended Act do not say 'served' at section 29(3), and it would be fairly difficult if not impossible for the landlord to discover, independently of the tenant, whether or not the tenant has in fact already made an application under section 24(1) (obviously, the landlord will know whether or not it has already made an application under section 24(1)).

7.5 TYPE OF PROCEDURAL CLAIM

Under the CPR, there are two main types of claim procedure: that under Part 7 and that under Part 8. The former is intended to deal with most types of claim (e.g. debt claims or injunctions, etc.) while Part 8 claims are intended to deal with disputes which are unlikely to involve disputed evidence (e.g. claims about the interpretation of a contract).

As mentioned above, the Part 56 regime pre-RRO 2003 requires the tenant to issue its renewal proceedings using the Part 8 procedure, as modified by Part 56.

The Part 56 regime post-RRO 2003 has to address the new types of claim, but it also distinguishes between cases where the landlord opposes renewal under one or more of the grounds of opposition under section 30(1) or for some other reason (an 'opposed claim') and those where the landlord does not object to the tenant having a new tenancy (although there may be a dispute about the terms of the new tenancy (an 'unopposed claim').

By virtue of the provisions of the revised Part 56.3, where there is an unopposed claim the Part 8 procedure is to be applied, and where there is an opposed claim the Part 7 procedure is to be adopted. In both cases, the procedure is then modified by Part 56 and its Practice Direction (PD).

It seems odd to have different types of claim (Part 8 for unopposed claims and Part 7 for opposed claims) since the basic contents of the claim form in each case will be the same (see below), and in both cases the usual Part 7 or Part 8 procedure is disapplied by Part 56.

One would have thought that consistency is required. The more options there are for commencing the claim, the more likely it is that mistakes will be made. While it is possible that could be corrected, it will involve wasted time on the part of someone (whether it be the practitioner or the court or the parties).

One cannot see why one would not have a Part 8 claim in both cases followed by a modified acknowledgement of service form with which practitioners have already become familiar. As will be seen below, where there is an opposed claim, an acknowledgement of service form and then a defence is required (a defence being a requirement of Part 7 but not Part 8 CPR). It is difficult to see that anything is added to the process by having a defence, since the procedural form for acknowledging service of Part 8 proceedings carries with it a statement of truth which is one of the most important features of the CPR. In signing a statement of truth, the signatory is asserting that he or she has an honest belief in the veracity of the factual statements made in the document of which the statement of truth forms part. Although perhaps less of an issue in relation to proceedings under the Act, the requirement to sign a statement of truth has generally led to a reduction in some rather extreme statements in the statements of case which are the documents in which the dispute is described. There is no obvious difference between a defence and an acknowledgement of service in business tenancy cases under the Act because Part 56 specifies what matters are to be addressed by either an acknowedgement of service or a defence.

Further, although a section 25 notice or a landlord's counternotice to a section 26 request might state that the landlord will oppose the tenant having a new tenancy under the Act, until it has said so again in the acknowledgement of service form (the present requirement), there is no certainty (procedurally) that the landlord will object for the purposes of the court proceedings. The landlord could have legitimately changed its mind or the landlord could have changed and the new landlord might not want to oppose.

7.6 COMMENCING THE CLAIM

The scheme of the revisions to Part 56 and its PD is to set out the matters that must be addressed when any of the three types of claim are made under Part II of the Act (tenant and landlord renewals and landlord termination proceedings) and then to set out the matters to be dealt with in respect of the different types of claim.

The requirements for the claim form are given in paras. 7.6.1 to 7.6.3.

7.6.1 All cases

The claim form will either be N208 (the Part 8 claim form) or N1 (the Part 7 claim form). While the landlord will know which to use if it is initiating the renewal or termination proceedings (because, say, it will know whether or not it is pursuing an objection under the grounds in section 30(1)), the tenant will have to make an assumption about whether the proceedings are going to be an unopposed claim or an opposed claim based on either the landlord's section 25 notice or the landlord's counternotice to the tenant's section 26 request (it may turn out, depending on how the landlord responds to the claim once served, that an inappropriate procedure is being used by the tenant, effectively through no fault of its own). One would assume the revisions to Part 56 and its PD intend that, if the landlord has indicated at the notice or counternotice stage that it will object, the tenant will use the Part 7 procedure. But the possibility for confusion arises because, while there is reference in the revised Part 56 and its PD to 'grounds of opposition', that phrase is not used in the passages which explain what procedure is to be used.

In all cases the following must be addressed:

- a description of the property to which the claim relates;
- the particulars of the current tenancy (including the date, parties and duration), the current rent (if not the original rent) and the date and method of termination;
- every notice or request made under sections 25 and 26;
- the expiry of the 'statutory period' or any agreed period (see above under Chapter 2).

As under the Part 56 provisions pre-RRO 2003, the claim form in any of the different types of case must be served within two months of issue.

7.6.2 Tenant's claim for renewal

In addition to the matters required in all cases, the following must be addressed where the tenant commences renewal proceedings under section 24(1):

- the nature of the business carried on at the property;
- whether the tenant relies on section 23(1A) (see para. 5.2 above), section 41 (which relates to trusts and occupation of the property by beneficiaries of trusts), or section 42 (which relates to occupation by group companies), and if so, on what basis;
- whether the tenant relies on section 31A (by which the tenant can try and obtain a new tenancy by making certain 'concessions', even though the landlord would otherwise satisfy the court about its intended redevelopment under section 30(1)(f) and successfully oppose the tenant having a new tenancy), and if so, on what basis;
- whether any, and if so, what part of the property comprised in the tenancy is occupied neither by the tenant nor by a person employed by it for the purpose of a business;

- the tenant's proposals for the new tenancy;
- the name and address of anyone known to the tenant who has an interest in the reversion in the property (whether immediate or in not more than 15 years) on the termination of the tenant's current tenancy, and who is likely to be affected by the grant of a new tenancy; or if the tenant does not so know of anyone, the tenant must give the name and address of any person having a freehold interest in the property (the claim form must be served on anyone named under these procedural provisions).

7.6.3 Landlord's claim for renewal

In addition to the matters required in all cases, the following must be addressed where the landlord commences renewal proceedings under section 24(1):

- the landlord's proposals for the new tenancy;
- whether the landlord is aware that the tenancy is one to which section 32(2) applies (where the tenant does not occupy all of the property comprised in the tenancy), and if so, whether the landlord requires any new tenancy to be of the whole of the property comprised in the current tenancy, or just of the holding (in essence, the part actually occupied by the tenant);
- the name and address of anyone known to the landlord who has an interest in the reversion in the property (whether immediate or in not more than 15 years) on the termination of the tenant's current tenancy and who is likely to be affected by the grant of a new tenancy; or if the landlord does not so know of anyone, the landlord must give the name and address of any person having a freehold interest in the property (the claim form must be served on anyone named under these procedural provisions).

It should be noted that, while it may be likely that a landlord opposing a new tenancy will commence termination proceedings, the landlord is not precluded from commencing renewal proceedings and may still oppose. If so, one would have expected there to a be a requirement as in the landlord's termination proceedings that, if it is objecting to the tenant having a new tenancy, it specify its grounds of opposition and the details of those grounds (see para. 7.6.4). Further, while the concept of the landlord commencing renewal proceedings yet opposing the grant of a new tenancy has been considered to be theoretical (see section 6.1.3 above), it may be that due to the effect of the revisions to Part 56 CPR, the definition (in rule 56.3(2)) of an opposed claim, and the nature of the tenant's response to an opposed claim being limited to a landlord's termination proceedings (see section 7.7.4 below), where the landlord does oppose for reasons other than those set out in section 30(1) of the Act, it will be obliged to commence renewal proceedings (which is not precluded by rule 56.3(2)(c)(i) CPR).

7.6.4 Landlord's termination proceedings

In addition to the matters required in all cases, the following must be addressed where the landlord commences termination proceedings under section 29(2):

- the landlord's grounds of opposition (it should be noted that these are only the grounds of opposition set out in section 30(1) of the Act. The provisions do not cover the situation where the landlord asserts that the tenant is not entitled to a new tenancy at all, e.g. because it is or was not in occupation, either at all or for the purposes of a business, although such a situation is contemplated by the definition of 'grounds of opposition' at paragraph 3.1(3) of the practice direction to Part 56 CPR);
- the details of those grounds of opposition (one can only assume that this means 'spelling out' the grounds relied on as they appear in section 30(1));
- the terms of the new tenancy proposed by the landlord if the termination claim fails.

7.7 RESPONDING TO THE CLAIM

7.7.1 Unopposed claims where the claimant is the tenant

An acknowledgement of service form must be given, using the procedural form (CPR Form N210) that relates to a Part 8 claim. As was noted above in section 7.5, it is possible that the tenant could commence the renewal claim using either the Part 8 procedure (which would be appropriate if it is an unopposed claim) or the Part 7 procedure (which would be appropriate if it is an opposed claim). In theory, the landlord cannot change the type of procedure; so if the tenant has used the Part 7 procedure believing the claim to be opposed, but the landlord, having at the notice or counternotice stage previously indicated that it would oppose the tenant having a new tenancy, has in fact changed its mind, the landlord must still use the Part 7 acknowledgement of service form, form N9 (see section 7.7.3 below). It is possible that the landlord must then continue using the procedure that relates to the response required in opposed claims, even though it does not oppose. As seen below in para. 7.7.3, it will then require the service of a defence.

If the tenant has used the Part 8 procedure, because the landlord indicated at the notice or counternotice stage that it would not oppose the tenant having a new tenancy (and it is prevented from later opposing if it had not done so at the notice or counternotice stage, although a decision to 'oppose' after serving the notice or counternotice could have an impact on the length of new tenancy the tenant obtains), then the landlord must use form N210 to acknowledge service.

Using the correct procedural form, the matters to be addressed (by modifying the acknowledgement of service form) are as follows:

- whether, if a new tenancy is granted, the landlord objects to any of the terms proposed by the tenant and if so, the terms to which there is objection and the landlord's proposals insofar as they differ from those proposed by the tenant;
- whether the landlord is a tenant under a lease having less than 15 years unexpired at the date of termination of the tenant's current tenancy, and if so, the name and address of any person who, to the knowledge of the landlord, has an interest in the reversion in the property expectant (whether immediately or in not more than 15 years from that date) on the termination of the landlord's tenancy;
- the name and address of any person having an interest in the property who is likely to be affected by the grant of a new tenancy (this requirement is not limited to such persons of whom the landlord has knowledge, but it is submitted that must be the implication);
- whether the tenant's current tenancy is one to which section 32(2) applies (where the tenant does not occupy all of the property comprised in the tenancy), and if so, whether the landlord requires any new tenancy to be of the whole of the property comprised in the current tenancy.

The acknowledgement of service must be filed within 14 days of the service of the claim form, as calculated under the CPR.

7.7.2 Unopposed claims where the claimant is the landlord

The matters to be addressed (by modifying the acknowledgement of service form N210) are as follows:

- the nature of the business carried on at the property;
- whether the tenant relies on section 23(1A) (see para. 5.2 above), section 41 (which relates to trusts and occupation of the property by beneficiaries of trusts), or section 42 (which relates to occupation by group companies), and if so, on what basis;
- whether any, and if so what part of the property comprised in the tenancy is occupied neither by the tenant nor by a person employed by it for the purpose of a business;
- the name and address of anyone known to the tenant who has an interest in the reversion in the property (whether immediate or in not more than 15 years) on the termination of the tenant's current tenancy and who is likely to be affected by the grant of a new tenancy; or if the tenant does not so know of anyone, the tenant must give the name and address of any person having a freehold interest in the property;
- whether, if a new tenancy is granted, the tenant objects to any of the terms proposed by the landlord, and if so, to which terms there is objection, and the tenant's proposals insofar as they differ from those proposed by the landlord.

The acknowledgement of service must be filed within 14 days of the service of the claim form as calculated under the CPR.

7.7.3 Opposed claims where the claimant is the tenant

There is a two-stage process in the case of opposed claims: firstly, there is a requirement to file an acknowledgement of service form; and secondly, there is a requirement to put in a defence.

There is an assumption that in cases where the claim is opposed as envisaged by the revisions to Part 56 and its PD, the tenant will commence the claim using the Part 7 procedure. For the reasons explained above in section 7.5, the tenant may believe that the claim is not opposed and commence the claim using the Part 8 procedure.

Alternatively, the landlord may have indicated at the notice or counternotice stage that it would object to the tenant having a new tenancy, but it may subsequently have legitimately changed its mind. Notwithstanding this change of mind resulting in the claim no longer being opposed, it would seem that the procedure to be applied will continue to be that for opposed claims where the claimant is the tenant.

By virtue of paragraph 3.12 of the PD to Part 56, whatever the procedure used by the tenant in opposed claims, and even though the claim may no longer be opposed, the landlord must respond using an acknowledgement of service in form N9. It must be filed within 14 days of the service of the claim form (as calculated under the CPR) and there are no requirements to modify it, unlike the procedure for unopposed claims.

The landlord must also file a defence to the claim. Under the CPR, the provisions that address how to respond to a claim explain that the defendant to the claim can either file an acknowledgement of service or a defence within 14 days of service of the claim form. But if the defendant to the claim does file an acknowledgement of service, then it effectively has further time to put in the defence which must be done within 28 days of the service of the claim form (or particulars of claim, if they were served later). That choice, i.e. to file a defence earlier (and if so, not to file an acknowledgement of service), seems not to apply under the revised provisions of Part 56 and its PD. In practice, one would have thought that the landlord would have wanted as much time as possible to put in a defence in any case, and would have filed an acknowledgement of service if it had the choice and then filed a defence, so the point is probably only of academic interest.

Thus, the landlord is also required to file a defence and it must do so within 28 days of the service of the claim form. That period can be extended by agreement, but only within the limitations of Part 15 CPR, i.e. by no more than 28 days.

The matters to be addressed in the defence are as follows:

- the landlord's grounds of opposition;
- full details of those grounds of opposition;
- whether, if a new tenancy is granted, the landlord objects to any of the terms proposed by the tenant, and if so, to which terms there is objection, and the landlord's proposals insofar as they differ from those proposed by the tenant;
- whether the landlord is a tenant under a lease having less than 15 years unexpired at the date of termination of the tenant's current tenancy, and if so, the name and address of any person who, to the knowledge of the landlord, has an interest in the reversion in the property expectant (whether immediately or in not more than 15 years from that date) on the termination of the landlord's tenancy;
- the name and address of any person having an interest in the property who is likely to be affected by the grant of a new tenancy (this requirement is not limited to persons of whom the landlord has knowledge, but that appears to be the implication);
- whether the tenant's current tenancy is one to which section 32(2) applies (where the tenant does not occupy all of the property comprised in the tenancy), and if so, whether the landlord requires any new tenancy to be of the whole of the property comprised in the current tenancy.

7.7.4 Opposed claims where the claimant is the landlord

It should be noted that the procedure described in this section is limited only to claims where the landlord has initiated termination proceedings under section 29(2). It does not, on the face of it, address landlord's renewal claims where the landlord objects to the tenant having a new tenancy. In addition, the procedure (which is set out at paragraph 3.13 of the practice direction to Part 56 CPR) is preceded by a heading which suggests it is limited to responses to a landlord's termination proceedings under section 29(2) of the Act. Consequently, it will only apply where the landlord has stated that it relies on one or more of the grounds of opposition in section 30(1) of the Act; it will not apply where the landlord opposes a new tenancy for some other reason.

As explained above, there is a two-stage process in the case of opposed claims: firstly, there is a requirement to file an acknowledgement of service form; and, secondly, there is a requirement to put in a defence.

The acknowledgement of service must be in form N9: it must be filed within 14 days of the service of the claim form, and there are no requirements to modify it, unlike the procedure for unopposed claims.

The tenant is required to file a defence, and it must do so within 28 days of the service of the claim form. That period can be extended by agreement, but only within the limitations of Part 15 CPR, i.e. by no more than 28 days.

The matters to be addressed in the defence are as follows:

- whether the tenant relies on section 23(1A) (see para. 5.2 above), section 41 (which relates to trusts and occupation of the property by beneficiaries of trusts), or section 42 (which relates to occupation by group companies); and if so, on what basis;
- whether the tenant relies on section 31A (by which the tenant can try and obtain a new tenancy by making certain 'concessions' even though the landlord would otherwise satisfy the court about its intended redevelopment under section 30(1)(f) and successfully oppose the tenant having a new tenancy); and, if so, on what basis;
- the terms of the new tenancy proposed by the tenant if the landlord's termination claim fails.

Strangely, the tenant, in its defence, is not required to address some of the matters required of it where the claim is unopposed, even though the issues concerned are just as relevant to the operation of the Act. For example, the tenant is not required to state the nature of the business carried on at the property, nor whether any part of the property comprised in the tenancy is occupied neither by the tenant nor by a person employed by it for the purpose of a business. Further, the tenant is not required to state the name and address of anyone known to have an interest in the reversion in the property (whether immediate or in not more than 15 years) on the termination of the tenant's current tenancy, and who is likely to be affected by the grant of a new tenancy; or if the tenant does not so know of anyone, the name and address of any person having a freehold interest in the property. There is no obvious explanation for this.

7.8 THE MANAGEMENT OF THE CLAIM

The manner in which the revised Part 56 and its PD guide the management of the claim differs according to whether the claim is unopposed or opposed.

7.8.1 Unopposed claims

Whether the claim is initiated by the tenant or the landlord, once the acknowledgement of service form is filed, the court will give directions about the conduct of the claim (see rule 56.3(3)(c) CPR). It has a free hand. Indeed, under paragraph 3.14 of the practice direction to Part 56 CPR, no evidence is to be filed until the court so directs. However, as mentioned above under the discussion of the pre-RRO 2003 Part 56 procedure, the approach to case management may well be similar post-RRO 2003. The guidance offered in the Post-Action Protocol for Business Tenancy Renewals developed by the Property Litigation Association and the Central London County Court would still seem relevant.

7.8.2 Opposed claims

Unlike unopposed claims, rule 56.3 CPR makes no provision for the giving of directions. That is probably deliberate because, by virtue of the Part 7 procedure being required, a defence will be filed that will be the trigger for the court to require the parties to complete a procedural document known as an allocation questionnaire. This document will act as a prompt to the court to make directions for the conduct of the proceedings.

Paragraphs 3.15 and 3.16 of the practice direction to Part 56 CPR give the court guidance as to the directions to be ordered.

It has a free hand as to evidence, but it must require the landlord to file its evidence first. It may also direct that any grounds of opposition (see section 7.6.4 above) may be tried as a preliminary issue.

7.9 INTERIM RENT

The revisions to Part 56 and its PD make provision for interim rent in a number of ways.

Where proceedings for the renewal of a tenancy are commenced, an application for interim rent can be made in the claim form itself, in the acknowledgement of service or by an ordinary procedural application under the CPR (in fact, under Part 23). What seems slightly odd is that while under the revised procedures there will always be an acknowledgement of service, there will, in opposed cases, be a defence too; one would therefore have thought that interim rent could also be sought in that document. However, to allow such a course of action would effectively create a counterclaim, and it was perhaps thought desirable to avoid such an outcome.

It will be recalled that under section 24D(3) (see section 3.5.2 above), where the court has ordered a new tenancy and an interim rent under section 24C, but either the new tenancy order is subsequently revoked under section 36(2) of the Act (see Appendix B) or the landlord and the tenant agree not to act on the order, the court, on the application of either the landlord or the tenant, shall determine the interim rent in accordance with section 24D(1) and (2) without the need for any new application for interim rent having to be made under section 24A(1). An application for such a determination is to be made using the Part 23 CPR procedure in the original proceedings.

Where no other proceedings have been commenced for the grant of a new tenancy or for termination or where such proceedings have been disposed of, a claim for interim rent should be made by stand-alone proceedings using the Part 8 CPR procedure as modified by the revised PD to Part 56.

In the latter case, the claim form is required to address the following matters:

- the property to which the claim relates;
- the particulars of the current tenancy (including the date, parties and duration) and the current rent (if not the original rent);
- every notice or request made under sections 25 and 26;
- if the relevant tenancy has terminated, the date and mode of termination;
- if the relevant tenancy has terminated and the landlord has granted a new tenancy of the property to the tenant:
  (a) particulars of the new tenancy (including date, parties and duration) and the rent; and
  (b) in a case to which section 24C(2) applies (i.e. that the interim rent will be the same as the new rent) but the claimant seeks a different rent under section 24C(3), particulars of the matters on which the claimant relies as satisfying section 24C(3).

Appendix A
REGULATORY REFORM (BUSINESS TENANCIES) (ENGLAND AND WALES) ORDER 2003, SI 2003/3096

Approved by both Houses of Parliament
Made 1st December 2003
Coming into force 1st June 2004

Whereas

(a) the First Secretary of State has consulted –
  (i) such organisations as appear to him to be representative of interests substantially affected by his proposals for this Order,
  (ii) the National Assembly for Wales,
  (iii) the Law Commission, and
  (iv) such other persons as he considered appropriate;
(b) as a result of that consultation it appeared to the First Secretary of State that it was appropriate to vary part of his proposals, and he undertook such further consultation with respect to the variations as appeared to him appropriate;
(c) following the consultation mentioned in recitals (a) and (b) the First Secretary of State considered it appropriate to proceed with the making of this Order;
(d) a document containing the First Secretary of State's proposals was laid before Parliament as required by section 6 of the Regulatory Reform Act 2001 and the period for Parliamentary consideration under section 8 of that Act expired;
(e) the First Secretary of State had regard to the representations made during that period and, in particular, to the reports of the House of Commons Regulatory Reform Committee (Second Report, Session 2002–03, HC182) and the House of Lords Select Committee on Delegated Powers and Regulatory Reform (Fourth Report, Session 2002–03), HL Paper 22);
(f) a draft of this Order was laid before Parliament with a statement giving details of those representations and the changes to the First Secretary of State's proposals in the light of them;
(g) the draft was approved by a resolution of each of House of Parliament;
(h) this Order modifies a function of the National Assembly for Wales and the Assembly has agreed that it be made;
(i) the First Secretary of State is of the opinion that this Order does not remove any necessary protection or prevent any person from continuing to exercise any right or freedom which he might reasonably expect to continue to exercise; and
(j) this Order creates burdens affecting persons in the carrying on of certain activities, and the First Secretary of State is of the opinion that –
  (i) the provisions of this Order, taken as a whole, strike a fair balance between the public interest and the interests of the persons affected by the burdens being created, and

(ii) the extent to which this Order removes or reduces one or more burdens, or has other beneficial effects for persons affected by the burdens imposed by the existing law, makes it desirable for this Order to be made;

Now therefore the First Secretary of State, in exercise of the powers conferred by sections 1 and 4 of the Regulatory Reform Act 2001, hereby makes the following Order:

Introduction

1. Citation, commencement and interpretation

(1) This Order may be cited as the Regulatory Reform (Business Tenancies) (England and Wales) Order 2003.
(2) This Order extends to England and Wales only.
(3) This Order shall come into force at the end of the period of 6 months beginning with the day on which it is made.
(4) In this Order, 'the Act' means the Landlord and Tenant Act 1954.

2. Amendment of the Landlord and Tenant Act 1954

The Act shall be amended as follows.

Applications to court by landlord or tenant

3. Amendments to section 24

(1) In section 24(1) (continuation of business tenancies), for the words 'provisions of section twenty-nine of this Act, the tenant under such a tenancy may apply to the court for' substitute the words 'following provisions of this Act either the tenant or the landlord under such a tenancy may apply to the court for an order for the grant of'.
(2) Insert the following subsections after section 24(2) –
  '(2A) Neither the tenant nor the landlord may make an application under subsection (1) above if the other has made such an application and the application has been served.
  (2B) Neither the tenant nor the landlord may make such an application if the landlord has made an application under section 29(2) of this Act and the application has been served.
  (2C) The landlord may not withdraw an application under subsection (1) above unless the tenant consents to its withdrawal.'.

4. Amendments to section 25

(1) Omit section 25(5) (requirement for tenant to notify landlord whether he is willing to give up possession).
(2) For section 25(6) substitute –
  '(6) A notice under this section shall not have effect unless it states whether the landlord is opposed to the grant of a new tenancy to the tenant.
  (7) A notice under this section which states that the landlord is opposed to the grant of a new tenancy to the tenant shall not have effect unless it also specifies one or more of the grounds specified in section 30(1) of this Act as the ground or grounds for his opposition.
  (8) A notice under this section which states that the landlord is not opposed to the grant of a new tenancy to the tenant shall not have effect unless it sets out the landlord's proposals as to –

(a) the property to be comprised in the new tenancy (being either the whole or part of the property comprised in the current tenancy);
(b) the rent to be payable under the new tenancy; and
(c) the other terms of the new tenancy.'.

5. Landlord's application to terminate tenancy

For section 29 (order by court for grant of a new tenancy) and the cross-heading immediately preceding it substitute –

'Applications to court

29. Order by court for grant of new tenancy or termination of current tenancy

(1) Subject to the provisions of this Act, on an application under section 24(1) of this Act, the court shall make an order for the grant of a new tenancy and accordingly for the termination of the current tenancy immediately before the commencement of the new tenancy.
(2) Subject to the following provisions of this Act, a landlord may apply to the court for an order for the termination of a tenancy to which this Part of this Act applies without the grant of a new tenancy –
   (a) if he has given notice under section 25 of this Act that he is opposed to the grant of a new tenancy to the tenant; or
   (b) if the tenant has made a request for a new tenancy in accordance with section 26 of this Act and the landlord has given notice under subsection (6) of that section.
(3) The landlord may not make an application under subsection (2) above if either the tenant or the landlord has made an application under section 24(1) of this Act.
(4) Subject to the provisions of this Act, where the landlord makes an application under subsection (2) above –
   (a) if he establishes, to the satisfaction of the court, any of the grounds on which he is entitled to make the application in accordance with section 30 of this Act, the court shall make an order for the termination of the current tenancy in accordance with section 64 of this Act without the grant of a new tenancy; and
   (b) if not, it shall make an order for the grant of a new tenancy and accordingly for the termination of the current tenancy immediately before the commencement of the new tenancy.
(5) The court shall dismiss an application by the landlord under section 24(1) of this Act if the tenant informs the court that he does not want a new tenancy.
(6) The landlord may not withdraw an application under subsection (2) above unless the tenant consents to its withdrawal.'.

6. Amendments to section 30

(1) In section 30(1) (grounds of opposition by landlord to renewal of tenancy), for the words 'subsection (1) of section twenty-four of this Act' substitute 'section 24(1) of this Act, or make an application under section 29(2) of this Act,'.
(2) In section 30(2), after the words 'oppose an application' insert 'under section 24(1) of this Act, or make an application under section 29(2) of this Act,'.

7. Amendment to section 31

In section 31(2) (declaration and order of the court in certain cases where landlord opposes renewal) for the words from the beginning to 'any of those grounds' substitute 'Where the landlord opposes an application under section 24(1) of this Act, or makes an application under section 29(2) of this Act, on one or more of the grounds specified in section 30(1)(d) to (f) of this Act but establishes none of those grounds, and none of the other grounds specified in section 30(1) of this Act, to the satisfaction of the court, then if the court would have been satisfied on any of the grounds specified in section 30(1)(d) to (f) of this Act'.

8. Amendment to section 31A

In section 31A(1) (grant of new tenancy in some cases where section 30(1)(f) applies), after the words '30(1) of this Act' insert ', or makes an application under section 29(2) of this Act on that ground,'.

9. Amendment to section 34

In section 34(2)(a) (rent under new tenancy), for the words 'for the new tenancy' substitute the words 'to the court'.

10. Time limits for applications to court

After section 29 insert the following sections –

'29A. Time limits for applications to court

(1) Subject to section 29B of this Act, the court shall not entertain an application –
  (a) by the tenant or the landlord under section 24(1) of this Act; or
  (b) by the landlord under section 29(2) of this Act,

  if it is made after the end of the statutory period.

(2) In this section and section 29B of this Act 'the statutory period' means a period ending –
  (a) where the landlord gave a notice under section 25 of this Act, on the date specified in his notice; and
  (b) where the tenant made a request for a new tenancy under section 26 of this Act, immediately before the date specified in his request.

(3) Where the tenant has made a request for a new tenancy under section 26 of this Act, the court shall not entertain an application under section 24(1) of this Act which is made before the end of the period of two months beginning with the date of the making of the request, unless the application is made after the landlord has given a notice under section 26(6) of this Act.

29B. Agreements extending time limits

(1) After the landlord has given a notice under section 25 of this Act, or the tenant has made a request under section 26 of this Act, but before the end of the statutory period, the landlord and tenant may agree that an application such as is mentioned in section 29A(1) of this Act, may be made before the end of a period specified in the agreement which will expire after the end of the statutory period.
(2) The landlord and tenant may from time to time by agreement further extend the period for making such an application, but any such agreement must be made before the end of the period specified in the current agreement.
(3) Where an agreement is made under this section, the court may entertain an application such as is mentioned in section 29A(1) of this Act if it is made before the end of the period specified in the agreement.
(4) Where an agreement is made under this section, or two or more agreements are made under this section, the landlord's notice under section 25 of this Act or tenant's request under section 26 of this Act shall be treated as terminating the tenancy at the end of the period specified in the agreement or, as the case may be, at the end of the period specified in the last of those agreements.'.

11. Amendment to section 25

In section 25(1) (termination of tenancy subject to provisions of Part 4) after 'subject to' insert 'the provisions of section 29B(4) of this Act and'.

12. Amendment to section 26

In section 26(5) (termination of tenancy subject to section 36(2) and Part 4) for 'subsection (2) of section thirty-six' substitute 'sections 29B(4) and 36(2)'.

Companies and their controlling shareholders

13. Amendment to section 23

After section 23(1) (tenancies to which Part 2 applies) insert –

'(1A) Occupation or the carrying on of a business –

(a) by a company in which the tenant has a controlling interest; or
(b) where the tenant is a company, by a person with a controlling interest in the company,

shall be treated for the purposes of this section as equivalent to occupation or, as the case may be, the carrying on of a business by the tenant.

(1B) Accordingly references (however expressed) in this Part of this Act to the business of, or to use, occupation or enjoyment by, the tenant shall be construed as including references to the business of, or to use, occupation or enjoyment by, a company falling within subsection (1A)(a) above or a person falling within subsection (1A)(b) above.'.

14. Amendments to section 30

(1) After section 30(1) (opposition by landlord to renewal of tenancy) insert –

'(1A) Where the landlord has a controlling interest in a company, the reference in subsection (1)(g) above to the landlord shall be construed as a reference to the landlord or that company.

(1B) Subject to subsection (2A) below, where the landlord is a company and a person has a controlling interest in the company, the reference in subsection (1)(g) above to the landlord shall be construed as a reference to the landlord or that person.'

(2) After section 30(2) insert –

'(2A) Subsection (1B) above shall not apply if the controlling interest was acquired after the beginning of the period of five years which ends with the termination of the current tenancy, and at all times since the acquisition of the controlling interest the holding has been comprised in a tenancy or successive tenancies of the description specified in section 23(1) of this Act.'.

15. Amendment to section 34

After section 34(2) (improvements to which subsection (1)(c) applies) insert –

'(2A) If this Part of this Act applies by virtue of section 23(1A) of this Act, the reference in subsection (1)(d) above to the tenant shall be construed as including –

(a) a company in which the tenant has a controlling interest, or
(b) where the tenant is a company, a person with a controlling interest in the company.'.

16. Amendment to section 42

At the end of the first paragraph of section 42(1) (groups of companies) add 'or the same person has a controlling interest in both'.

17. Amendments to section 46

(1) Section 46 (interpretation of Part 2) shall become section 46(1).
(2) After that subsection add –

'(2) For the purposes of this Part of this Act, a person has a controlling interest in a company, if, had he been a company, the other company would have been its subsidiary; and in this Part –

"company" has the meaning given by section 735 of the Companies Act 1985; and "subsidiary" has the meaning given by section 736 of that Act.'.

Interim rent

18. Rent while tenancy continues by virtue of section 24

For section 24A (interim rent) substitute –

'24A. Applications for determination of interim rent while tenancy continues

(1) Subject to subsection (2) below, if –

(a) the landlord of a tenancy to which this Part of this Act applies has given notice under section 25 of this Act to terminate the tenancy; or
(b) the tenant of such a tenancy has made a request for a new tenancy in accordance with section 26 of this Act,

either of them may make an application to the court to determine a rent (an "interim rent") which the tenant is to pay while the tenancy ("the relevant tenancy") continues by virtue of section 24 of this Act and the court may order payment of an interim rent in accordance with section 24C or 24D of this Act.
(2) Neither the tenant nor the landlord may make an application under subsection (1) above if the other has made such an application and has not withdrawn it.
(3) No application shall be entertained under subsection (1) above if it is made more than six months after the termination of the relevant tenancy.

24B. Date from which interim rent is payable

(1) The interim rent determined on an application under section 24A(1) of this Act shall be payable from the appropriate date.
(2) If an application under section 24A(1) of this Act is made in a case where the landlord has given a notice under section 25 of this Act, the appropriate date is the earliest date of termination that could have been specified in the landlord's notice.
(3) If an application under section 24A(1) of this Act is made in a case where the tenant has made a request for a new tenancy under section 26 of this Act, the appropriate date is the earliest date that could have been specified in the tenant's request as the date from which the new tenancy is to begin.

24C. Amount of interim rent where new tenancy of whole premises granted and landlord not opposed

(1) This section applies where –

(a) the landlord gave a notice under section 25 of this Act at a time when the tenant was in occupation of the whole of the property comprised in the relevant tenancy for purposes such as are mentioned in section 23(1) of this

Act and stated in the notice that he was not opposed to the grant of a new tenancy; or

(b) the tenant made a request for a new tenancy under section 26 of this Act at a time when he was in occupation of the whole of that property for such purposes and the landlord did not give notice under subsection (6) of that section,

and the landlord grants a new tenancy of the whole of the property comprised in the relevant tenancy to the tenant (whether as a result of an order for the grant of a new tenancy or otherwise).

(2) Subject to the following provisions of this section, the rent payable under and at the commencement of the new tenancy shall also be the interim rent.

(3) Subsection (2) above does not apply where –

(a) the landlord or the tenant shows to the satisfaction of the court that the interim rent under that subsection differs substantially from the relevant rent; or

(b) the landlord or the tenant shows to the satisfaction of the court that the terms of the new tenancy differ from the terms of the relevant tenancy to such an extent that the interim rent under that subsection is substantially different from the rent which (in default of such agreement) the court would have determined under section 34 of this Act to be payable under a tenancy which commenced on the same day as the new tenancy and whose other terms were the same as the relevant tenancy.

(4) In this section "the relevant rent" means the rent which (in default of agreement between the landlord and the tenant) the court would have determined under section 34 of this Act to be payable under the new tenancy if the new tenancy had commenced on the appropriate date (within the meaning of section 24B of this Act).

(5) The interim rent in a case where subsection (2) above does not apply by virtue only of subsection (3)(a) above is the relevant rent.

(6) The interim rent in a case where subsection (2) above does not apply by virtue only of subsection (3)(b) above, or by virtue of subsection (3)(a) and (b) above, is the rent which it is reasonable for the tenant to pay while the relevant tenancy continues by virtue of section 24 of this Act.

(7) In determining the interim rent under subsection (6) above the court shall have regard –

(a) to the rent payable under the terms of the relevant tenancy; and

(b) to the rent payable under any sub-tenancy of part of the property comprised in the relevant tenancy,

but otherwise subsections (1) and (2) of section 34 of this Act shall apply to the determination as they would apply to the determination of a rent under that section if a new tenancy of the whole of the property comprised in the relevant tenancy were granted to the tenant by order of the court and the duration of that new tenancy were the same as the duration of the new tenancy which is actually granted to the tenant.

(8) In this section and section 24D of this Act "the relevant tenancy" has the same meaning as in section 24A of this Act.

24D. Amount of interim rent in any other case

(1) The interim rent in a case where section 24C of this Act does not apply is the rent which it is reasonable for the tenant to pay while the relevant tenancy continues by virtue of section 24 of this Act.

(2) In determining the interim rent under subsection (1) above the court shall have regard –

(a) to the rent payable under the terms of the relevant tenancy; and
(b) to the rent payable under any sub-tenancy of part of the property comprised in the relevant tenancy,

but otherwise subsections (1) and (2) of section 34 of this Act shall apply to the determination as they would apply to the determination of a rent under that section if a new tenancy from year to year of the whole of the property comprised in the relevant tenancy were granted to the tenant by order of the court.

(3) If the court –

(a) has made an order for the grant of a new tenancy and has ordered payment of interim rent in accordance with section 24C of this Act, but
(b) either –

(i) it subsequently revokes under section 36(2) of this Act the order for the grant of a new tenancy; or
(ii) the landlord and tenant agree not to act on the order,

the court on the application of the landlord or the tenant shall determine a new interim rent in accordance with subsections (1) and (2) above without a further application under section 24A(1) of this Act.'.

Compensation

19. Compensation for refusal of new tenancy

(1) For section 37(1) (compensation where new tenancy precluded on certain grounds) substitute –

'(1) Subject to the provisions of this Act, in a case specified in subsection (1A), (1B) or (1C) below (a "compensation case") the tenant shall be entitled on quitting the holding to recover from the landlord by way of compensation an amount determined in accordance with this section.

(1A) The first compensation case is where on the making of an application by the tenant under section 24(1) of this Act the court is precluded (whether by subsection (1) or subsection (2) of section 31 of this Act) from making an order for the grant of a new tenancy by reason of any of the grounds specified in paragraphs (e), (f) and (g) of section 30(1) of this Act (the "compensation grounds") and not of any grounds specified in any other paragraph of section 30(1).

(1B) The second compensation case is where on the making of an application under section 29(2) of this Act the court is precluded (whether by section 29(4)(a) or section 31(2) of this Act) from making an order for the grant of a new tenancy by reason of any of the compensation grounds and not of any other grounds specified in section 30(1) of this Act.

(1C) The third compensation case is where –

(a) the landlord's notice under section 25 of this Act or, as the case may be, under section 26(6) of this Act, states his opposition to the grant of a new tenancy on any of the compensation grounds and not on any other grounds specified in section 30(1) of this Act; and
(b) either –

(i) no application is made by the tenant under section 24(1) of this Act or by the landlord under section 29(2) of this Act; or
(ii) such an application is made but is subsequently withdrawn.'.

(2) In section 37(2) –

(a) for the words 'subsections (5A) to (5E) of this section the said amount' substitute 'the following provisions of this section, compensation under this section'; and

(b) in paragraph (a), after the word 'satisfied' insert 'in relation to the whole of the holding'.

(3) After section 37(3) insert –

'(3A) If the conditions specified in subsection (3) above are satisfied in relation to part of the holding but not in relation to the other part, the amount of compensation shall be the aggregate of sums calculated separately as compensation in respect of each part, and accordingly, for the purpose of calculating compensation in respect of a part any reference in this section to the holding shall be construed as a reference to that part.

(3B) Where section 44(1A) of this Act applies, the compensation shall be determined separately for each part and compensation determined for any part shall be recoverable only from the person who is the owner of an interest in that part which fulfils the conditions specified in section 44(1) of this Act.'.

(4) In section 37(4), for the words 'the circumstances mentioned in subsection (1) of this section' substitute 'a compensation case'.

20. Compensation for misrepresentation

After section 37 insert –

'37A. Compensation for possession obtained by misrepresentation

(1) Where the court –

(a) makes an order for the termination of the current tenancy but does not make an order for the grant of a new tenancy, or

(b) refuses an order for the grant of a new tenancy,

and it subsequently made to appear to the court that the order was obtained, or the court was induced to refuse the grant, by misrepresentation or the concealment of material facts, the court may order the landlord to pay to the tenant such sum as appears sufficient as compensation for damage or loss sustained by the tenant as the result of the order or refusal.

(2) Where –

(a) the tenant has quit the holding –

(i) after making but withdrawing an application under section 24(1) of this Act; or

(ii) without making such an application; and

(b) it is made to appear to the court that he did so by reason of misrepresentation or the concealment of material facts,

the court may order the landlord to pay to the tenant such sum as appears sufficient as compensation for damage or loss sustained by the tenant as the result of quitting the holding.'.

Agreements to exclude security of tenure

21. Amendments to section 38

(1) In section 38(1) (restrictions on agreements excluding provisions of Part 2) for 'subsection (4) of this section' substitute 'section 38A of this Act'.

(2) Omit section 38(4).

22. Agreements to exclude sections 24 to 28

(1) After section 38 insert –

'38A. Agreements to exclude provisions of Part 2

(1) The persons who will be the landlord and the tenant in relation to a tenancy to be granted for a term of years certain which will be a tenancy to which this Part of this Act applies may agree that the provisions of sections 24 to 28 of this Act shall be excluded in relation to that tenancy.

(2) The persons who are the landlord and the tenant in relation to a tenancy to which this Part of this Act applies may agree that the tenancy shall be surrendered on such date or in such circumstances as may be specified in the agreement and on such terms (if any) as may be so specified.

(3) An agreement under subsection (1) above shall be void unless –

- (a) the landlord has served on the tenant a notice in the form, or substantially in the form, set out in Schedule 1 to the Regulatory Reform (Business Tenancies) (England and Wales) Order 2003 ("the 2003 Order"); and
- (b) the requirements specified in Schedule 2 to that Order are met.

(4) An agreement under subsection (2) above shall be void unless –

- (a) the landlord has served on the tenant a notice in the form, or substantially in the form, set out in Schedule 3 to the 2003 Order; and
- (b) the requirements specified in Schedule 4 to that Order are met.'

(2) Schedules 1 to 4 to this Order shall have effect.

Duties to give information

23. Provision of information

For section 40 substitute –

'40. Duties of tenants and landlords of business premises to give information to each other

(1) Where a person who is an owner of an interest in reversion expectant (whether immediately or not) on a tenancy of any business premises has served on the tenant a notice in the prescribed form requiring him to do so, it shall be the duty of the tenant to give the appropriate person in writing the information specified in subsection (2) below.

(2) That information is –

- (a) whether the tenant occupies the premises or any part of them wholly or partly for the purposes of a business carried on by him;
- (b) whether his tenancy has effect subject to any sub-tenancy on which his tenancy is immediately expectant and, if so –
  - (i) what premises are comprised in the sub-tenancy;
  - (ii) for what term it has effect (or, if it is terminable by notice, by what notice it can be terminated);
  - (iii) what is the rent payable under it;
  - (iv) who is the sub-tenant;
  - (v) (to the best of his knowledge and belief) whether the sub-tenant is in occupation of the premises or of part of the premises comprised in the sub-tenancy and, if not, what is the sub-tenant's address;
  - (vi) whether an agreement is in force excluding in relation to the sub-tenancy the provisions of sections 24 to 28 of this Act; and
  - (vii) whether a notice has been given under section 25 or 26(6) of this Act, or a request has been made under section 26 of this Act, in relation to the sub-tenancy and, if so, details of the notice or request; and
- (c) (to the best of his knowledge and belief) the name and address of any other person who owns an interest in reversion in any part of the premises.

(3) Where the tenant of any business premises who is a tenant under such a tenancy as is mentioned in section 26(1) of this Act has served on a reversioner or a reversioner's mortgagee in possession a notice in the prescribed form requiring him to do so, it shall be the duty of the person on whom the notice is served to give the appropriate person in writing the information specified in subsection (4) below.

(4) That information is –

(a) whether he is the owner of the fee simple in respect of the premises or any part of them or the mortgagee in possession of such an owner,

(b) if he is not, then (to the best of his knowledge and belief) –

(i) the name and address of the person who is his or, as the case may be, his mortgagor's immediate landlord in respect of those premises or of the part in respect of which he or his mortgagor is not the owner in fee simple;

(ii) for what term his or his mortgagor's tenancy has effect and what is the earliest date (if any) at which that tenancy is terminable by notice to quit given by the landlord; and

(iii) whether a notice has been given under section 25 or 26(6) of this Act, or a request has been made under section 26 of this Act, in relation to the tenancy and, if so, details of the notice or request;

(c) (to the best of his knowledge and belief) the name and address of any other person who owns an interest in reversion in any part of the premises; and

(d) if he is a reversioner, whether there is a mortgagee in possession of his interest in the premises and, if so, (to the best of his knowledge and belief) what is the name and address of the mortgagee.

(5) A duty imposed on a person by this section is a duty –

(a) to give the information concerned within the period of one month beginning with the date of service of the notice; and

(b) if within the period of six months beginning with the date of service of the notice that person becomes aware that any information which has been given in pursuance of the notice is not, or is no longer, correct, to give the appropriate person correct information within the period of one month beginning with the date on which he becomes aware.

(6) This section shall not apply to a notice served by or on the tenant more than two years before the date on which apart from this Act his tenancy would come to an end by effluxion of time or could be brought to an end by notice to quit given by the landlord.

(7) Except as provided by section 40A of this Act, the appropriate person for the purposes of this section and section 40A(1) of this Act is the person who served the notice under subsection (1) or (3) above.

(8) In this section –

"business premises" means premises used wholly or partly for the purposes of a business;

"mortgagee in possession" includes a receiver appointed by the mortgagee or by the court who is in receipt of the rents and profits, and "his mortgagor" shall be construed accordingly;

"reversioner" means any person having an interest in the premises, being an interest in reversion expectant (whether immediately or not) on the tenancy;

"reversioner's mortgagee in possession" means any person being a mortgagee in possession in respect of such an interest; and

"sub-tenant" includes a person retaining possession of any premises by virtue of the Rent (Agriculture) Act 1976 or the Rent Act 1977 after the coming to an end of a sub-tenancy, and "sub-tenancy" includes a right so to retain possession.'.

24. Section 40 duties in transfer cases

After section 40 insert the following sections –

'40A. Duties in transfer cases

(1) If a person on whom a notice under section 40(1) or (3) of this Act has been served has transferred his interest in the premises or any part of them to some other person and gives the appropriate person notice in writing –

(a) of the transfer of his interest; and

(b) of the name and address of the person to whom he transferred it,

on giving the notice he ceases in relation to the premises or (as the case may be) to that part to be under any duty imposed by section 40 of this Act.

(2) If –

(a) the person who served the notice under section 40(1) or (3) of this Act ("the transferor") has transferred his interest in the premises to some other person ("the transferee"); and

(b) the transferor or the transferee has given the person required to give the information notice in writing –

(i) of the transfer; and

(ii) of the transferee's name and address,

the appropriate person for the purposes of section 40 of this Act and subsection (1) above is the transferee.

(3) If –

(a) a transfer such as is mentioned in paragraph (a) of subsection (2) above has taken place; but

(b) neither the transferor nor the transferee has given a notice such as is mentioned in paragraph (b) of that subsection,

any duty imposed by section 40 of this Act may be performed by giving the information either to the transferor or to the transferee.

40B. Proceedings for breach of duties to give information

A claim that a person has broken any duty imposed by section 40 of this Act may be made the subject of civil proceedings for breach of statutory duty; and in any such proceedings a court may order that person to comply with that duty and may make an award of damages.'.

Miscellaneous amendments

25. Termination by tenant of tenancy

(1) After section 27(1) (termination by tenant of fixed term tenancy at end of term) insert –

'(1A) Section 24 of this Act shall not have effect in relation to a tenancy for a term of years certain where the tenant is not in occupation of the property comprised in the tenancy at the time when, apart from this Act, the tenancy would come to an end by effluxion of time.'.

(2) In section 27(2) (termination by tenant of fixed term tenancy continuing by virtue of section 24) –

(a) after 'of this Act' insert 'shall not come to an end by reason only of the tenant ceasing to occupy the property comprised in the tenancy but'; and

(b) omit the word 'quarter'.

(3) After that subsection insert –

'(3) Where a tenancy is terminated under subsection (2) above, any rent payable in respect of a period which begins before, and ends after, the tenancy is terminated shall be apportioned, and any rent paid by the tenant in excess of the amount apportioned to the period before termination shall be recoverable by him.'.

26. Maximum duration of new tenancy

In section 33 (duration of new tenancy) for the word 'fourteen' substitute the word 'fifteen'.

27. Divided reversions

(1) In section 44(1) (meaning of 'landlord'), for 'the next following subsection,' substitute 'subsections (1A) and (2) below,'.

(2) After section 44(1) insert –

'(1A) The reference in subsection (1) above to a person who is the owner of an interest such as is mentioned in that subsection is to be construed, where different persons own such interests in different parts of the property, as a reference to all those persons collectively.'.

(3) In section 35(1) (other terms of new tenancy), after the word 'thereunder)' insert ', including, where different persons own interests which fulfil the conditions specified in section 44(1) of this Act in different parts of it, terms as to the apportionment of the rent,'.

Final provisions

28. Consequential amendments, repeals and subordinate provisions

(1) Schedule 5 to this Order, which contains amendments consequential on the provisions of this Order, shall have effect.

(2) The enactments specified in Schedule 6 to this Order are repealed to the extent mentioned in the third column of that Schedule.

(3) Schedules 1 to 4 to this Order are designated as subordinate provisions for the purposes of section 4 of the Regulatory Reform Act 2001.

(4) A subordinate provisions order relating to the subordinate provisions designated by paragraph (3) above shall be subject to annulment in pursuance of a resolution of either House of Parliament.

(5) The power to make a subordinate provisions order relating to those provisions is to be exercisable in relation to Wales by the National Assembly for Wales concurrently with a Minister of the Crown.

(6) Paragraph (4) above does not apply to a subordinate provisions order made by the National Assembly for Wales.

(7) The notices and statutory declarations set out in Schedules 1 to 4 to this Order shall be treated for the purposes of section 26 of the Welsh Language Act 1993 (power to prescribe Welsh forms) as if they were specified by an Act of Parliament; and accordingly the power conferred by section 26(2) of that Act may be exercised in relation to those notices and declarations.

29. Transitional provisions

(1) Where, before this Order came into force –

(a) the landlord gave the tenant notice under section 25 of the Act; or

(b) the tenant made a request for a new tenancy in accordance with section 26 of the Act,

nothing in this Order has effect in relation to the notice or request or anything done in consequence of it.

(2) Nothing in this Order has effect in relation –

(a) to an agreement –

(i) for the surrender of a tenancy which was made before this Order came into force and which fell within section 24(2)(b) of the Act; or

(ii) which was authorised by the court under section 38(4) of the Act before this Order came into force; or

(b) to a notice under section 27(2) of the Act which was given by the tenant to the immediate landlord before this Order came into force.

(3) Any provision in a tenancy which requires an order under section 38(4) of the Act to be obtained in respect of any subtenancy shall, so far as is necessary after the coming into force of this Order, be construed as if it required the procedure mentioned in section 38A of the Act to be followed, and any related requirement shall be construed accordingly.

(4) If a person has, before the coming into force of this Order, entered into an agreement to take a tenancy, any provision in that agreement which requires an order under section 38(4) of the Act to be obtained in respect of the tenancy shall continue to be effective, notwithstanding the repeal of that provision by Article 21(2) of this Order, and the court shall retain jurisdiction to make such an order.

(5) Article 20 above does not have effect where the tenant quit the holding before this Order came into force.

(6) Nothing in Articles 23 and 24 above applies to a notice under section 40 of the Act served before this Order came into force.

Signed by authority of the First Secretary of State

Keith Hill
Minister of State, Office of the Deputy Prime Minister
1st December 2003

SCHEDULE 1

Article 22(2) FORM OF NOTICE THAT SECTIONS 24 TO 28 OF THE LANDLORD AND TENANT ACT 1954 ARE NOT TO APPLY TO A BUSINESS TENANCY

To:

____

____

____

[*Name and address of tenant*]

From:

____

____

____

[*Name and address of landlord*]

IMPORTANT NOTICE

You are being offered a lease without security of tenure. Do not commit yourself to the lease unless you have read this message carefully and have discussed it with a professional adviser.

Business tenants normally have security of tenure – the right to stay in their business premises when the lease ends.

If you commit yourself to the lease you will be giving up these important legal rights.

- You will have **no right** to stay in the premises when the lease ends.
- Unless the landlord chooses to offer you another lease, you will need to leave the premises.
- You will be unable to claim compensation for the loss of your business premises, unless the lease specifically gives you this right.
- If the landlord offers you another lease, you will have no right to ask the court to fix the rent.

It is therefore important to get professional advice – from a qualified surveyor, lawyer or accountant – before agreeing to give up these rights.

If you want to ensure that you can stay in the same business premises when the lease ends, you should consult your adviser about another form of lease that does not exclude the protection of the Landlord and Tenant Act 1954.

If you receive this notice at least 14 days before committing yourself to the lease, you will need to sign a simple declaration that you have received this notice and have accepted its consequences, before signing the lease.

But if you do not receive at least 14 days notice, you will need to sign a 'statutory' declaration. To do so, you will need to visit an independent solicitor (or someone else empowered to administer oaths).

Unless there is a special reason for committing yourself to the lease sooner, you may want to ask the landlord to let you have at least 14 days to consider whether you wish to give up your statutory rights. If you then decided to go ahead with the agreement to exclude the protection of the Landlord and Tenant Act 1954, you would only need to make a simple declaration, and so you would not need to make a separate visit to an independent solicitor.

SCHEDULE 2

Article 22(2) **REQUIREMENTS FOR A VALID AGREEMENT THAT SECTIONS 24 TO 28 OF THE LANDLORD AND TENANT ACT 1954 ARE NOT TO APPLY TO A BUSINESS TENANCY**

1. The following are the requirements referred to in section 38A(3)(b) of the Act.
2. Subject to paragraph 4, the notice referred to in section 38A(3)(a) of the Act must be served on the tenant not less than 14 days before the tenant enters into the tenancy to which it applies, or (if earlier) becomes contractually bound to do so.
3. If the requirement in paragraph 2 is met, the tenant, or a person duly authorised by him to do so, must, before the tenant enters into the tenancy to which the notice applies, or (if earlier) becomes contractually bound to do so, make a declaration in the form, or substantially in the form, set out in paragraph 7.
4. If the requirement in paragraph 2 is not met, the notice referred to in section 38A(3)(a) of the Act must be served on the tenant before the tenant enters into the tenancy to which it applies, or (if earlier) becomes contractually bound to do so, and the tenant, or a person duly authorised by him to do so, must before that time make a statutory declaration in the form, or substantially in the form, set out in paragraph 8.
5. A reference to the notice and, where paragraph 3 applies, the declaration or, where paragraph 4 applies, the statutory declaration must be contained in or endorsed on the instrument creating the tenancy.
6. The agreement under section 38A(1) of the Act, or a reference to the agreement, must be contained in or endorsed upon the instrument creating the tenancy.
7. The form of declaration referred to in paragraph 3 is as follows: –

I

____

(*name of declarant*) of

____

(*address*) declare that –

1. I/

   ____

   (*name of tenant*) propose(s) to enter into a tenancy of premises at

   ____

   (*address of premises*) for a term commencing on

   ____

2. I/The tenant propose(s) to enter into an agreement with

   ____

   (name of landlord) that the provisions of sections 24 to 28 of the Landlord and Tenant Act 1954 (security of tenure) shall be excluded in relation to the tenancy.
3. The landlord has, not less than 14 days before I/the tenant enter(s) into the tenancy, or (if earlier) become(s) contractually bound to do so served on me/the tenant a notice in the form, or substantially in the form, set out in Schedule 1 to the Regulatory Reform (Business Tenancies) (England and Wales) Order 2003. The form of notice set out in that Schedule is reproduced below.
4. I have/The tenant has read the notice referred to in paragraph 3 above and accept(s) the consequences of entering into the agreement referred to in paragraph 2 above.
5. (as appropriate) I am duly authorised by the tenant to make this declaration.

DECLARED this

____

day of

____

To:

____

____

____

[*Name and address of tenant*]

From:

____

____

____

[*Name and address of landlord*]

IMPORTANT NOTICE

You are being offered a lease without security of tenure. Do not commit yourself to the lease unless you have read this message carefully and have discussed it with a professional adviser.

Business tenants normally have security of tenure – the right to stay in their business premises when the lease ends.

If you commit yourself to the lease you will be giving up these important legal rights.

- You will have **no right** to stay in the premises when the lease ends.
- Unless the landlord chooses to offer you another lease, you will need to leave the premises.
- You will be unable to claim compensation for the loss of your business premises, unless the lease specifically gives you this right.
- If the landlord offers you another lease, you will have no right to ask the court to fix the rent.

It is therefore important to get professional advice – from a qualified surveyor, lawyer or accountant – before agreeing to give up these rights.

If you want to ensure that you can stay in the same business premises when the lease ends, you should consult your adviser about another form of lease that does not exclude the protection of the Landlord and Tenant Act 1954.

If you receive this notice at least 14 days before committing yourself to the lease, you will need to sign a simple declaration that you have received this notice and have accepted its consequences, before signing the lease.

But if you do not receive at least 14 days notice, you will need to sign a 'statutory' declaration. To do so, you will need to visit an independent solicitor (or someone else empowered to administer oaths).

Unless there is a special reason for committing yourself to the lease sooner, you may want to ask the landlord to let you have at least 14 days to consider whether you wish to give up your statutory rights. If you then decided to go ahead with the agreement to exclude the protection of the Landlord and Tenant Act 1954, you would only need to make a simple declaration, and so you would not need to make a separate visit to an independent solicitor.

8. The form of statutory declaration referred to in paragraph 4 is as follows: –

I

____

(*name of declarant*) of

____

(*address*) do solemnly and sincerely declare that –

1. I

   ____

   (*name of tenant*) propose(s) to enter into a tenancy of premises at

   ____

   (*address of premises*) for a term commencing on

   ____

2. I/The tenant propose(s) to enter into an agreement with (name of landlord) that the provisions of sections 24 to 28 of the Landlord and Tenant Act 1954 (security of tenure) shall be excluded in relation to the tenancy.
3. The landlord has served on me/the tenant a notice in the form, or substantially in the form, set out in Schedule 1 to the Regulatory Reform (Business Tenancies) (England and Wales) Order 2003. The form of notice set out in that Schedule is reproduced below.
4. I have/The tenant has read the notice referred to in paragraph 3 above and accept(s) the consequences of entering into the agreement referred to in paragraph 2 above.
5. (*as appropriate*) I am duly authorised by the tenant to make this declaration.

To:

____

____

____

[*Name and address of tenant*]

From:

____

____

____

[*Name and address of landlord*]

IMPORTANT NOTICE

You are being offered a lease without security of tenure. Do not commit yourself to the lease unless you have read this message carefully and have discussed it with a professional adviser.

Business tenants normally have security of tenure – the right to stay in their business premises when the lease ends.

If you commit yourself to the lease you will be giving up these important legal rights.

- You will have **no right** to stay in the premises when the lease ends.
- Unless the landlord chooses to offer you another lease, you will need to leave the premises.
- You will be unable to claim compensation for the loss of your business premises, unless the lease specifically gives you this right.
- If the landlord offers you another lease, you will have no right to ask the court to fix the rent.

It is therefore important to get professional advice – from a qualified surveyor, lawyer or accountant – before agreeing to give up these rights.

If you want to ensure that you can stay in the same business premises when the lease ends, you should consult your adviser about another form of lease that does not exclude the protection of the Landlord and Tenant Act 1954.

If you receive this notice at least 14 days before committing yourself to the lease, you will need to sign a simple declaration that you have received this notice and have accepted its consequences, before signing the lease.

But if you do not receive at least 14 days notice, you will need to sign a 'statutory' declaration. To do so, you will need to visit an independent solicitor (or someone else empowered to administer oaths).

Unless there is a special reason for committing yourself to the lease sooner, you may want to ask the landlord to let you have at least 14 days to consider whether you wish to give up your statutory rights. If you then decided to go ahead with the agreement to exclude the protection of the Landlord and Tenant Act 1954, you would only need to make a simple declaration, and so you would not need to make a separate visit to an independent solicitor.

AND I make this solemn declaration conscientiously believing the same to be true and by virtue of the Statutory Declaration Act 1835.

DECLARED at

____

this

____

day of

____

Before me

(signature of person before whom declaration is made)

A commissioner for oaths or A solicitor empowered to administer oaths or (*as appropriate*)

SCHEDULE 3

Article 22(2) FORM OF NOTICE THAT AN AGREEMENT TO SURRENDER A BUSINESS TENANCY IS TO BE MADE

To:

____

____

____

[Name and address of tenant]

From:

____

____

____

[Name and address of landlord]

IMPORTANT NOTICE FOR TENANT

You are being offered a lease without security of tenure. Do not commit yourself to the lease unless you have read this message carefully and have discussed it with a professional adviser.

Business tenants normally have security of tenure – the right to stay in their business premises when the lease ends.

If you commit yourself to the lease you will be giving up these important legal rights.

- You will have **no right** to stay in the premises when the lease ends.
- Unless the landlord chooses to offer you another lease, you will need to leave the premises.
- You will be unable to claim compensation for the loss of your business premises, unless the lease specifically gives you this right.
- If the landlord offers you another lease, you will have no right to ask the court to fix the rent.

It is therefore important to get professional advice – from a qualified surveyor, lawyer or accountant – before agreeing to give up these rights.

If you want to ensure that you can stay in the same business premises when the lease ends, you should consult your adviser about another form of lease that does not exclude the protection of the Landlord and Tenant Act 1954.

If you receive this notice at least 14 days before committing yourself to the lease, you will need to sign a simple declaration that you have received this notice and have accepted its consequences, before signing the lease.

But if you do not receive at least 14 days notice, you will need to sign a 'statutory' declaration. To do so, you will need to visit an independent solicitor (or someone else empowered to administer oaths).

Unless there is a special reason for committing yourself to the lease sooner, you may want to ask the landlord to let you have at least 14 days to consider whether you wish to give up your statutory rights. If you then decided to go ahead with the agreement to exclude the protection of the Landlord and Tenant Act 1954, you would only need to make a simple declaration, and so you would not need to make a separate visit to an independent solicitor.

SCHEDULE 4

Article 22(2) REQUIREMENTS FOR A VALID AGREEMENT TO SURRENDER A BUSINESS TENANCY

1. The following are the requirements referred to in section 38A(4)(b) of the Act.
2. Subject to paragraph 4, the notice referred to in section 38A(4)(a) of the Act must be served on the tenant not less than 14 days before the tenant enters into the agreement under section 38A(2) of the Act, or (if earlier) becomes contractually bound to do so.
3. If the requirement in paragraph 2 is met, the tenant or a person duly authorised by him to do so, must, before the tenant enters into the agreement under section 38A(2) of the Act, or (if earlier) becomes contractually bound to do so, make a declaration in the form, or substantially in the form, set out in paragraph 6.
4. If the requirement in paragraph 2 is not met, the notice referred to in section 38A(4)(a) of the Act must be served on the tenant before the tenant enters into the agreement under section 38A(2) of the Act, or (if earlier) becomes contractually bound to do so, and the tenant, or a person duly authorised by him to do so, must before that time make a statutory declaration in the form, or substantially in the form, set out in paragraph 7.
5. A reference to the notice and, where paragraph 3 applies, the declaration or, where paragraph 4 applies, the statutory declaration must be contained in or endorsed on the instrument creating the agreement under section 38A(2).
6. The form of declaration referred to in paragraph 3 is as follows: –

   I

   ____

   (*name of declarant*) of

   ____

   (*address*) declare that –

   1. I have/

      ____

      (*name of tenant*) has a tenancy of premises at

      ____

      (*address of premises*) for a term commencing on

      ____

   2. I/The tenant propose(s) to enter into an agreement with

      ____

      (*name of landlord*) to surrender the tenancy on a date or in circumstances specified in the agreement.
   3. The landlord has not less than 14 days before I/the tenant enter(s) into the agreement referred to in paragraph 2 above, or (if earlier) become(s) contractually bound to do so, served on me/the tenant a notice in the form, or substantially in the form, set out in Schedule 3 to Regulatory Reform (Business Tenancies) (England and Wales) Order 2003. The form of notice set out in that Schedule is reproduced below.
   4. I have/The tenant has read the notice referred to in paragraph 3 above and accept(s) the consequences of entering into the agreement referred to in paragraph 2 above.
   5. (*as appropriate*) I am duly authorised by the tenant to make this declaration.

   DECLARED this

   ____

   day of

   ____

To:

____

____

____

[*Name and address of tenant*]

From:

____

____

____

[*Name and address of landlord*]

IMPORTANT NOTICE FOR TENANT

Do not commit to any agreement to surrender your lease unless you have read this message carefully and discussed it with a professional adviser.

Normally, you have the right to renew your lease when it expires. By committing yourself to an agreement to surrender, ***you will be giving up this important statutory right***.

- You will **not** be able to continue occupying the premises beyond the date provided for under the agreement for surrender, **unless** the landlord chooses to offer you a further term (in which case you would lose the right to ask the court to determine the new rent). You will need to leave the premises.
- You will be unable to claim compensation for the loss of your premises, unless the lease or agreement for surrender gives you this right.

A qualified surveyor, lawyer or accountant would be able to offer you professional advice on your options.

You do not have to commit yourself to the agreement to surrender your lease unless you want to.

If you receive this notice at least 14 days before committing yourself to agreement to surrender, you will need to sign a simple declaration that you have received this notice and have accepted its consequences, before signing the lease.

But if you do not receive at least 14 days notice, you will need to sign a 'statutory' declaration. To do so, you will need to visit an independent solicitor (or someone else empowered to administer oaths).

Unless there is a special reason for committing yourself to the agreement to surrender sooner, you may want to ask the landlord to let you have at least 14 days to consider whether you wish to give up your statutory rights. If you then decided to go ahead with the agreement to end your lease, you would only need to make a simple declaration, and so you would not need to make a separate visit to an independent solicitor.

7. The form of statutory declaration referred to in paragraph 4 is as follows: –

I

____

(*name of declarant*) of

____

(*address*) do solemnly and sincerely declare that –

1. I have/

____

(*name of tenant*) has a tenancy of premises at

____

(*address of premises*) for a term commencing on

____

2. I/The tenant propose(s) to enter into an agreement with

____

(*name of landlord*) to surrender the tenancy on a date or in circumstances specified in the agreement.

3. The landlord has served on me/the tenant a notice in the form, or substantially in the form, set out in Schedule 3 to the Regulatory Reform (Business Tenancies) (England and Wales) Order 2003. The form of notice set out in that Schedule is reproduced below.

4. I have/The tenant has read the notice referred to in paragraph 3 above and accept(s) the consequences of entering into the agreement referred to in paragraph 2 above.

5. (*as appropriate*) I am duly authorised by the tenant to make this declaration.

To:

____

____

____

[*Name and address of tenant*]

From:

____

____

____

[*Name and address of landlord*]

IMPORTANT NOTICE FOR TENANT

Do not commit to any agreement to surrender your lease unless you have read this message carefully and discussed it with a professional adviser.

Normally, you have the right to renew your lease when it expires. By committing yourself to an agreement to surrender, ***you will be giving up this important statutory right***.

- You will **not** be able to continue occupying the premises beyond the date provided for under the agreement for surrender, **unless** the landlord chooses to offer you a further term (in which case you would lose the right to ask the court to determine the new rent). You will need to leave the premises.
- You will be unable to claim compensation for the loss of your premises, unless the lease or agreement for surrender gives you this right.

A qualified surveyor, lawyer or accountant would be able to offer you professional advice on your options.

You do not have to commit yourself to the agreement to surrender your lease unless you want to.

If you receive this notice at least 14 days before committing yourself to agreement to surrender, you will need to sign a simple declaration that you have received this notice and have accepted its consequences, before signing the lease.

But if you do not receive at least 14 days notice, you will need to sign a 'statutory' declaration. To do so, you will need to visit an independent solicitor (or someone else empowered to administer oaths).

Unless there is a special reason for committing yourself to the agreement to surrender sooner, you may want to ask the landlord to let you have at least 14 days to consider whether you wish to give up your statutory rights. If you then decided to go ahead with the agreement to end your lease, you would only need to make a simple declaration, and so you would not need to make a separate visit to an independent solicitor.

AND I make this solemn declaration conscientiously believing the same to be true and by virtue of the Statutory Declaration Act 1835.

DECLARED at

____

this

____

day of

____

Before me

(*signature of person before whom declaration is made*)

A commissioner for oaths or A solicitor empowered to administer oaths or (*as appropriate*)

SCHEDULE 5

Article 28(1) CONSEQUENTIAL AMENDMENTS

Landlord and Tenant Act 1954

1. The Act shall be amended as follows.
2. After section 14 insert –

'Compensation for possession obtained by misrepresentation

14A. Where an order is made for possession of the property comprised in a tenancy to which section 1 of this Act applies and it is subsequently made to appear to the court that the order was obtained by misrepresentation or the concealment of material facts, the court may order the landlord to pay to the tenant such a sum as appears sufficient as compensation for damage or loss sustained by the tenant as the result of the order.'.

3. In section 26(1), for the words 'tenancy under which he holds for the time being (hereinafter referred to as 'the current tenancy')' substitute 'current tenancy'.
4. In section 38(2) and (3) for the words 'the last foregoing section' substitute the words 'section 37 of this Act'.
5. In section 41A(6) for the words from 'section 29(1)' to 'jointly' substitute 'section 29 of this Act for the grant of a new tenancy it may order the grant to be made to the business tenants or to them jointly'.
6. In section 46 –

(a) for the definition of 'current tenancy' substitute –

'"current tenancy" means the tenancy under which the tenant holds for the time being;' and

(b) after the definition of 'the holding' insert –

'"interim rent" has the meaning given by section 24A(1) of this Act;';

7. In sections 57(3)(a) and 58(1)(a) –

for the words 'subsection (5) and' substitute the word 'subsection'; and
after the word 'under', in the second place where it occurs, insert the words 'subsection (1) of'.

8. In section 59(1), after '(3)' insert the words 'to (3B)'.
9. In section 64(1)(b), for the words 'the said part II' substitute the words 'under section 24(1) or 29(2) of this Act'.

Leasehold Reform Act 1967

10. Schedule 3 to the Leasehold Reform Act 1967 shall be amended as follows.
11. For paragraph 2(1) substitute –

'(1) Sub-paragraphs (1A) to (1E) below apply where a landlord's notice terminating the tenancy of any property has been given under section 4 or 25 of the Landlord and Tenant Act 1954 or served under paragraph 4(1) of Schedule 10 to the Local Government and Housing Act 1989 (whether or not that notice has effect to terminate the tenancy).

(1A) A claim to acquire the freehold or an extended lease of the property shall be of no effect if made after the relevant time, but this sub-paragraph is subject to sub-paragraphs (1D) and (1E) below.

(1B) In this paragraph (but subject to sub-paragraph (1C) below) "the relevant time" is the end of the period of two months beginning with the date on which the landlord's notice terminating the tenancy has been given or served.

(1C) Where –

(a) a landlord's notice terminating the tenancy has been given under section 25 of the Landlord and Tenant Act 1954, and

(b) the tenant applies to the court under section 24(1) of that Act for an order for the grant of a new tenancy before the end of the period of two months mentioned in sub-paragraph (1B) above,

"the relevant time" is the time when the application is made.

(1D) Sub-paragraph (1A) above shall not apply where the landlord gives his written consent to the claim being made after the relevant time.

(1E) Where a tenant, having given notice of a desire to have the freehold, gives after the relevant time a further notice under section 9(3) of this Act of his inability or unwillingness to acquire the house and premises at the price he must pay, he may with the notice under section 9(3) give a notice of his desire to have an extended lease (if he then has a right to such a lease).'.

12. After paragraph 2 insert –

'2A (1) If –

(a) the landlord commences proceedings under Part 2 of the Landlord and Tenant Act 1954; and

(b) the tenant subsequently makes a claim to acquire the freehold or an extended lease of the property; and

(c) paragraph 2 above does not render the claim of no effect, no further steps shall be taken in the proceedings under Part 2 otherwise than for their dismissal and for the making of any consequential order.

(2) Section 64 of the Landlord and Tenant Act 1954 shall have no effect in a case to which sub-paragraph (1) above applies.'.

13. After paragraph 10(2) insert –

'(2A) If the landlord's notice is under section 25 of the Landlord and Tenant Act 1954, sub-paragraph (2) above shall effect in relation to it as if in paragraph (b), after the word "operate" there were inserted the words "and no further proceedings may be taken by him under Part 2 of the Landlord and Tenant Act 1954."'.

SCHEDULE 6

Article 28(2) ENACTMENTS REPEALED

Chapter	*Short title*	*Extent of repeal*
2 and 3 Eliz. 2 c. 56	Landlord and Tenant Act 1954	Section 24(2)(b) and the word 'or' immediately preceding it.
		Section 25(5).
		In section 27(2), the word 'quarter'.
		Section 30(3).
		Section 38(4).
		In section 42(1), the second paragraph.
		Section 55.
		In section 67, the words '(2) or'.
1967 c. 88	Leasehold Reform Act 1967	In Schedule 3, paragraph 2(4)(b) and the word 'and' immediately preceding it.
1969 c. 59	Law of Property Act 1969	Section 6.
1989 c. 40	Companies Act 1989	In Schedule 18, paragraph 3.

Appendix B
LANDLORD AND TENANT ACT 1954

[*Editorial Note*: This 'Keeling Schedule' of the Act shows the changes made by RRO 2003 and a version was first published on the ODPM website. For this publication, new text is highlighted in italic; text which has been either superseded or repealed is given in square brackets and quotation marks.]

PART I SECURITY OF TENURE FOR RESIDENTIAL TENANTS

Provisions as to possession on termination of a long tenancy

14A. Compensation for possession obtained by misrepresentation

Where an order is made for possession of the property comprised in a tenancy to which section 1 of this Act applies and it is subsequently made to appear to the court that the order was obtained by misrepresentation or the concealment of material facts, the court may order the landlord to pay to the tenant such a sum as appears sufficient as compensation for damage or loss sustained by the tenant as the result of the order.

PART II SECURITY OF TENURE FOR BUSINESS, PROFESSIONAL AND OTHER TENANTS

Tenancies to which Part II applies

23. Tenancies to which Part II applies

(1) Subject to the provisions of this Act, this Part of this Act applies to any tenancy where the property comprised in the tenancy is or includes premises which are occupied by the tenant and are so occupied for the purposes of a business carried on by him or for those and other purposes.

(1A) *Occupation or the carrying on of a business –*

(a) by a company in which the tenant has a controlling interest; or

(b) where the tenant is a company, by a person with a controlling interest in the company,

shall be treated for the purposes of this section as equivalent to occupation or, as the case may be, the carrying on of a business by the tenant.

(1B) *Accordingly references (however expressed) in this Part of this Act to the business of, or to use, occupation or enjoyment by, the tenant shall be construed as including references to the business of, or to use, occupation or enjoyment by, a company falling within subsection (1A)(a) above or a person falling within subsection (1A)(b) above.*

(2) In this Part of this Act the expression 'business' includes a trade, profession or employment and includes any activity carried on by a body of persons, whether corporate or unincorporate.

(3) In the following provisions of this Part of this Act the expression 'the holding', in relation to a tenancy to which this Part of this Act applies, means the property comprised

in the tenancy, there being excluded any part thereof which is occupied neither by the tenant nor by a person employed by the tenant and so employed for the purposes of a business by reason of which the tenancy is one to which this Part of this Act applies.

(4) Where the tenant is carrying on a business, in all or any part of the property comprised in a tenancy, in breach of a prohibition (however expressed) of use for business purposes which subsists under the terms of the tenancy and extends to the whole of that property, this Part of this Act shall not apply to the tenancy unless the immediate landlord or his predecessor in title has consented to the breach or the immediate landlord has acquiesced therein.

In this subsection the reference to a prohibition of use for business purposes does not include a prohibition of use for the purposes of a specified business, or of use for purposes of any but a specified business, but save as aforesaid includes a prohibition of use for the purposes of some one or more only of the classes of business specified in the definition of that expression in subsection (2) of this section.

Continuation and renewal of tenancies

24. Continuation of tenancies to which Part II applies and grant of new tenancies

(1) A tenancy to which this Part of this Act applies shall not come to an end unless terminated in accordance with the provisions of this Part of this Act; and, subject to the [**pre-RRO**: 'provisions of section twenty-nine of this Act, the tenant under such a tenancy may apply to the court for'] *following provisions of this Act either the tenant or the landlord under such a tenancy may apply to the court for an order for the grant of* a new tenancy –

(a) if the landlord has given notice under section 25 of this Act to terminate the tenancy, or

(b) if the tenant has made a request for a new tenancy in accordance with section 26 of this Act.

(2) The last foregoing subsection shall not prevent the coming to an end of a tenancy by notice to quit given by the tenant, by surrender or forfeiture, or by the forfeiture of a superior tenancy unless –

(a) in the case of a notice to quit, the notice was given before the tenant had been in occupation in right of the tenancy for one month;

[**Pre-RRO**:

(b) 'in the case of an instrument of surrender, the instrument was executed before, or was executed in pursuance of an agreement made before, the tenant had been in occupation in right of the tenancy for one month.']

(2A) Neither the tenant nor the landlord may make an application under subsection (1) above if the other has made such an application and the application has been served.

(2B) Neither the tenant nor the landlord may make such an application if the landlord has made an application under section 29(2) of this Act and the application has been served.

(2C) The landlord may not withdraw an application under subsection (1) above unless the tenant consents to its withdrawal.

(3) Notwithstanding anything in subsection (1) of this section –

(a) where a tenancy to which this Part of this Act applies ceases to be such a tenancy, it shall not come to an end by reason only of the cesser, but if it was granted for a term of years certain and has been continued by subsection (1) of this section then (without prejudice to the termination thereof in accordance with any terms of the tenancy) it may be terminated by not less than three nor more than six months' notice in writing given by the landlord to the tenant;

(b) where, at a time when a tenancy is not one to which this Part of this Act applies, the landlord gives notice to quit, the operation of the notice shall not be affected by reason that the tenancy becomes one to which this Part of this Act applies after the giving of the notice.

24A. Applications for determination of interim rent while tenancy continues

[**Pre-RRO**:

'(1) The landlord of a tenancy to which this Part of this Act applies may, –

(a) if he has given notice under section 25 of this Act to terminate the tenancy; or

(b) if the tenant has made a request for a new tenancy in accordance with section 26 of this Act;

apply to the court to determine a rent which it would be reasonable for the tenant to pay while the tenancy continues by virtue of section 24 of this Act, and the court may determine a rent accordingly.

(2) A rent determined in proceedings under this section shall be deemed to be the rent payable under the tenancy from the date on which the proceedings were commenced or the date specified in the landlord's notice or the tenant's request, whichever is the later.

(3) In determining a rent under this section the court shall have regard to the rent payable under the terms of the tenancy, but otherwise subsections (1) and (2) of section 34 of this Act shall apply to the determination as they would apply to the determination of a rent under that section if a new tenancy from year to year of the whole of the property comprised in the tenancy were granted to the tenant by order of the court.']

(1) Subject to subsection (2) below, if –

(a) the landlord of a tenancy to which this Part of this Act applies has given notice under section 25 of this Act to terminate the tenancy; or

(b) the tenant of such a tenancy has made a request for a new tenancy in accordance with section 26 of this Act,

either of them may make an application to the court to determine a rent (an 'interim rent') which the tenant is to pay while the tenancy ('the relevant tenancy') continues by virtue of section 24 of this Act and the court may order payment of an interim rent in accordance with section 24C or 24D of this Act.

(2) Neither the tenant nor the landlord may make an application under subsection (1) above if the other has made such an application and has not withdrawn it.

(3) No application shall be entertained under subsection (1) above if it is made more than six months after the termination of the relevant tenancy.

24B. Date from which interim rent is payable

(1) The interim rent determined on an application under section 24A(1) of this Act shall be payable from the appropriate date.

(2) If an application under section 24A(1) of this Act is made in a case where the landlord has given a notice under section 25 of this Act, the appropriate date is the earliest date of termination that could have been specified in the landlord's notice.

(3) If an application under section 24A(1) of this Act is made in a case where the tenant has made a request for a new tenancy under section 26 of this Act, the appropriate date is the earliest date that could have been specified in the tenant's request as the date from which the new tenancy is to begin.

24C. Amount of interim rent where new tenancy of whole premises granted and landlord not opposed

(1) This section applies where –

(a) the landlord gave a notice under section 25 of this Act at a time when the tenant was in occupation of the whole of the property comprised in the relevant tenancy for pur-

poses such as are mentioned in section 23(1) of this Act and stated in the notice that he was not opposed to the grant of a new tenancy; or

(b) *the tenant made a request for a new tenancy under section 26 of this Act at a time when he was in occupation of the whole of that property for such purposes and the landlord did not give notice under subsection (6) of that section,*

and the landlord grants a new tenancy of the whole of the property comprised in the relevant tenancy to the tenant (whether as a result of an order for the grant of a new tenancy or otherwise).

(2) *Subject to the following provisions of this section, the rent payable under and at the commencement of the new tenancy shall also be the interim rent.*

(3) *Subsection (2) above does not apply where –*

(a) *the landlord or the tenant shows to the satisfaction of the court that the interim rent under that subsection differs substantially from the relevant rent; or*

(b) *the landlord or the tenant shows to the satisfaction of the court that the terms of the new tenancy differ from the terms of the relevant tenancy to such an extent that the interim rent under that subsection is substantially different from the rent which (in default of such agreement) the court would have determined under section 34 of this Act to be payable under a tenancy which commenced on the same day as the new tenancy and whose other terms were the same as the relevant tenancy.*

(4) *In this section 'the relevant rent' means the rent which (in default of agreement between the landlord and the tenant) the court would have determined under section 34 of this Act to be payable under the new tenancy if the new tenancy had commenced on the appropriate date (within the meaning of section 24B of this Act).*

(5) *The interim rent in a case where subsection (2) above does not apply by virtue only of subsection (3)(a) above is the relevant rent.*

(6) *The interim rent in a case where subsection (2) above does not apply by virtue only of subsection (3)(b) above, or by virtue of subsection (3)(a) and (b) above, is the rent which it is reasonable for the tenant to pay while the relevant tenancy continues by virtue of section 24 of this Act.*

(7) *In determining the interim rent under subsection (6) above the court shall have regard –*

(a) *to the rent payable under the terms of the relevant tenancy; and*

(b) *to the rent payable under any sub-tenancy of part of the property comprised in the relevant tenancy,*

but otherwise subsections (1) and (2) of section 34 of this Act shall apply to the determination as they would apply to the determination of a rent under that section if a new tenancy of the whole of the property comprised in the relevant tenancy were granted to the tenant by order of the court and the duration of that new tenancy were the same as the duration of the new tenancy which is actually granted to the tenant.

(8) *In this section and section 24D of this Act 'the relevant tenancy' has the same meaning as in section 24A of this Act.*

24D. Amount of interim rent in any other case

(1) *The interim rent in a case where section 24C of this Act does not apply is the rent which it is reasonable for the tenant to pay while the relevant tenancy continues by virtue of section 24 of this Act.*

(2) *In determining the interim rent under subsection (1) above the court shall have regard –*

(a) *to the rent payable under the terms of the relevant tenancy; and*

(b) *to the rent payable under any sub-tenancy of part of the property comprised in the relevant tenancy, but otherwise subsections (1) and (2) of section 34 of this Act shall apply to the determination as they would apply to the determination of a rent under that section if a new tenancy from year to year of the whole of the property comprised in the relevant tenancy were granted to the tenant by order of the court.*

(3) *If the court –*

(a) *has made an order for the grant of a new tenancy and has ordered payment of interim rent in accordance with section 24C of this Act, but*

(b) *either –*

(i) *it subsequently revokes under section 36(2) of this Act the order for the grant of a new tenancy; or*

(ii) *the landlord and tenant agree not to act on the order, the court on the application of the landlord or the tenant shall determine a new interim rent in accordance with subsections (1) and (2) above without a further application under section 24A(1) of this Act.*

25. Termination of tenancy by the landlord

(1) The landlord may terminate a tenancy to which this Part of this Act applies by a notice given to the tenant in the prescribed form specifying the date at which the tenancy is to come to an end (hereinafter referred to as 'the date of termination'):

Provided that this subsection has effect subject *to the provisions of section 29B(4) of this Act and* Part IV of this Act as to the interim continuation of tenancies pending the disposal of applications to the court.

(2) Subject to the provisions of the next following subsection, a notice under this section shall not have effect unless it is given not more than twelve nor less than six months before the date of termination specified therein.

(3) In the case of a tenancy which apart from this Act could have been brought to an end by notice to quit given by the landlord –

(a) the date of termination specified in a notice under this section shall not be earlier than the earliest date on which apart from this Part of this Act the tenancy could have been brought to an end by notice to quit given by the landlord on the date of the giving of the notice under this section; and

(b) where apart from this Part of this Act more than six months' notice to quit would have been required to bring the tenancy to an end, the last foregoing subsection shall have effect with the substitution for twelve months of a period six months longer than the length of notice to quit which would have been required as aforesaid.

(4) In the case of any other tenancy, a notice under this section shall not specify a date of termination earlier than the date on which apart from this Part of this Act the tenancy would have come to an end by effluxion of time.

[**Pre-RRO**:

'(5) A notice under this section shall not have effect unless it requires the tenant, within two months after the giving of the notice, to notify the landlord in writing whether or not, at the date of termination, the tenant will be willing to give up possession of the property comprised in the tenancy.

(6) A notice under this section shall not have effect unless it states whether the landlord would oppose an application to the court under this Part of this Act for the grant of a new tenancy and, if so, also states on which of the grounds mentioned in section 30 of this Act he would do so.']

(6) *A notice under this section shall not have effect unless it states whether the landlord is opposed to the grant of a new tenancy to the tenant.*

(7) *A notice under this section which states that the landlord is opposed to the grant of a new tenancy to the tenant shall not have effect unless it also specifies one or more of the grounds specified in section 30(1) of this Act as the ground or grounds for his opposition.*

(8) *A notice under this section which states that the landlord is not opposed to the grant of a new tenancy to the tenant shall not have effect unless it sets out the landlord's proposals as to –*

(a) *the property to be comprised in the new tenancy (being either the whole or part of the property comprised in the current tenancy);*
(b) *the rent to be payable under the new tenancy; and*
(c) *the other terms of the new tenancy.*

26. Tenant's request for a new tenancy

(1) A tenant's request for a new tenancy may be made where the [**pre-RRO**: 'tenancy under which he holds for the time being (hereinafter referred to as 'the current tenancy')'] *current tenancy* is a tenancy granted for a term of years certain exceeding one year, whether or not continued by section 24 of this Act, or granted for a term of years certain and thereafter from year to year.

(2) A tenant's request for a new tenancy shall be for a tenancy beginning with such date, not more than twelve nor less than six months after the making of the request, as maybe specified therein;

Provided that the said date shall not be earlier than the date on which apart from this Act the current tenancy would come to an end by effluxion of time or could be brought to an end by notice to quit given by the tenant.

(3) A tenant's request for a new tenancy shall not have effect unless it is made by notice in the prescribed form given to the landlord and sets out the tenant's proposals as to the property to be comprised in the new tenancy (being either the whole or part of the property comprised in the current tenancy), as to the rent to be payable under the new tenancy and as to the other terms of the new tenancy.

(4) A tenant's request for a new tenancy shall not be made if the landlord has already given notice under the last foregoing section to terminate the current tenancy, or if the tenant has already given notice to quit or notice under the next following section; and no such notice shall be given by the landlord or the tenant after the making by the tenant of a request for a new tenancy.

(5) Where the tenant makes a request for a new tenancy in accordance with the foregoing provisions of this section, the current tenancy shall, subject to the provisions of [**pre-RRO**: 'subsection (2) of section thirty-six'] *sections 29B(4) and 36(2)* of this Act and the provisions of Part IV of this Act as to the interim continuation of tenancies, terminate immediately before the date specified in the request for the beginning of the new tenancy.

(6) Within two months of the making of a tenant's request for a new tenancy the landlord may give notice to the tenant that he will oppose an application to the court for the grant of a new tenancy, and any such notice shall state on which of the grounds mentioned in section 30 of this Act the landlord will oppose the application.

27. Termination by tenant of tenancy for fixed term

(1) Where the tenant under a tenancy to which this Part of this Act applies, being a tenancy granted for a term of years certain, gives to the immediate landlord, not later than three months before the date on which apart from this Act the tenancy would come to an end by effluxion of time, a notice in writing that the tenant does not desire the tenancy to be continued, section 24 of this Act shall not have effect in relation to the tenancy, unless the notice is given before the tenant has been in occupation in right of the tenancy for one month.

(1A) *Section 24 of this Act shall not have effect in relation to a tenancy for a term of years certain where the tenant is not in occupation of the property comprised in the tenancy at the time when, apart from this Act, the tenancy would come to an end by effluxion of time.*

(2) A tenancy granted for a term of years certain which is continuing by virtue of section 24 of this Act *shall not come to an end by reason only of the tenant ceasing to occupy the property comprised in the tenancy but* may be brought to an end on any day by not less than three months' notice in writing given by the tenant to the immediate landlord, whether the notice is given after the date on which apart from

this Act the tenancy would have come to an end or before that date, but not before the tenant has been in occupation in right of the tenancy for one month.

(3) *Where a tenancy is terminated under subsection (2) above, any rent payable in respect of a period which begins before, and ends after, the tenancy is terminated shall be apportioned, and any rent paid by the tenant in excess of the amount apportioned to the period before termination shall be recoverable by him.*

28. Renewal of tenancies by agreement

Where the landlord and tenant agree for the grant to the tenant of a future tenancy of the holding, or of the holding with other land, on terms and from a date specified in the agreement, the current tenancy shall continue until that date but no longer, and shall not be a tenancy to which this Part of this Act applies.

Applications to court

29. Order by court for grant of new tenancy or termination of current tenancy

[**Pre-RRO**:

'(1) Subject to the provisions of this Act, on an application under subsection (1) of section 24 of this Act for a new tenancy the court shall make an order for the grant of a tenancy comprising such property, at such rent and on such other terms, as are hereinafter provided.

(2) Where such an application is made in consequence of a notice given by the landlord under section 25 of this Act, it shall not be entertained unless the tenant has duly notified the landlord that he will not be willing at the date of termination to give up possession of the property comprised in the tenancy.

(3) No application under subsection (1) of section 24 of this Act shall be entertained unless it is made not less than two nor more than four months after the giving of the landlord's notice under section 25 of this Act or, as the case may be, after the making of the tenant's request for a new tenancy.']

(1) *Subject to the provisions of this Act, on an application under section 24(1) of this Act, the court shall make an order for the grant of a new tenancy and accordingly for the termination of the current tenancy immediately before the commencement of the new tenancy.*

(2) *Subject to the following provisions of this Act, a landlord may apply to the court for an order for the termination of a tenancy to which this Part of this Act applies without the grant of a new tenancy –*

 (a) *if he has given notice under section 25 of this Act that he is opposed to the grant of a new tenancy to the tenant; or*

 (b) *if the tenant has made a request for a new tenancy in accordance with section 26 of this Act and the landlord has given notice under subsection (6) of that section.*

(3) *The landlord may not make an application under subsection (2) above if either the tenant or the landlord has made an application under section 24(1) of this Act.*

(4) *Subject to the provisions of this Act, where the landlord makes an application under subsection (2) above –*

 (a) *if he establishes, to the satisfaction of the court, any of the grounds on which he is entitled to make the application in accordance with section 30 of this Act, the court shall make an order for the termination of the current tenancy <u>in accordance with section 64 of this Act</u> without the grant of a new tenancy; and*

 (b) *if not, it shall make an order for the grant of a new tenancy and accordingly for the termination of the current tenancy immediately before the commencement of the new tenancy.*

(5) *The court shall dismiss an application by the landlord under section 24(1) of this Act if the tenant informs the court that he does not want a new tenancy.*

(6) *The landlord may not withdraw an application under subsection (2) above unless the tenant consents to its withdrawal.*

29A. Time limits for applications to court

(1) *Subject to section 29B of this Act, the court shall not entertain an application –*

(a) *by the tenant or the landlord under section 24(1) of this Act; or*

(b) *by the landlord under section 29(2) of this Act,*

if it is made after the end of the statutory period.

(2) *In this section and section 29B of this Act 'the statutory period' means a period ending –*

(a) *where the landlord gave a notice under section 25 of this Act, on the date specified in his notice; and*

(b) *where the tenant made a request for a new tenancy under section 26 of this Act, immediately before the date specified in his request.*

(3) *Where the tenant has made a request for a new tenancy under section 26 of this Act, the court shall not entertain an application under section 24(1) of this Act which is made before the end of the period of two months beginning with the date of the making of the request, unless the application is made after the landlord has given a notice under section 26(6) of this Act.*

29B. Agreements extending time limits

(1) *After the landlord has given a notice under section 25 of this Act, or the tenant has made a request under section 26 of this Act, but before the end of the statutory period, the landlord and tenant may agree that an application such as is mentioned in section 29A(1) of this Act may be made before the end of a period specified in the agreement which will expire after the end of the statutory period.*

(2) *The landlord and tenant may from time to time by agreement further extend the period for making such an application, but any such agreement must be made before the end of the period specified in the current agreement.*

(3) *Where an agreement is made under this section, the court may entertain an application such as is mentioned in section 29A(1) of this Act if it is made before the end of the period specified in the agreement.*

(4) *Where an agreement is made under this section, or two or more agreements are made under this section, the landlord's notice under section 25 of this Act or tenant's request under section 26 of this Act shall be treated as terminating the tenancy at the end of the period specified in the agreement or, as the case may be, at the end of the period specified in the last of those agreements.*

30. Opposition by landlord to application for new tenancy

(1) The grounds on which a landlord may oppose an application under [**pre-RRO**: 'subsection (1) of section twenty-four of this Act'] *section 24(1) of this Act, or make an application under section 29(2) of this Act*, are such of the following grounds as may be stated in the landlord's notice under section 25 of this Act or, as the case may be, under subsection (6) of section 26 thereof, that is to say:

(a) where under the current tenancy the tenant has any obligations as respects the repair and maintenance of the holding, that the tenant ought not to be granted a new tenancy in view of the state of repair of the holding, being a state resulting from the tenant's failure to comply with the said obligations;

(b) that the tenant ought not to be granted a new tenancy in view of his persistent delay in paying rent which has become due;

(c) that the tenant ought not to be granted a new tenancy in view of other substantial breaches by him of his obligations under the current tenancy, or for any other reason connected with the tenant's use or management of the holding;

(d) that the landlord has offered and is willing to provide or secure the provision of alternative accommodation for the tenant, that the terms on which the alternative accommodation is available are reasonable having regard to the terms of the current tenancy and to all other relevant circumstances, and that the accommodation and the time at which it will be available are suitable for the tenant's requirements (including the requirement to preserve goodwill) having regard to the nature and class of his business and to the situation and extent of, and facilities afforded by, the holding;
(e) where the current tenancy was created by the sub-letting of part only of the property comprised in a superior tenancy and the landlord is the owner of an interest in reversion expectant on the termination of that superior tenancy, that the aggregate of the rents reasonably obtainable on separate lettings of the holding and the remainder of that property would be substantially less than the rent reasonably obtainable on a letting of that property as a whole, that on the termination of the current tenancy the landlord requires possession of the holding for the purpose of letting or otherwise disposing of the said property as a whole, and that in view thereof the tenant ought not to be granted a new tenancy;
(f) that on the termination of the current tenancy the landlord intends to demolish or reconstruct the premises comprised in the holding or a substantial part of those premises or to carry out substantial work of construction on the holding or part thereof and that he could not reasonably do so without obtaining possession of the holding;
(g) subject as hereinafter provided, that on the termination of the current tenancy the landlord intends to occupy the holding for the purposes, or partly for the purposes, of a business to be carried on by him therein, or as his residence.

(1A) Where the landlord has a controlling interest in a company, the reference in subsection (1)(g) above to the landlord shall be construed as a reference to the landlord or that company.

(1B) Subject to subsection (2A) below, where the landlord is a company and a person has a controlling interest in the company, the reference in subsection (1)(g) above to the landlord shall be construed as a reference to the landlord or that person.

(2) The landlord shall not be entitled to oppose an application *under section 24(1) of this Act, or make an application under section 29(2) of this Act*, on the ground specified in paragraph (g) of the last foregoing subsection if the interest of the landlord, or an interest which has merged in that interest and but for the merger would be the interest of the landlord, was purchased or created after the beginning of the period of five years which ends with the termination of the current tenancy, and at all times since the purchase or creation thereof the holding has been comprised in a tenancy or successive tenancies of the description specified in subsection (1) of section 23 of this Act.

(2A) Subsection (1B) above shall not apply if the controlling interest was acquired after the beginning of the period of five years which ends with the termination of the current tenancy, and at all times since the acquisition of the controlling interest the holding has been comprised in a tenancy or successive tenancies of the description specified in section 23(1) of this Act.

[**Pre-RRO**:

'(3) Where the landlord has a controlling interest in a company any business to be carried on by the company shall be treated for the purposes of subsection (1)(g) of this section as a business to be carried on by him.

For the purposes of this subsection, a person has a controlling interest in a company if and only if either –

(a) he is a member of it and able, without the consent of any other person, to appoint or remove the holders of at least a majority of the directorships; or

(b) he holds more than one-half of its equity share capital, there being disregarded any shares held by him in a fiduciary capacity or as nominee for another person;

and in this subsection 'company' and 'share' have the meanings assigned to them by section 455(l) of the Companies Act 1948 and 'equity share capital' the meaning assigned to it by section 154(5) of that Act.']

31. Dismissal of application for new tenancy where landlord successfully opposes

(1) If the landlord opposes an application under subsection (1) of section 24 of this Act on grounds on which he is entitled to oppose it in accordance with the last foregoing section and establishes any of those grounds to the satisfaction of the court, the court shall not make an order for the grant of a new tenancy.

(2) [**Pre-RRO**: 'Where in a case not falling within the last foregoing subsection the landlord opposes an application under the said subsection (1) on one or more of the grounds specified in paragraphs (d), (e) and (f) of subsection (1) of the last foregoing section but establishes none of those grounds to the satisfaction of the court; then if the court would have been satisfied of any of those grounds'] *Where the landlord opposes an application under section 24(1) of this Act, or makes an application under section 29(2) of this Act, on one or more of the grounds specified in section 30(1)(d) to (f) of this Act but establishes none of those grounds, and none of the other grounds specified in section 30(1) of this Act, to the satisfaction of the court, then if the court would have been satisfied on any of the grounds specified in section 30(1)(d) to (f) of this Act* if the date of termination specified in the landlord's notice or, as the case may be, the date specified in the tenant's request for a new tenancy as the date from which the new tenancy is to begin, had been such later date as the court may determine, being a date not more than one year later than the date so specified, –

(a) the court shall make a declaration to that effect, stating of which of the said grounds the court would have been satisfied as aforesaid and specifying the date determined by the court as aforesaid, but shall not make an order for the grant of a new tenancy;

(b) if, within fourteen days after the making of the declaration, the tenant so requires the court shall make an order substituting the said date for the date specified in the said landlord's notice or tenant's request, and thereupon that notice or request shall have effect accordingly.

31A. Grant of new tenancy in some cases where section 30(1)(f) applies

(1) Where the landlord opposes an application under section 24(1) of this Act on the ground specified in paragraph (f) of section 30(1) of this Act, *or makes an application under section 29(2) of this Act on that ground*, the court shall not hold that the landlord could not reasonably carry out the demolition, reconstruction or work of construction intended without obtaining possession of the holding if –

(a) the tenant agrees to the inclusion in the terms of the new tenancy of terms giving the landlord access and other facilities for carrying out the work intended and, given that access and those facilities, the landlord could reasonably carry out the work without obtaining possession of the holding and without interfering to a substantial extent or for a substantial time with the use of the holding for the purposes of the business carried on by the tenant; or

(b) the tenant is willing to accept a tenancy of an economically separable part of the holding and either paragraph (a) of this section is satisfied with respect to that part or possession of the remainder of the holding would be reasonably sufficient to enable the landlord to carry out the intended work.

(2) For the purposes of subsection (1)(b) of this section a part of a holding shall be deemed to be an economically separate part if, and only if, the aggregate of the rents which, after the completion of the intended work, would be reasonably obtainable on

separate lettings of that part and the remainder of the premises affected by or resulting from the work would not be substantially less than the rent which would then be reasonably obtainable on a letting of those premises as a whole.

32. Property to be comprised in new tenancy

(1) Subject to the following provisions of this section, an order under section 29 of this Act for the grant of a new tenancy shall be an order for the grant of a new tenancy of the holding; and in the absence of agreement between the landlord and the tenant as to the property which constitutes the holding the court shall in the order designate that property by reference to the circumstances existing at the date of the order.

(1A) Where the court, by virtue of paragraph (b) of section 31A(1) of this Act, makes an order under section 29 of this Act for the grant of a new tenancy in a case where the tenant is willing to accept a tenancy of part of the holding, the order shall be an order for the grant of a new tenancy of that part only.

(2) The foregoing provisions of this section shall not apply in a case where the property comprised in the current tenancy includes other property besides the holding and the landlord requires any new tenancy ordered to be granted under section 29 of this Act to be a tenancy of the whole of the property comprised in the current tenancy; but in any such case –

- (a) any order under the said section 29 for the grant of a new tenancy shall be an order for the grant of a new tenancy of the whole of the property comprised in the current tenancy, and
- (b) references in the following provisions of this Part of this Act to the holding shall be construed as references to the whole of that property.

(3) Where the current tenancy includes rights enjoyed by the tenant in connection with the holding, those rights shall be included in a tenancy ordered to be granted under section 29 of this Act, except as otherwise agreed between the landlord and the tenant or, in default of such agreement, determined by the court.

33. Duration of new tenancy

Where on an application under this Part of this Act the court makes an order for the grant of a new tenancy, the new tenancy shall be such tenancy as may be agreed between the landlord and the tenant, or, in default of such an agreement, shall be such a tenancy as may be determined by the court to be reasonable in all the circumstances, being, if it is a tenancy for a term of years certain, a tenancy for a term not exceeding [**pre-RRO**: 'fourteen'] *fifteen* years, and shall begin on the coming to an end of the current tenancy.

34. Rent under new tenancy

(1) The rent payable under a tenancy granted by order of the court under this Part of this Act shall be such as may be agreed between the landlord and the tenant or as, in default of such agreement, may be determined by the court to be that at which, having regard to the terms of the tenancy (other than those relating to rent), the holding might reasonably be expected to be let in the open market by a willing lessor, there being disregarded –

- (a) any effect on rent of the fact that the tenant has or his predecessors in title have been in occupation of the holding,
- (b) any goodwill attached to the holding by reason of the carrying on thereat of the business of the tenant (whether by him or by a predecessor of his in that business),
- (c) any effect on rent of an improvement to which this paragraph applies,
- (d) in the case of a holding comprising licensed premises, any addition to its value attributable to the licence, if it appears to the court that having regard to the terms of the current tenancy and any other relevant circumstances the benefit of the licence belongs to the tenant.

(2) Paragraph (c) of the foregoing subsection applies to any improvement carried out by a person who at the time it was carried out was the tenant, but only if it was carried out otherwise than in pursuance of an obligation to his immediate landlord, and either it was carried out during the current tenancy or the following conditions are satisfied, that is to say –

(a) that it was completed not more than twenty-one years before the application [**pre-RRO**: 'for the new tenancy'] *to the court* was made; and

(b) that the holding or any part of it affected by the improvement has at all times since the completion of the improvement been comprised in tenancies of the description specified in section 23(1) of this Act; and

(c) that at the termination of each of those tenancies the tenant did not quit.

(2A) If this Part of this Act applies by virtue of section 23(1A) of this Act, the reference in subsection (1)(d) above to the tenant shall be construed as including –

(a) a company in which the tenant has a controlling interest, or

(b) where the tenant is a company, a person with a controlling interest in the company.

(3) Where the rent is determined by the court the court may, if it thinks fit, further determine that the terms of the tenancy shall include such provision for varying the rent as may be specified in the determination.

(4) It is hereby declared that the matters which are to be taken into account by the court in determining the rent include any effect on rent of the operation of the provisions of the Landlord and Tenant (Covenants) Act 1995.

35. Other terms of new tenancy

(1) The terms of a tenancy granted by order of the court under this Part of this Act (other than terms as to the duration thereof and as to the rent payable thereunder), *including, where different persons own interests which fulfil the conditions specified in section 44(1) of this Act in different parts of it, terms as to the apportionment of the rent,* shall be such as may be agreed between the landlord and the tenant or as, in default of such agreement, may be determined by the court; and in determining those terms the court shall have regard to the terms of the current tenancy and to all relevant circumstances.

(2) In subsection (1) of this section the reference to all relevant circumstances includes (without prejudice to the generality of that reference) a reference to the operation of the provisions of the Landlord and Tenant (Covenants) Act 1995.

36. Carrying out of order for new tenancy

(1) Where under this Part of this Act the court makes an order for the grant of a new tenancy, then, unless the order is revoked under the next following subsection or the landlord and the tenant agree not to act upon the order, the landlord shall be bound to execute or make in favour of the tenant, and the tenant shall be bound to accept, a lease or agreement for a tenancy of the holding embodying the terms agreed between the landlord and the tenant or determined by the court in accordance with the foregoing provisions of this Part of this Act; and where the landlord executes or makes such a lease or agreement the tenant shall be bound, if so required by the landlord, to execute a counterpart or duplicate thereof.

(2) If the tenant, within fourteen days after the making of an order under this Part of this Act for the grant of a new tenancy, applies to the court for the revocation of the order the court shall revoke the order; and where the order is so revoked, then, if it is so agreed between the landlord and the tenant or determined by the court, the current tenancy shall continue, beyond the date at which it would have come to an end apart from this subsection, for such period as may be so agreed or determined to be necessary to afford to the landlord a reasonable opportunity for reletting or otherwise disposing of the premises which would have been comprised in the new

tenancy; and while the current tenancy continues by virtue of this subsection it shall not be a tenancy to which this Part of this Act applies.

(3) Where an order is revoked under the last foregoing subsection any provision thereof as to payment of costs shall not cease to have effect by reason only of the revocation; but the court may, if it thinks fit, revoke or vary any such provision or, where no costs have been awarded in the proceedings for the revoked order, award such costs.

(4) A lease executed or agreement made under this section, in a case where the interest of the lessor is subject to a mortgage, shall be deemed to be one authorised by section 99 of the Law of Property Act 1925 (which confers certain powers of leasing on mortgagors in possession), and subsection (13) of that section (which allows those powers to be restricted or excluded by agreement) shall not have effect in relation to such a lease or agreement.

37. Compensation where order for new tenancy precluded on certain grounds

[**Pre-RRO**:

'(1) Where on the making of an application under section 24 of this Act the court is precluded (whether by subsection (1) or subsection (2) of section 31 of this Act) from making an order for the grant of a new tenancy by reason of any of the grounds specified in paragraphs (e), (f) and (g) of subsection (1) of section 30 of this Act and not of any grounds specified in any other paragraph of that subsection, or where no other ground is specified in the landlord's notice under section 25 of this Act or, as the case may be, under section 26(6) thereof, than those specified in the said paragraphs (e), (f) and (g) and either no application under the said section 24 is made or such an application is withdrawn, then, subject to the provisions of this Act, the tenant shall be entitled on quitting the holding to recover from the landlord by way of compensation an amount determined in accordance with the following provisions of this section.']

(1) *Subject to the provisions of this Act, in a case specified in subsection (1A), (1B) or (1C) below (a 'compensation case') the tenant shall be entitled on quitting the holding to recover from the landlord by way of compensation an amount determined in accordance with this section.*

(1A) *The first compensation case is where on the making of an application by the tenant under section 24(1) of this Act the court is precluded (whether by subsection (1) or subsection (2) of section 31 of this Act) from making an order for the grant of a new tenancy by reason of any of the grounds specified in paragraphs (e), (f) and (g) of section 30(1) of this Act (the 'compensation grounds') and not of any grounds specified in any other paragraph of section 30(1).*

(1B) *The second compensation case is where on the making of an application under section 29(2) of this Act the court is precluded (whether by section 29(4)(a) or section 31(2) of this Act) from making an order for the grant of a new tenancy by reason of any of the compensation grounds and not of any other grounds specified in section 30(1) of this Act.*

(1C) *The third compensation case is where –*

- (a) *the landlord's notice under section 25 of this Act or, as the case may be, under section 26(6) of this Act, states his opposition to the grant of a new tenancy on any of the compensation grounds and not on any other grounds specified in section 30(1) of this Act; and*
- (b) *either –*
  - (i) *no application is made by the tenant under section 24(1) of this Act or by the landlord under section 29(2) of this Act; or*
  - (ii) *such an application is made but is subsequently withdrawn.*

(2) Subject to [**pre-RRO**: 'subsections (5A) to (5E) of this section the said amount'] *the following provisions of this section, compensation under this section* shall be as follows, that is to say –

(a) where the conditions specified in the next following subsection are satisfied in *relation to the whole of the holding* it shall be the product of the appropriate multiplier and twice the rateable value of the holding,
(b) in any other case it shall be the product of the appropriate multiplier and the rateable value of the holding.

(3) The said conditions are –

(a) that, during the whole of the fourteen years immediately preceding the termination of the current tenancy, premises being or comprised in the holding have been occupied for the purposes of a business carried on by the occupier or for those and other purposes;
(b) that, if during those fourteen years there was a change in the occupier of the premises, the person who was the occupier immediately after the change was the successor to the business carried on by the person who was the occupier immediately before the change.

(3A) If the conditions specified in subsection (3) above are satisfied in relation to part of the holding but not in relation to the other part, the amount of compensation shall be the aggregate of sums calculated separately as compensation in respect of each part, and accordingly, for the purpose of calculating compensation in respect of a part any reference in this section to the holding shall be construed as a reference to that part.

(3B) Where section 44(1A) of this Act applies, the compensation shall be determined separately for each part and compensation determined for any part shall be recoverable only from the person who is the owner of an interest in that part which fulfils the conditions specified in section 44(1) of this Act.

(4) Where the court is precluded from making an order for the grant of a new tenancy under this Part of this Act in [**pre-RRO**: 'the circumstances mentioned in subsection (1) of this section'] *a compensation case*, the court shall on the application of the tenant certify that fact.

(5) For the purposes of subsection (2) of this section the rateable value of the holding shall be determined as follows: –

(a) where in the valuation list in force at the date on which the landlord's notice under section 25 or, as the case may be, subsection (6) of section 26 of this Act is given a value is then shown as the annual value (as hereinafter defined) of the holding, the rateable value of the holding shall be taken to be that value;
(b) where no such value is so shown with respect to the holding but such a value or such values is or are so shown with respect to premises comprised in or comprising the holding or part of it, the rateable value of the holding shall betaken to be such value as is found by a proper apportionment or aggregation of the value or values so shown;
(c) where the rateable value of the holding cannot be ascertained in accordance with the foregoing paragraphs of this subsection, it shall be taken to be the value which, apart from any exemption from assessment to rates, would on a proper assessment be the value to be entered in the said valuation list as the annual value of the holding;

and any dispute arising, whether in proceedings before the court or otherwise, as to the determination for those purposes of the rateable value of the holding shall be referred to the Commissioners of Inland Revenue for decision by the valuation officer.

An appeal shall lie to the Lands Tribunal from any decision of a valuation officer under this subsection, but subject thereto any such decision shall be final.

(5A) If part of the holding is domestic property, as defined in section 66 of the Local Government Finance Act 1988 –

(a) the domestic property shall be disregarded in determining the rateable value of the holding under subsection (5) of this section; and

(b) if, on the date specified in subsection (5)(a) of this section, the tenant occupied the whole or any part of the domestic property, the amount of compensation to which he is entitled under subsection (1) of this section shall be increased by the addition of a sum equal to his reasonable expenses in removing from the domestic property.

(5B) Any question as to the amount of the sum referred to in paragraph (b) of subsection (5A) of this section shall be determined by agreement between the landlord and the tenant or, in default of agreement, by the court.

(5C) If the whole of the holding is domestic property, as defined in section 66 of the Local Government Finance Act 1988, for the purposes of subsection (2) of this section the rateable value of the holding shall be taken to be an amount equal to the rent at which it is estimated the holding might reasonably be expected to let from year to year if the tenant undertook to pay all usual tenant's rates and taxes and to bear the cost of the repairs and insurance and the other expenses (if any) necessary to maintain the holding in a state to command that rent.

(5D) The following provisions shall have effect as regards a determination of an amount mentioned in subsection (5C) of this section –

(a) the date by reference to which such a determination is to be made is the date on which the landlord's notice under section 25 or, as the case may be, subsection (6) of section 26 of this Act is given;
(b) any dispute arising, whether in proceedings before the court or otherwise, as to such a determination shall be referred to the Commissioners of Inland Revenue for decision by a valuation officer;
(c) an appeal shall lie to the Lands Tribunal from such a decision, but subject to that, such a decision shall be final.

(5E) Any deduction made under paragraph 2A of Schedule 6 to the Local Government Finance Act 1988 (deduction from valuation of hereditaments used for breeding horses etc.) shall be disregarded, to the extent that it relates to the holding, in determining the rateable value of the holding under subsection (5) of this section.

(6) The Commissioners of Inland Revenue may by statutory instrument make rules prescribing the procedure in connection with references under this section.

(7) In this section –

the reference to the termination of the current tenancy is a reference to the date of termination specified in the landlord's notice under section 25 of this Act or, as the case may be, the date specified in the tenant's request for a new tenancy as the date from which the new tenancy is to begin;

the expression 'annual value' means rateable value except that where the rateable value differs from the net annual value the said expression means net annual value;

the expression 'valuation officer' means any officer of the Commissioners of Inland Revenue for the time being authorised by a certificate of the Commissioners to act in relation to a valuation list.

(8) In subsection (2) of this section 'the appropriate multiplier' means such multiplier as the Secretary of State may by order made by statutory instrument prescribe and different multipliers may be so prescribed in relation to different cases.

(9) A statutory instrument containing an order under subsection (8) of this section shall be subject to annulment in pursuance of a resolution of either House of Parliament.

37A. Compensation for possession obtained by misrepresentation

(1) *Where the court –*

(a) *makes an order for the termination of the current tenancy but does not make an order for the grant of a new tenancy, or*
(b) *refuses an order for the grant of a new tenancy,*

and it is subsequently made to appear to the court that the order was obtained, or the court was induced to refuse the grant, by misrepresentation or the concealment of material facts, the court may order the landlord to pay to the tenant such sum as appears sufficient as compensation for damage or loss sustained by the tenant as the result of the order or refusal.

(2) *Where –*

(*a*) *the tenant has quit the holding –*

(*i*) *after making but withdrawing an application under section 24(1) of this Act; or*
(*ii*) *without making such an application; and*

(*b*) *it is made to appear to the court that he did so by reason of misrepresentation or the concealment of material facts, the court may order the landlord to pay to the tenant such sum as appears sufficient as compensation for damage or loss sustained by the tenant as the result of quitting the holding.*

38. Restriction on agreements excluding provisions of Part II

(1) Any agreement relating to a tenancy to which this Part of this Act applies (whether contained in the instrument creating the tenancy or not) shall be void (except as provided by [**pre-RRO**: 'subsection (4) of this section'] *section 38A of this Act*) in so far as it purports to preclude the tenant from making an application or request under this Part of this Act or provides for the termination or the surrender of the tenancy in the event of his making such an application or request or for the imposition of any penalty or disability on the tenant in that event.

(2) Where –

(a) during the whole of the five years immediately preceding the date on which the tenant under a tenancy to which this Part of this Act applies is to quit the holding, premises being or comprised in the holding have been occupied for the purposes of a business carried on by the occupier or for those and other purposes, and

(b) if during those five years there was a change in the occupier of the premises, the person who was the occupier immediately after the change was the successor to the business carried on by the person who was the occupier immediately before the change,

any agreement (whether contained in the instrument creating the tenancy or not and whether made before or after the termination of that tenancy) which purports to exclude or reduce compensation under [**pre-RRO**: 'the last foregoing section'] *section 37 of this Act* shall to that extent be void, so however that this subsection shall not affect any agreement as to the amount of any such compensation which is made after the right to compensation has accrued.

(3) In a case not falling within the last foregoing subsection the right to compensation conferred by [**pre-RRO**: 'the last foregoing section'] *section 37 of this Act* may be excluded or modified by agreement.

[**Pre-RRO**:

'(4) The court may –

(a) on the joint application of the persons who will be the landlord and the tenant in relation to a tenancy to be granted for a term of years certain which will be a tenancy to which this Part of this Act applies, authorise an agreement excluding in relation to that tenancy the provisions of sections 24 to 28 of this Act; and

(b) on the joint application of the persons who are the landlord and the tenant in relation to a tenancy to which this Part of this Act applies, authorise an agreement for the surrender of the tenancy on such date or in such circumstances as may be specified in the agreement and on such terms (if any) as may be so specified;

if the agreement is contained in or endorsed on the instrument creating the tenancy or such other instrument as the court may specify; and an agreement contained in or endorsed on an instrument in pursuance of an authorisation given under this sub-section shall be valid notwithstanding anything in the preceding provisions of this section.']

38A. Agreements to exclude provisions of Part II

(1) *The persons who will be the landlord and the tenant in relation to a tenancy to be granted for a term of years certain which will be a tenancy to which this Part of this Act applies may agree that the provisions of sections 24 to 28 of this Act shall be excluded in relation to that tenancy.*

(2) *The persons who are the landlord and the tenant in relation to a tenancy to which this Part of this Act applies may agree that the tenancy shall be surrendered on such date or in such circumstances as may be specified in the agreement and on such terms (if any) as may be so specified.*

(3) *An agreement under subsection (1) above shall be void unless –*

  (a) *the landlord has served on the tenant a notice in the form, or substantially in the form, set out in Schedule 1 to the Regulatory Reform (Business Tenancies) (England and Wales) Order 2003 ('the 2003 Order'); and*

  (b) *the requirements specified in Schedule 2 to that Order are met.*

(4) *An agreement under subsection (2) above shall be void unless –*

  (a) *the landlord has served on the tenant a notice in the form, or substantially in the form, set out in Schedule 3 to the 2003 Order; and*

  (b) *the requirements specified in Schedule 4 to that Order are met.*

General and supplementary provisions

39. Saving for compulsory acquisitions

(1) [*Repealed*]

(2) If the amount of the compensation which would have been payable under section 37 of this Act if the tenancy had come to an end in circumstances giving rise to compensation under that section and the date at which the acquiring authority obtained possession had been the termination of the current tenancy exceeds the amount of the compensation payable under section 121 of the Lands Clauses Consolidation Act 1845 or section 20 of the Compulsory Purchase Act 1965 in the case of a tenancy to which this Part of this Act applies, that compensation shall be increased by the amount of the excess.

(3) Nothing in section 24 of this Act shall affect the operation of the said section 121.

40. Duty of tenants and landlords of business premises to give information to each other

[**Pre-RRO**:

'(1) Where any person having an interest in any business premises, being an interest in reversion expectant (whether immediately or not) on a tenancy of those premises, serves on the tenant a notice in the prescribed form requiring him to do so, it shall be the duty of the tenant to notify that person in writing within one month of the service of the notice –

  (a) whether he occupies the premises or any part thereof wholly or partly for the purposes of a business carried on him, and

  (b) whether his tenancy has effect subject to any sub-tenancy on which his tenancy is immediately expectant and, if so, what premises are comprised in the sub-tenancy, for what term it has effect (or, if it is terminable by notice, by what notice it can be terminated), what is the rent payable thereunder, who is the subtenant, and (to the best of his knowledge and belief) whether the sub-tenant is in occupation of the premises or of part of the premises comprised in the subtenancy and, if not, what is the sub-tenant's address.

(2) Where the tenant of any business premises, being a tenant under such a tenancy as is mentioned in subsection (1) of section 26 of this Act, serves on any persons mentioned in the next following subsection a notice in the prescribed form requiring him to do so, it shall be the duty of that person to notify the tenant in writing within one month after the service of the notice –

(a) whether he is the owner of the fee simple in respect of those premises or any part thereof or the mortgagee in possession of such an owner and, if not,

(b) (to the best of his knowledge and belief) the name and address of the person who is his or, as the case may be, his mortgagor's immediate landlord in respect of those premises or of the part in respect of which he or his mortgagor is not the owner in fee simple, for what term his or his mortgagor's tenancy thereof has effect and what is the earliest date (if any) at which that tenancy is terminable by notice to quit given by the landlord.

(3) The persons referred to in the last foregoing subsection are, in relation to the tenant of any business premises –

(a) any person having an interest in the premises, being an interest in reversion expectant (whether immediately or not) on the tenant's, and

(b) any person being a mortgagee in possession in respect of such an interest in reversion as is mentioned in paragraph (a) of this subsection;

and the information which any such person as is mentioned in paragraph (a) of this subsection is required to give under the last foregoing subsection shall include information whether there is a mortgagee in possession of his interest in the premises and, if so, what is the name and address of the mortgagee.

(4) The foregoing provisions of this section shall not apply to a notice served by or on the tenant more than two years before the date on which apart from this Act his tenancy would come to an end by effluxion of time or could be brought to an end by notice to quit given by the landlord.

(5) In this section –

the expression "business premises" means premises used wholly or partly for the purposes of a business;

the expression "mortgagee in possession" includes a receiver appointed by the mortgagee or by the court who is in receipt of the rents and profits, and the expression "his mortgagor" shall be construed accordingly;

the expression "sub-tenant" includes a person retaining possession of any premises by virtue of the Rent Act 1977 after the coming to an end of a sub-tenancy, and the expression "sub-tenancy" includes a right so to retain possession.']

(1) Where a person who is an owner of an interest in reversion expectant (whether immediately or not) on a tenancy of any business premises has served on the tenant a notice in the prescribed form requiring him to do so, it shall be the duty of the tenant to give the appropriate person in writing the information specified in subsection (2) below.

(2) That information is –

(a) whether the tenant occupies the premises or any part of them wholly or partly for the purposes of a business carried on by him;

(b) whether his tenancy has effect subject to any sub-tenancy on which his tenancy is immediately expectant and, if so –

(i) what premises are comprised in the sub-tenancy;

(ii) for what term it has effect (or, if it is terminable by notice, by what notice it can be terminated);

(iii) *what is the rent payable under it;*
(iv) *who is the sub-tenant;*
(v) *(to the best of his knowledge and belief) whether the sub-tenant is in occupation of the premises or of part of the premises comprised in the sub-tenancy and, if not, what is the sub-tenant's address;*
(vi) *whether an agreement is in force excluding in relation to the sub-tenancy the provisions of sections 24 to 28 of this Act; and*
(vii) *whether a notice has been given under section 25 or 26(6) of this Act, or a request has been made under section 26 of this Act, in relation to the sub-tenancy and, if so, details of the notice or request; and(c) (to the best of his knowledge and belief) the name and address of any other person who owns an interest in reversion in any part of the premises.*

(3) *Where the tenant of any business premises who is a tenant under such a tenancy as is mentioned in section 26(1) of this Act has served on a reversioner or a reversioner's mortgagee in possession a notice in the prescribed form requiring him to do so, it shall be the duty of the person on whom the notice is served to give the appropriate person in writing the information specified in subsection (4) below.*

(4) *That information is –*
(a) *whether he is the owner of the fee simple in respect of the premises or any part of them or the mortgagee in possession of such an owner,*
(b) *if he is not, then (to the best of his knowledge and belief) –*
(i) *the name and address of the person who is his or, as the case may be, his mortgagor's immediate landlord in respect of those premises or of the part in respect of which he or his mortgagor is not the owner in fee simple;*
(ii) *for what term his or his mortgagor's tenancy has effect and what is the earliest date (if any) at which that tenancy is terminable by notice to quit given by the landlord; and*
(iii) *whether a notice has been given under section 25 or 26(6) of this Act, or a request has been made under section 26 of this Act, in relation to the tenancy and, if so, details of the notice or request;*
(c) *(to the best of his knowledge and belief) the name and address of any other person who owns an interest in reversion in any part of the premises; and*
(d) *if he is a reversioner, whether there is a mortgagee in possession of his interest in the premises and, if so, (to the best of his knowledge and belief) what is the name and address of the mortgagee.*

(5) *A duty imposed on a person by this section is a duty –*
(a) *to give the information concerned within the period of one month beginning with the date of service of the notice; and*
(b) *if within the period of six months beginning with the date of service of the notice that person becomes aware that any information which has been given in pursuance of the notice is not, or is no longer, correct, to give the appropriate person correct information within the period of one month beginning with the date on which he becomes aware.*

(6) *This section shall not apply to a notice served by or on the tenant more than two years before the date on which apart from this Act his tenancy would come to an end by effluxion of time or could be brought to an end by notice to quit given by the landlord.*

(7) *Except as provided by section 40A of this Act, the appropriate person for the purposes of this section and section 40A(1) of this Act is the person who served the notice under subsection (1) or (3) above.*

(8) *In this section –*
'business premises' means premises used wholly or partly for the purposes of a business;

'mortgagee in possession' includes a receiver appointed by the mortgagee or by the court who is in receipt of the rents and profits, and 'his mortgagor' shall be construed accordingly;

'reversioner' means any person having an interest in the premises, being an interest in reversion expectant (whether immediately or not) on the tenancy;

'reversioner's mortgagee in possession' means any person being a mortgagee in possession in respect of such an interest; and

'sub-tenant' includes a person retaining possession of any premises by virtue of the Rent (Agriculture) Act 1976 or the Rent Act 1977 after the coming to an end of a sub-tenancy, and 'sub-tenancy' includes a right so to retain possession.

40A. Duties in transfer cases

(1) *If a person on whom a notice under section 40(1) or (3) of this Act has been served has transferred his interest in the premises or any part of them to some other person and gives the appropriate person notice in writing –*

(a) *of the transfer of his interest; and*

(b) *of the name and address of the person to whom he transferred it,*

on giving the notice he ceases in relation to the premises or (as the case may be) to that part to be under any duty imposed by section 40 of this Act.

(2) *If –*

(a) *the person who served the notice under section 40(1) or (3) of this Act ('the transferor') has transferred his interest in the premises to some other person ('the transferee'); and*

(b) *the transferor or the transferee has given the person required to give the information notice in writing –*

(i) *of the transfer; and*

(ii) *of the transferee's name and address, the appropriate person for the purposes of section 40 of this Act and subsection (1) above is the transferee.*

(3) *If –*

(a) *a transfer such as is mentioned in paragraph (a) of subsection (2) above has taken place; but*

(b) *neither the transferor nor the transferee has given a notice such as is mentioned in paragraph (b) of that subsection,*

any duty imposed by section 40 of this Act may be performed by giving the information either to the transferor or to the transferee.

40B. Proceedings for breach of duties to give information

A claim that a person has broken any duty imposed by section 40 of this Act may be made the subject of civil proceedings for breach of statutory duty; and in any such proceedings a court may order that person to comply with that duty and may make an award of damages.

41. Trusts

(1) Where a tenancy is held on trust, occupation by all or any of the beneficiaries under the trust, and the carrying on of a business by all or any of the beneficiaries, shall be treated for the purposes of section 23 of this Act as equivalent to occupation or the carrying on of a business by the tenant; and in relation to a tenancy to which this Part of this Act applies by virtue of the foregoing provisions of this subsection –

(a) references (however expressed) in this Part of this Act and in the Ninth Schedule to this Act to the business of, or to carrying on of business, use, occupation or enjoyment by, the tenant shall be construed as including references to the business of, or to carrying on of business, use, occupation or enjoyment by, the beneficiaries or beneficiary;

(b) the reference in paragraph (d) of subsection (1) of section 34 of this Act to the tenant shall be construed as including the beneficiaries or beneficiary; and
(c) a change in the persons of the trustees shall not be treated as a change in the person of the tenant.

(2) Where the landlord's interest is held on trust the references in paragraph (g) of subsection (1) of section 30 of this Act to the landlord shall be construed as including references to the beneficiaries under the trust or any of them; but, except in the case of a trust arising under a will or on the intestacy of any person, the reference in subsection (2) of that section to the creation of the interest therein mentioned shall be construed as including the creation of the trust.

41A. Partnerships

(1) The following provisions of this section shall apply where –
(a) a tenancy is held jointly by two or more persons (in this section referred to as the joint tenants); and
(b) the property comprised in the tenancy is or includes premises occupied for the purposes of a business; and
(c) the business (or some other business) was at some time during the existence of the tenancy carried on in partnership by all the persons who were then the joint tenants or by those and other persons and the joint tenants' interest in the premises was then partnership property; and
(d) the business is carried on (whether alone or in partnership with other persons) by one or some only of the joint tenants and no part of the property comprised in the tenancy is occupied, in right of the tenancy, for the purposes of a business carried on (whether alone or in partnership with other persons) by the other or others.

(2) In the following provisions of this section those of the joint tenants who for the time being carry on the business are referred to as the business tenants and the others as the other joint tenants.

(3) Any notice given by the business tenants which, had it been given by all the joint tenants, would have been –
(a) a tenant's request for a new tenancy made in accordance with section 26 of this Act; or
(b) a notice under subsection (1) or subsection (2) of section 27 of this Act; shall be treated as such if it states that it is given by virtue of this section and sets out the facts by virtue of which the persons giving it are the business tenants;

and references in those sections and in section 24A of this Act to the tenant shall be construed accordingly.

(4) A notice given by the landlord to the business tenants which, had it been given to all the joint tenants, would have been a notice under section 25 of this Act shall be treated as such a notice, and references in that section to the tenant shall be construed accordingly.

(5) An application under section 24(1) of this Act for a new tenancy may, instead of being made by all the joint tenants, be made by the business tenants alone; and where it is so made –
(a) this Part of this Act shall have effect, in relation to it, as if the references therein to the tenant included references to the business tenants alone; and
(b) the business tenants shall be liable, to the exclusion of the other joint tenants, for the payment of rent and the discharge of any other obligation under the current tenancy for any rental period beginning after the date specified in the landlord's notice under section 25 of this Act or, as the case may be, beginning on or after the date specified in their request for a new tenancy.

(6) Where the court makes an order under [**pre-RRO**: 'section 29(1) of this Act for the grant of a new tenancy on an application made by the business tenants it may order the grant to be made to them or to them jointly'] *section 29 of this Act for the grant of a new tenancy it may order the grant to be made to the business tenants or to them jointly* with the persons carrying on the business in partnership with them, and may order the grant to be made subject to the satisfaction, within a time specified by the order, of such conditions as to guarantors, sureties or otherwise as appear to the court equitable, having regard to the omission of the other joint tenants from the persons who will be the tenants under the new tenancy.

(7) The business tenants shall be entitled to recover any amount payable by way of compensation under section 37 or section 59 of this Act.

42. Groups of companies

(1) For the purposes of this section two bodies corporate shall be taken to be members of a group if and only if one is a subsidiary of the other or both are subsidiaries of the third body corporate *or the same person has a controlling interest in both.*

[**Pre-RRO**: 'In this subsection "subsidiary" has the meaning given by section 736 of the Companies Act 1985.']

(2) Where a tenancy is held by a member of a group, occupation by another member of the group, and the carrying on of a business by another member of the group, shall be treated for the purposes of section 23 of this Act as equivalent to occupation or the carrying on of a business by the member of the group holding the tenancy; and in relation to a tenancy to which this Part of this Act applies by virtue of the foregoing provisions of this subsection –

(a) references (however expressed) in this Part of this Act and in the Ninth Schedule to this Act to the business of or to use occupation or enjoyment by the tenant shall be construed as including references to the business of or to use occupation or enjoyment by the said other member;

(b) the reference in paragraph (d) of subsection (1) of section 34 of this Act to the tenant shall be construed as including the said other member; and

(c) an assignment of the tenancy from one member of the group to another shall not be treated as a change in the person of the tenant.

(3) Where the landlord's interest is held by a member of a group –

(a) the reference in paragraph (g) of subsection (1) of section 30 of this Act to intended occupation by the landlord for the purposes of a business to be carried on by him shall be construed as including intended occupation by any member of the group for the purposes of a business to be carried on by that member; and

(b) the reference in subsection (2) of that section to the purchase or creation of any interest shall be construed as a reference to a purchaser from or creation by a person other than a member of the group.

43. Tenancies excluded from Part II

(1) This Part of this Act does not apply –

(a) to a tenancy of an agricultural holding which is a tenancy in relation to which the Agricultural Holdings Act 1986 applies or a tenancy which would be a tenancy of an agricultural holding in relation to which that Act applied if subsection (3) of section 2 of that Act did not have effect or, in a case where approval was given under subsection (1) of that section, if that approval had not been given;

(aa) to a farm business tenancy;

(b) to a tenancy created by a mining lease; or

(c) [*Repealed*]

(d) [*Repealed*]

(2) This Part of this Act does not apply to a tenancy granted by reason that the tenant was the holder of an office, appointment or employment from the grantor thereof and continuing only so long as the tenant holds the office, appointment or employment, or terminable by the grantor on the tenant's ceasing to hold it, or coming to an end at a time fixed by reference to the time at which the tenant ceases to hold it:

Provided that this subsection shall not have effect in relation to a tenancy granted after the commencement of this Act unless the tenancy was granted by an instrument in writing which expressed the purpose for which the tenancy was granted.

(3) This Part of this Act does not apply to a tenancy granted for a term certain not exceeding six months unless –

(a) the tenancy contains provision for renewing the term or for extending it beyond six months from its beginning; or

(b) the tenant has been in occupation for a period which, together with any period during which any predecessor in the carrying on of the business carried on by the tenant was in occupation, exceeds twelve months.

43A. Jurisdiction of county court to make declaration

Where the rateable value of the holding is such that the jurisdiction conferred on the court by any other provision of this Part of this Act is, by virtue of section 63 of this Act, exercisable by the county court, the county court shall have jurisdiction (but without prejudice to the jurisdiction of the High Court) to make any declaration as to any matter arising under this Part of this Act, whether or not any other relief is sought in the proceedings.

44. Meaning of 'the landlord' in Part II, and provisions as to mesne landlords, etc.

(1) Subject to [**pre-RRO**: 'the next following subsection'] *subsections (1A) and (2) below*, in this Part of this Act the expression 'the landlord' in relation to a tenancy (in this section referred to as 'the relevant tenancy'), means the person (whether or not he is the immediate landlord) who is the owner of that interest in the property comprised in the relevant tenancy which for the time being fulfils the following conditions, that is to say –

(a) that it is an interest in reversion expectant (whether immediately or not) on the termination of the relevant tenancy, and

(b) that it is either the fee simple or a tenancy which will not come to an end within fourteen months by effluxion of time and, if it is such a tenancy, that no notice has been given by virtue of which it will come to an end within fourteen months or any further time by which it may be continued under section 36(2) or section 64 of this Act, and is not itself in reversion expectant (whether immediately or not) on an interest which fulfils those conditions.

(1A) The reference in subsection (1) above to a person who is the owner of an interest such as is mentioned in that subsection is to be construed, where different persons own such interests in different parts of the property, as a reference to all those persons collectively.

(2) References in this Part of this Act to a notice to quit given by the landlord are references to a notice to quit given by the immediate landlord.

(3) The provisions of the Sixth Schedule to this Act shall have effect for the application of this Part of this Act to cases where the immediate landlord of the tenant is not the owner of the fee simple in respect of the holding.

45. [*Repealed*]

46. Interpretation of Part II

(1) In this Part of this Act: –

'business' has the meaning assigned to it by subsection (2) of section 23 of this Act;

[**Pre-RRO**: '"current tenancy" has the meaning assigned to it by subsection (1) of section 26 of this Act'] *'current tenancy' means the tenancy under which the tenant holds for the time being;*

'date of termination' has the meaning assigned to it by subsection (1) of section 25 of this Act;

subject to the provisions of section 32 of this Act, 'the holding' has the meaning assigned to it by subsection (3) of section 23of this Act;

'interim rent' has the meaning given by section 24A(1) of this Act;

'mining lease' has the same meaning as in the Landlord and Tenant Act 1927.

(2) *For the purposes of this Part of this Act, a person has a controlling interest in a company if, had he been a company, the other company would have been its subsidiary; and in this Part –*

'company' has the meaning given by section 735 of the Companies Act 1985; and 'subsidiary' has the meaning given by section 736 of that Act.

PART III COMPENSATION FOR IMPROVEMENTS

47. Time for making claims for compensation for improvements

(1) Where a tenancy is terminated by notice to quit, whether given by the landlord or by the tenant, or by a notice given by any person under Part I or Part II of this Act, the time for making a claim for compensation at the termination of the tenancy shall be a time falling within the period of three months beginning on the date on which the notice is given:

Provided that where the tenancy is terminated by a tenant's request for a new tenancy under section 26 of this Act, the said time shall be a time falling within the period of three months beginning on the date on which the landlord gives notice, or (if he has not given such a notice) the latest date on which he could have given notice, under subsection (6) of the said section 26 or, as the case may be, paragraph (a) of subsection (4) of section57 or paragraph (b) of subsection (1) of section 58 of this Act.

(2) Where a tenancy comes to an end by effluxion of time, the time for making such a claim shall be a time not earlier than six nor later than three months before the coming to an end of the tenancy.

(3) Where a tenancy is terminated by forfeiture or re-entry, the time for making such a claim shall be a time falling within the period of three months beginning with the effective date of the order of the court for the recovery of possession of the land comprised in the tenancy or, if the tenancy is terminated by re-entry without such an order, the period of three months beginning with the date of the re-entry.

(4) In the last foregoing subsection the reference to the effective date of an order is a reference to the date on which the order is to take effect according to the terms thereof or the date on which it ceases to be subject to appeal, whichever is the later.

(5) In subsection (1) of section one of the Act of 1927, for paragraphs (a) and (b) (which specify the time for making claims for compensation) there shall be substituted the words 'and within the time limited by section 47 of the Landlord and Tenant Act 1954.'

48. Amendments as to limitations on tenant's right to compensation

(1) So much of paragraph (b) of subsection (1) of section 2 of the Act of 1927 as provides that a tenant shall not be entitled to compensation in respect of any improvement made in pursuance of a statutory obligation shall not apply to any improvement begun after the commencement of this Act, but section 3 of the Act of 1927 (which enables a landlord to object to a proposed improvement) shall not have

effect in relation to an improvement made in pursuance of a statutory obligation except so much thereof as –

(a) requires the tenant to serve on the landlord notice of his intention to make the improvement together with such a plan and specification as are mentioned in that section and to supply copies of the plan and specification at the request of any superior landlord; and
(b) enables the tenant to obtain at his expense a certificate from the landlord or the tribunal that the improvement has been duly executed.

(2) Paragraph (c) of the said subsection (1) (which provides that a tenant shall not be entitled to compensation in respect of any improvement made less than three years before the termination of the tenancy) shall not apply to any improvement begun after the commencement of this Act.
(3) No notice shall be served after the commencement of this Act under paragraph (d) of the said subsection (1) (which excludes rights to compensation where the landlord serves on the tenant notice offering a renewal of the tenancy on reasonable terms).

49. Restrictions on contracting out

In section 9 of the Act of 1927 (which provides that Part I of that Act shall apply notwithstanding any contract to the contrary made after the date specified in that section) the proviso (which requires effect to be given to such a contract where it appears to the tribunal that the contract was made for adequate consideration) shall cease to have effect except as respects a contract made before the tenth day of December, nineteen hundred and fifty-three.

50. Interpretation of Part III

In this Part of this Act the expression 'Act of 1927' means the Landlord and Tenant Act 1927, the expression 'compensation' means compensation under Part I of that Act in respect of an improvement, and other expressions used in this Part of this Act and in the Act of 1927 have the same meanings in this Part of this Act as in that Act.

PART IV MISCELLANEOUS AND SUPPLEMENTARY

[*Sections 51 to 54 not reproduced here*]

[Pre-RRO:

'55. Compensation for possession obtained by misrepresentation

(1) Where under Part I of this Act an order is made for possession of the property comprised in a tenancy, or under Part II of this Act the court refuses an order for the grant of a new tenancy, and it is subsequently made to appear to the court that the order was obtained, or the court induced to refuse the grant, by misrepresentation or the concealment of material facts, the court may order the landlord to pay to the tenant such sum as appears sufficient as compensation for damage or loss sustained by the tenant as the result of the order or refusal.
(2) In this section the expression "the landlord" means the person applying for possession or opposing an application for the grant of a new tenancy and the expression "the tenant" means the person against whom the order for possession was made or to whom the grant of a new tenancy was refused.']

56. Application to Crown

(1) Subject to the provisions of this and the four next following sections, Part II of this Act shall apply where there is an interest belonging to Her Majesty in right of the Crown or the Duchy of Lancaster or belonging to the Duchy of Cornwall, or belong-

ing to a Government department or held on behalf of Her Majesty for the purposes of a Government department, in like manner as if that interest were an interest not so belonging or held.

(2) The provisions of the Eighth Schedule to this Act shall have effect as respects the application of Part II of this Act to cases where the interest of the landlord belongs to Her Majesty in right of the Crown or the Duchy of Lancaster or to the Duchy of Cornwall.

(3) Where a tenancy is held by or on behalf of a Government department and the property comprised therein is or includes premises occupied for any purposes of a Government department, the tenancy shall be one to which Part II of this Act applies; and for the purposes of any provision of the said Part II or the Ninth Schedule to this Act which is applicable only if either or both of the following conditions are satisfied, that is to say –

(a) that any premises have during any period been occupied for the purposes of the tenant's business;

(b) that on any change of occupier of any premises the new occupier succeeded to the business of the former occupier,

the said conditions shall be deemed to be satisfied respectively, in relation to such a tenancy, if during that period or, as the case may be, immediately before and immediately after the change, the premises were occupied for the purposes of a Government department.

(4) The last foregoing subsection shall apply in relation to any premises provided by a Government department without any rent being payable to the department therefor as if the premises were occupied for the purposes of a Government department.

(5) The provisions of Parts III and IV of this Act, amending any other enactment which binds the Crown or applies to land belonging to Her Majesty in right of the Crown or the Duchy of Lancaster, or land belonging to the Duchy of Cornwall, or to land belonging to any Government department, shall bind the Crown or apply to such land.

(6) Sections 53 and 54 of this Act shall apply where the interest of the landlord, or any other interest in the land in question, belongs to Her Majesty in right of the Crown or the Duchy of Lancaster or to the Duchy of Cornwall, or belongs to a Government department or is held on behalf of Her Majesty for the purposes of a Government department, in like manner as if that interest were an interest not so belonging or held.

(7) Part I of this Act shall apply where –

(a) there is an interest belonging to Her Majesty in right of the Crown and that interest is under the management of the Crown Estate Commissioners; or

(b) there is an interest belonging to Her Majesty in right of the Duchy of Lancaster or belonging to the Duchy of Cornwall; as if it were an interest not so belonging.

57. Modification on grounds of public interest of rights under Part II

(1) Where the interest of the landlord or any superior landlord in the property comprised in any tenancy belongs to or is held for the purposes of a Government department or is held by a local authority, statutory undertakers or a development corporation, the Minister or Board in charge of any Government department may certify that it is requisite for the purposes of the first-mentioned department, or, as the case may be, of the authority, undertakers or corporation, that the use or occupation of the property or a part thereof shall be changed by a specified date.

(2) A certificate under the last foregoing subsection shall not be given unless the owner of the interest belonging or held as mentioned in the last foregoing subsection has given to the tenant a notice stating –

(a) that the question of the giving of such a certificate is under consideration by the Minister or Board specified in the notice, and

(b) that if within twenty-one days of the giving of the notice the tenant makes to that Minister or Board representations in writing with respect to that question, they will be considered before the question is determined, and if the tenant makes any such representations within the said twenty-one days the Minister or Board shall consider them before determining whether to give the certificate.

(3) Where a certificate has been given under subsection (1) of this section in relation to any tenancy, then –

(a) if a notice given under subsection (1) of section 25 of this Act specifies as the date of termination a date not earlier than the date specified in the certificate and contains a copy of the certificate [**pre-RRO**: 'subsections (5) and'] *subsection* (6) of that section shall not apply to the notice and no application for a new tenancy shall be made by the tenant under *subsection (1) of* section 24 of this Act;

(b) if such a notice specifies an earlier date as the date of termination and contains a copy of the certificate, then if the court makes an order under Part II of this Act for the grant of a new tenancy the new tenancy shall be for a term expiring not later than the date specified in the certificate and shall not be a tenancy to which Part II of this Act applies.

(4) Where a tenant makes a request for a new tenancy under section 26 of this Act, and the interest of the landlord or any superior landlord in the property comprised in the current tenancy belongs or is held as mentioned in subsection (1) of this section, the following provisions shall have effect: –

(a) if a certificate has been given under the said subsection (1) in relation to the current tenancy, and within two months after the making of the request the landlord gives notice to the tenant that the certificate has been given and the notice contains a copy of the certificate, then, –

(i) if the date specified in the certificate is not later than that specified in the tenant's request for a new tenancy, the tenant shall not make an application under section 24 of this Act for the grant of a new tenancy;

(ii) if, in any other case, the court makes an order under Part II of this Act for the grant of a new tenancy the new tenancy shall be for a term expiring not later than the date specified in the certificate and shall not be a tenant to which Part II of this Act applies;

(b) if no such certificate has been given but notice under subsection (2) of this section has been given before the making of the request or within two months thereafter, the request shall not have effect, without prejudice however, to the making of a new request when the Minister or Board has determined whether to give a certificate.

(5) Where application is made to the court under Part II of this Act for the grant of a new tenancy and the landlord's interest in the property comprised in the tenancy belongs or is held as mentioned in subsection (1) of this section, the Minister or Board in charge of any Government department may certify that it is necessary in the public interest that if the landlord makes an application in that behalf the court shall determine as a term of the new tenancy that is shall be terminable by six months' notice to quit given by the landlord.

Subsection (2) of this section shall apply in relation to a certificate under this subsection, and if notice under the said subsection (2) has been given to the tenant –

(a) the court shall not determine the application for the grant of a new tenancy until the Minister or Board has determined whether to give a certificate,

(b) if a certificate is given, the court shall on the application of the landlord determine as a term of the new tenancy that it shall be terminable as aforesaid, and section 25 of this Act shall apply accordingly.

(6) The foregoing provisions of this section shall apply to an interest held by a Health Authority or Special Health Authority as they apply to an interest held by a local authority but with the substitution, for the reference to the purposes of the authority, of a reference to the purposes of the National Health Service Act 1977.

(7) Where the interest of the landlord or any superior landlord in the property comprised in any tenancy belongs to the National Trust the Minister of Works may certify that it is requisite, for the purpose of securing that the property will as from a specified date be used or occupied in a manner better suited to the nature thereof, that the use or occupation of the property should be changed; and subsections (2) to (4) of this section shall apply in relation to certificates under this subsection, and to cases where the interest of the landlord or any superior landlord belongs to the National Trust, as those subsections apply in relation to certificates under subsection (1) of this section and to cases where the interest of the landlord or any superior landlord belongs or is held as mentioned in that subsection.

(8) In this and the next following section the expression 'Government department' does not include the Commissioners of Crown Lands and the expression 'landlord' has the same meaning as in Part II of this Act; and in the last foregoing subsection the expression 'National Trust' means the National Trust for Places of Historic Interest or Natural Beauty.

58. Termination on special grounds of tenancies to which Part II applies

(1) Where the landlord's interest in the property comprised in any tenancy belongs to or is held for the purposes of a Government department, and the Minister or Board in charge of any Government department certifies that for reasons of national security it is necessary that the use or occupation of the property should be discontinued or changed, then –

(a) if the landlord gives a notice under subsection (1) of section 25 of this Act containing a copy of the certificate, [**pre-RRO**: 'subsections (5) and'] *subsection* (6) of that section shall not apply to the notice and no application for a new tenancy shall be made by the tenant under *subsection (1) of* section 24 of this Act;

(b) if (whether before or after the giving of the certificate) the tenant makes a request for a new tenancy under section 26 of this Act, and within two months after the making the request the landlord gives notice to the tenant that the certificate has been given and the notice contains a copy of the certificate –

(i) the tenant shall not make an application under section 24 of this Act for the grant of a new tenancy, and

(ii) if the notice specifies as the date on which the tenancy is to terminate a date earlier than that specified in the tenant's request as the date on which the new tenancy is to begin but neither earlier than six months from the giving of the notice nor earlier than the earliest date at which apart from this Act the tenancy would come to an end or could be brought to an end, the tenancy shall terminate on the date specified in the notice instead of that specified in the request.

(2) Where the landlord's interest in the property comprised in any tenancy belongs to or is held for the purposes of a Government department, nothing in this Act shall invalidate an agreement to the effect –

(a) that on the giving of such a certificate as is mentioned in the last foregoing subsection the tenancy may be terminated by notice to quit given by the landlord of such length as may be specified in the agreement, if the notice contains a copy of the certificate; and

(b) that after the giving of such a notice containing such a copy the tenancy shall not be one to which Part II of this Act applies.

(3) Where the landlord's interest in the property comprised in any tenancy is held by statutory undertakers, nothing in this Act shall invalidate an agreement to the effect –

(a) that where the Minister or Board in charge of a Government department certifies that possession of the property comprised in the tenancy or a part thereof is urgently required for carrying out repairs (whether on that property or elsewhere) which are needed for the proper operation of the landlord's undertaking, the tenancy may be terminated by notice to quit given by the landlord of such length as may be specified in the agreement, if the notice contains a copy of the certificate; and

(b) that after the giving of such a notice containing such a copy, the tenancy shall not be one to which Part II of this Act applies.

(4) Where the court makes an order under Part II of this Act for the grant of a new tenancy and the Minister or Board in charge of any Government department certifies that the public interest requires the tenancy to be subject to such a term as is mentioned in paragraph (a) or (b) of this subsection, as the case may be, then –

(a) if the landlord's interest in the property comprised in the tenancy belongs to or is held for the purposes of a Government department, the court shall on the application of the landlord determine as a term of the new tenancy that such an agreement as is mentioned in subsection (2) of this section and specifying such length of notice as is mentioned in the certificate shall be embodied in the new tenancy;

(b) if the landlord's interest in that property is held by statutory undertakers, the court shall on the application of the landlord determine as a term of the new tenancy that such an agreement as is mentioned in subsection (3) of this section and specifying such length of notice as is mentioned in the certificate shall be embodied in the new tenancy.

59. Compensation for exercise of powers under sections 57 and 58

(1) Where by virtue of any certificate given for the purposes of either of the two last foregoing sections or, subject to subsection (1A) below, section 60A below the tenant is precluded from obtaining an order for the grant of a new tenancy, or of a new tenancy for a term expiring later than a specified date, the tenant shall be entitled on quitting the premises to recover from the owner of the interest by virtue of which the certificate was given an amount by way of compensation, and subsections (2), (3) *to (3B)* and (5) to (7) of section 37 of this Act shall with the necessary modifications apply for the purposes of ascertaining the amount.

(1A) No compensation shall be recoverable under subsection (1) above where the certificate was given under section 60A below and either –

(a) the premises vested in the Welsh Development Agency under section 7 (property of Welsh Industrial Estates Corporation) or 8 (land held under Local Employment Act 1972) of the Welsh Development Agency Act 1975, or

(b) the tenant was not tenant of the premises when the said Agency acquired the interest by virtue of which the certificate was given.

(2) Subsections (2) and (3) of section 38 of this Act shall apply to compensation under this section as they apply to compensation under section 37 of this Act.

60. Special provisions as to premises in development or intermediate areas

(1) Where the property comprised in a tenancy consists of premises of which the Secretary of State or the Urban Regeneration Agency is the landlord, being premises situated in a locality which is either –

(a) a development area; or

(b) an intermediate area;

and the Secretary of State certifies that it is necessary or expedient for achieving the purpose mentioned in section 2(1) of the Local Employment Act 1972 that the use or occupation of the property should be changed, paragraphs (a) and (b) of subsection (1) of section 58 of this Act shall apply as they apply where such a certificate is given as is mentioned in that subsection.

(2) Where the court makes an order under Part II of this Act for the grant of a new tenancy of any such premises as aforesaid, and the Secretary of State certifies that it is necessary or expedient as aforesaid that the tenancy should be subject to a term, specified in the certificate, prohibiting or restricting the tenant from assigning the tenancy or sub-letting, charging or parting with possession of the premises or any part thereof or changing the use of the premises or any part thereof, the court shall determine that the terms of the tenancy shall include the terms specified in the certificate.

(3) In this section 'development area' and 'intermediate area' mean an area for the time being specified as a development area or, as the case may be, as an intermediate area by an order made, or having effect as if made, under section 1 of the Industrial Development Act 1982.

60A. Welsh Development Agency premises

(1) Where property comprised in a tenancy consists of premises of which the Welsh Development Agency is the landlord, and the Secretary of State certifies that it is necessary or expedient, for the purpose of providing employment appropriate to the needs of the area in which the premises are situated, that the use or occupation of the property should be changed, paragraphs (a) and (b) of section 58(l) above shall apply as they apply where such a certificate is given as is mentioned in that sub-section.

(2) Where the court makes an order under Part II of this Act for the grant of a new tenancy of any such premises as aforesaid, and the Secretary of State certifies that it is necessary or expedient as aforesaid that the tenancy should be subject to a term, specified in the certificate, prohibiting or restricting the tenant from assigning the tenancy or subletting, charging or parting with possession of the premises or any part of the premises or changing the use of the premises or any part of the premises, the court shall determine that the terms of the tenancy shall include the terms specified in the certificate.

60B to 62 [*Repealed*]

63. Jurisdiction of court for purposes of Parts I and II and of Part I of Landlord and Tenant Act 1927

(1) Any jurisdiction conferred on the court by any provision of Part I of this Act shall be exercised by the county court.

(2) Any jurisdiction conferred on the court by any provision of Part II of this Act or conferred on the tribunal by Part I of the Landlord and Tenant Act 1927, shall, subject to the provisions of this section, be exercised, by the High Court or a county court.

(3) [*Repealed*]

(4) The following provisions shall have effect as respects transfer of proceedings from or to the High Court or the county court, that is to say –

 (a) where an application is made to the one but by virtue of an Order under section 1 of the Courts and Legal Services Act 1990, cannot be entertained except by the other, the application shall not be treated as improperly made but any proceedings thereon shall be transferred to the other court;

 (b) any proceedings under the provisions of Part II of this Act or of Part I of the Landlord and Tenant Act 1927, which are pending before one of those courts may by order of that court made on the application of any person interested be transferred to the other court, if it appears to the court making the order that it is desirable that the proceedings and any proceedings before the other court should both be entertained by the other court.

(5) In any proceedings where in accordance with the foregoing provisions of this section the county court exercises jurisdiction the powers of the judge of summoning one or more assessors under subsection (1) of section 63(1) of the County Courts Act 1984, may be exercised notwithstanding that no application is made in that behalf by any party to the proceedings.

(6) Where in any such proceedings an assessor is summoned by a judge under the said subsection (1), –

(a) he may, if so directed by the judge, inspect the land to which the proceedings relate without the judge and report to the judge in writing thereon;

(b) the judge may on consideration of the report and any observations of the parties thereon give such judgment or make such order in the proceedings as may be just;

(c) the remuneration of the assessor shall be at such rate as may be determined by the Lord Chancellor with the approval of the Treasury and shall be defrayed out of moneys provided by Parliament.

(7) In this section the expression 'the holding' –

(a) in relation to proceedings under Part II of this Act, has the meaning assigned to it by subsection (3) of section 23 of this Act,

(b) in relation to proceedings under Part I of the Landlord and Tenant Act 1927, has the same meaning as in the said Part I.

(8) [*Repealed*]

(9) Nothing in this section shall prejudice the operation of section 41 of the County Courts Act 1984 (which relates to the removal into the High Court of proceedings commenced in a county court).

(10) In accordance with the foregoing provisions of this section, for section 21 of the Landlord and Tenant Act 1927, there shall be substituted the following section –

21 'The tribunal

The tribunal for the purposes of Part I of this Act shall be the court exercising jurisdiction in accordance with the provisions of section 63 of the Landlord and Tenant Act 1954'.

64. Interim continuation of tenancies pending determination by court

(1) In any case where –

(a) a notice to terminate a tenancy has been given under Part I or Part II of this Act or a request for a new tenancy has been made under Part II thereof, and

(b) an application to the court has been made under the said Part I or *under section 24(1) or 29(2) of this Act* as the case may be, and

(c) apart from this section the effect of the notice or request would be to terminate the tenancy before the expiration of the period of three months beginning with the date on which the application is finally disposed of,

the effect of the notice or request shall be to terminate the tenancy at the expiration of the said period of three months and not at any other time.

(2) The reference in paragraph (c) of subsection (1) of this section to the date on which an application is finally disposed of shall be construed as a reference to the earliest date by which the proceedings on the application (including any proceedings on or in consequence of an appeal) have been determined and any time for appealing or further appealing has expired, except that if the application is withdrawn or any appeal is abandoned the reference shall be construed as a reference to the date of the withdrawal or abandonment.

65. Provisions as to reversions

(1) Where by virtue of any provision of this Act a tenancy (in this sub-section referred to as 'the inferior tenancy') is continued for a period such as to extend to or beyond the end of the term of a superior tenancy, the superior tenancy shall, for the purposes of this Act and of any other enactment and of any rule of law, be deemed so long as it subsists to be an interest in reversion expectant upon the termination of the inferior tenancy and, if there is no intermediate tenancy, to be the interest in reversion immediately expectant upon the termination thereof.

(2) In the case of a tenancy continuing by virtue of any provision of this Act after the coming to an end of the interest in reversion immediately expectant upon the termination thereof, subsection (1) of section 139 of the Law of Property Act 1925 (which relates to the effect of the extinguishment of a reversion) shall apply as if references in the said subsection (1) to the surrender or merger of the reversion included references to the coming to an end of the reversion for any reason other than surrender or merger.

(3) Where by virtue of any provision of this Act a tenancy (in this subsection referred to as 'the continuing tenancy') is continued beyond the beginning of a reversionary tenancy which was granted (whether before or after the commencement of this Act) so as to begin on or after the date on which apart from this Act the continuing tenancy would have come to an end, the reversionary tenancy shall have effect as if it had been granted subject to the continuing tenancy.

(4) Where by virtue of any provision of this Act a tenancy (in this subsection referred to as 'the new tenancy') is granted for a period beginning on the same date as a reversionary tenancy or for a period such as to extend beyond the beginning of the term of a reversionary tenancy, whether the reversionary tenancy in question was granted before or after the commencement of this Act, the reversionary tenancy shall have effect as if it had been granted subject to the new tenancy.

66. Provisions as to notices

(1) Any form of notice required by this Act to be prescribed shall be prescribed by regulations made by the Secretary of State by statutory instrument.

(2) Where the form of a notice to be served on persons of any description is to be prescribed for any of the purposes of this Act, the form to be prescribed shall include such an explanation of the relevant provisions of this Act as appears to the Secretary of State requisite for informing persons of that description of their rights and obligations under those provisions.

(3) Different forms of notice may be prescribed for the purposes of the operation of any provision of this Act in relation to different cases.

(4) Section 23 of the Landlord and Tenant Act 1927 (which relates to the service of notices) shall apply for the purposes of this Act.

(5) Any statutory instrument under this section shall be subject to annulment in pursuance of a resolution of either House of Parliament.

67. Provisions as to mortgagees in possession

Anything authorised or required by the provisions of this Act, other than subsection (3) of section 40, to be done at any time by, to or with the landlord, or a landlord of a specified description, shall, if at that time the interest of the landlord in question is subject to a mortgage and the mortgagee is in possession or a receiver appointed by the mortgagee or by the courts is in receipt of the rents and profits, be deemed to be authorised or required to be done by, to or with the mortgagee instead of that landlord.

68. [*Not reproduced here*]

69. Interpretation

(1) In this Act, the following expressions have the meanings hereby assigned to them respectively, that is to say –

'agricultural holding' has the same meaning as in the Agricultural Holdings Act 1986;
'development corporation' has the same meaning as in the New Towns Act 1946;
'farm business tenancy' has the same meaning as in the Agricultural Tenancies Act 1995;
'local authority' means any local authority within the meaning of the Town and Country Planning Act 1990, any National Park Authority, the Broads Authority or joint authority established by Part 4 of the Local Government Act 1985;
'mortgage' includes a charge or lien and 'mortgagor' and 'mortgagee' shall be construed accordingly;
'notice to quit' means a notice to terminate a tenancy (whether a periodical tenancy or a tenancy for a term of years certain) given in accordance with the provisions (whether express or implied) of that tenancy;
'repairs' includes any work of maintenance, decoration or restoration, and references to repairing, to keeping or yielding up in repair and to state of repair shall be construed accordingly;
'statutory undertakers' has the same meaning as in the Town and Country Planning Act 1990;
'tenancy' means a tenancy created either immediately or derivatively out of the freehold, whether by a lease or underlease, by an agreement for a lease or underlease or by a tenancy agreement or in pursuance of any enactment (including this Act), but does not include a mortgage term or any interest arising in favour of a mortgagor by his attorning tenant to his mortgagee, and references to the granting of a tenancy and to demised property shall be construed accordingly;
'terms', in relation to a tenancy, includes conditions.

(2) References in this Act to an agreement between the landlord and the tenant (except in section 17 and subsections (1) and (2) of section 38 thereof) shall be construed as references to an agreement in writing between them.

(3) Reference in this Act to an action for any relief shall be construed as including references to a claim for that relief by way of counterclaim in any proceedings.

70. Short title and citation, commencement and extent

(1) This Act may be cited as the Landlord and Tenant Act 1954, and the Landlord and Tenant Act 1927, and this Act may be cited together as the Landlord and Tenant Acts 1927 and 1954.

(2) This Act shall come into operation on the first day of October, nineteen hundred and fifty-four.

(3) This Act shall not extend to Scotland or to Northern Ireland.

Appendix C
LANDLORD AND TENANT ACT 1954, PART 2 (NOTICES) REGULATIONS 2004, SI 2004/1005

Made 30th March 2004
Laid before Parliament 6th April 2004
Coming into force 1st June 2004

The First Secretary of State, as respects England, and the National Assembly for Wales, as respects Wales, in exercise of the powers conferred by section 66 of the Landlord and Tenant Act 1954 (including that section as it has effect as mentioned in section 22(5) of the Leasehold Reform Act 1967), and of all other powers enabling them in that behalf, hereby make the following Regulations:

1. Citation and commencement

These Regulations may be cited as the Landlord and Tenant Act 1954, Part 2 (Notices) Regulations 2004 and shall come into force on 1st June 2004.

2. Interpretation

(1) In these Regulations –

'the Act' means the Landlord and Tenant Act 1954; and
'the 1967 Act' means the Leasehold Reform Act 1967.

(2) Any reference in these Regulations to a numbered form (in whatever terms) is a reference to the form bearing that number in Schedule 2 to these Regulations or a form substantially to the same effect.

3. Prescribed forms, and purposes for which they are to be used.

The form with the number shown in column (1) of Schedule 1 to these Regulations is prescribed for use for the purpose shown in the corresponding entry in column (2) of that Schedule.

4. Revocation of Regulations

The Landlord and Tenant Act 1954, Part II (Notices) Regulations 1983 and the Landlord and Tenant Act 1954, Part II (Notices) (Amendment) Regulations 1989 are hereby revoked.

Signed by authority of the First Secretary of State

Keith Hill
Minister of State, Office of the Deputy Prime Minister
16th March 2004

Signed on behalf of the National Assembly for Wales

D. Elis-Thomas
Presiding Officer of the National Assembly
30th March 2004

SCHEDULE 1 PRESCRIBED FORMS, AND PURPOSES FOR WHICH THEY ARE TO BE USED

Regulations 2(2) and 3

(1) *Form number*	(2) *Purpose for which to be used*
1	Ending a tenancy to which Part 2 of the Act applies, where the landlord is not opposed to the grant of a new tenancy (notice under section 25 of the Act).
2	Ending a tenancy to which Part 2 of the Act applies, where – (a) the landlord is opposed to the grant of a new tenancy (notice under section 25 of the Act); and (b) the tenant is not entitled under the 1967 Act to buy the freehold or an extended lease.
3	Tenant's request for a new tenancy of premises where Part 2 of the Act applies (notice under section 26 of the Act).
4	Landlord's notice activating tenant's duty under section 40(1) of the Act to give information as to his or her occupation of the premises and as to any sub-tenancies.
5	Tenant's notice activating duty under section 40(3) of the Act of reversioner or reversioner's mortgagee in possession to give information about his or her interest in the premises.
6	Withdrawal of notice given under section 25 of the Act ending a tenancy to which Part 2 of the Act applies (notice under section 44 of, and paragraph 6 of Schedule 6 to, the Act).
7	Ending a tenancy to which Part 2 of the Act applies, where the landlord is opposed to the grant of a new tenancy but where the tenant may be entitled under the 1967 Act to buy the freehold or an extended lease (notice under section 25 of the Act and paragraph 10 of Schedule 3 to the 1967 Act).
8	Ending a tenancy to which Part 2 of the Act applies, where: (a) the notice under section 25 of the Act contains a copy of a certificate given under section 57 of the Act that the use or occupation of the property or part of it is to be changed by a specified date; (b) the date of termination of the tenancy specified in the notice is not earlier than the date specified in the certificate; and (c) the tenant is not entitled under the 1967 Act to buy the freehold or an extended lease.
9	Ending a tenancy to which Part 2 of the Act applies, where: (a) the notice under section 25 of the Act contains a copy of a certificate given under section 57 of the Act that the use or occupation of the property or part of it is to be changed at a future date; (b) the date of termination of the tenancy specified in the notice is earlier than the date specified in the certificate; (c) the landlord opposes the grant of a new tenancy; and (d) the tenant is not entitled under the 1967 Act to buy the freehold or an extended lease.

10	Ending a tenancy to which Part 2 of the Act applies, where: (a) the notice under section 25 of the Act contains a copy of a certificate given under section 57 of the Act that the use or occupation of the property or part of it is to be changed at a future date; (b) the date of termination of the tenancy specified in the notice is earlier than the date specified in the certificate; (c) the landlord does not oppose the grant of a new tenancy; and (d) the tenant is not entitled under the 1967 Act to buy the freehold or an extended lease.
11	Ending a tenancy to which Part 2 of the Act applies, where the notice under section 25 of the Act contains a copy of a certificate given under section 58 of the Act that for reasons of national security it is necessary that the use or occupation of the property should be discontinued or changed.
12	Ending a tenancy to which Part 2 of the Act applies, where – (a) the notice under section 25 of the Act contains a copy of a certificate given under section 58 of the Act (as applied by section 60 of the Act) that it is necessary or expedient for achieving the purpose mentioned in section 2(1) of the Local Employment Act 1972 that the use or occupation of the property should be changed; and (b) the tenant is not entitled under the 1967 Act to buy the freehold or an extended lease.
13	Ending a tenancy to which Part 2 of the Act applies, where: (a) the notice under section 25 of the Act contains a copy of a certificate given under section 57 of the Act that the use or occupation of the property or part of it is to be changed by a specified date; and (b) the date of termination of the tenancy specified in the notice is not earlier than the date specified in the certificate; and (c) the tenant may be entitled under the 1967 Act to buy the freehold or an extended lease.
14	Ending a tenancy to which Part 2 of the Act applies, where: (a) the notice under section 25 of the Act contains a copy of a certificate given under section 57 of the Act that the use or occupation of the property or part of it is to be changed at a future date; (b) the date of termination of the tenancy specified in the notice is earlier than the date specified in the certificate; and (c) the tenant may be entitled under the 1967 Act to buy the freehold or an extended lease the landlord opposes the grant of a new tenancy.
15	Ending a tenancy to which Part 2 of the Act applies, where: (a) the notice under section 25 of the Act contains a copy of a certificate given under section 58 of the Act (as applied by section 60 of the Act) that it is necessary or expedient for achieving the purpose mentioned in section 2(1) of the Local Employment Act 1972 that the use or occupation of the property should be changed; and (b) the tenant may be entitled under the 1967 Act to buy the freehold or an extended lease the landlord opposes the grant of a new tenancy.

(1) Form number	(2) Purpose for which to be used
16	Ending a tenancy of Welsh Development Agency premises where – (a) the notice under section 25 of the Act contains a copy of a certificate given under section 58 of the Act (as applied by section 60A of the Act) that it is necessary or expedient, for the purposes of providing employment appropriate to the needs of the area in which the premises are situated, that the use or occupation of the property should be changed; and (b) the tenant is not entitled under the 1967 Act to buy the freehold or an extended lease.
17	Ending a tenancy of Welsh Development Agency premises where: (a) the notice under section 25 of the Act contains a copy of a certificate given under section 58 of the Act (as applied by section 60A of the Act) that it is necessary or expedient, for the purposes of providing employment appropriate to the needs of the area in which the premises are situated, that the use or occupation of the property should be changed; and (b) the tenant may be entitled under the 1967 Act to buy the freehold or an extended lease.

SCHEDULE 2 PRESCRIBED FORMS

Regulation 2(2)

FORM 1 LANDLORD'S NOTICE ENDING A BUSINESS TENANCY WITH PROPOSALS FOR A NEW ONE

Section 25 of the Landlord and Tenant Act 1954

IMPORTANT NOTE FOR THE LANDLORD: If you are willing to grant a new tenancy, complete this form and send it to the tenant. If you wish to oppose the grant of a new tenancy, use form 2 in Schedule 2 to the Landlord and Tenant Act 1954, Part 2 (Notices) Regulations 2004 or, where the tenant may be entitled to acquire the freehold or an extended lease, form 7 in that Schedule, instead of this form.

To: (*insert name and address of tenant*)

From: (*insert name and address of landlord*)

1. This notice applies to the following property: (*insert address or description of property*).
2. I am giving you notice under section 25 of the Landlord and Tenant Act 1954 to end your tenancy on (*insert date*).
3. I am not opposed to granting you a new tenancy. You will find my proposals for the new tenancy, which we can discuss, in the Schedule to this notice.
4. If we cannot agree on all the terms of a new tenancy, either you or I may ask the court to order the grant of a new tenancy and settle the terms on which we cannot agree.
5. If you wish to ask the court for a new tenancy you must do so by the date in paragraph 2, unless we agree in writing to a later date and do so before the date in paragraph 2.
6. Please send all correspondence about this notice to:

Name:

Address:

Signed: Date:

*[Landlord] *[On behalf of the landlord] *[Mortgagee] *[On behalf of the mortgagee]

*(*delete if inapplicable*)

SCHEDULE

LANDLORD'S PROPOSALS FOR A NEW TENANCY

(*attach or insert proposed terms of the new tenancy*)

IMPORTANT NOTE FOR THE TENANT

This Notice is intended to bring your tenancy to an end. If you want to continue to occupy your property after the date specified in paragraph 2 you must act quickly. If you are in any doubt about the action that you should take, get advice immediately from a solicitor or a surveyor.

The landlord is prepared to offer you a new tenancy and has set out proposed terms in the Schedule to this notice. You are not bound to accept these terms. They are merely suggestions as a basis for negotiation. In the event of disagreement, ultimately the court would settle the terms of the new tenancy.

It would be wise to seek professional advice before agreeing to accept the landlord's terms or putting forward your own proposals.

NOTES

The sections mentioned below are sections of the Landlord and Tenant Act 1954, as amended, (most recently by the Regulatory Reform (Business Tenancies) (England and Wales) Order 2003).

Ending of tenancy and grant of new tenancy

This notice is intended to bring your tenancy to an end on the date given in paragraph 2. Section 25 contains rules about the date that the landlord can put in that paragraph.

However, your landlord is prepared to offer you a new tenancy and has set out proposals for it in the Schedule to this notice (section 25(8)). You are not obliged to accept these proposals and may put forward your own.

If you and your landlord are unable to agree terms either one of you may apply to the court. You may not apply to the court if your landlord has already done so (section 24(2A)). If you wish to apply to the court you must do so by the date given in paragraph 2 of this notice, unless you and your landlord have agreed in writing to extend the deadline (sections 29A and 29B).

The court will settle the rent and other terms of the new tenancy or those on which you and your landlord cannot agree (sections 34 and 35). If you apply to the court your tenancy will continue after the date shown in paragraph 2 of this notice while your application is being considered (section 24).

If you are in any doubt about what action you should take, get advice immediately from a solicitor or a surveyor.

Negotiating a new tenancy

Most tenancies are renewed by negotiation. You and your landlord may agree in writing to extend the deadline for making an application to the court while negotiations continue. Either you or your landlord can ask the court to fix the rent that you will have to pay while the tenancy continues (sections 24A to 24D).

You may only stay in the property after the date in paragraph 2 (or if we have agreed in writing to a later date, that date), if by then you or the landlord has asked the court to order the grant of a new tenancy.

If you do try to agree a new tenancy with your landlord remember:

- that your present tenancy will not continue after the date in paragraph 2 of this notice without the agreement in writing mentioned above, unless you have applied to the court or your landlord has done so, and
- that you will lose your right to apply to the court once the deadline in paragraph 2 of this notice has passed, unless there is a written agreement extending the deadline.

Validity of this notice

The landlord who has given you this notice may not be the landlord to whom you pay your rent (sections 44 and 67). This does not necessarily mean that the notice is invalid.

If you have any doubts about whether this notice is valid, get advice immediately from a solicitor or a surveyor.

Further information

An explanation of the main points to consider when renewing or ending a business tenancy, 'Renewing and Ending Business Leases: a Guide for Tenants and Landlords', can be found at **www.odpm.gov.uk**. Printed copies of the explanation, but not of this form, are available from 1st June 2004 from Free Literature, PO Box 236, Wetherby, West Yorkshire, LS23 7NB (0870 1226 236).

FORM 2 LANDLORD'S NOTICE ENDING A BUSINESS TENANCY AND REASONS FOR REFUSING A NEW ONE

Section 25 of the Landlord and Tenant Act 1954

IMPORTANT NOTE FOR THE LANDLORD: If you wish to oppose the grant of a new tenancy on any of the grounds in section 30(1) of the Landlord and Tenant Act 1954, complete this form and send it to the tenant. If the tenant may be entitled to acquire the freehold or an extended lease, use form 7 in Schedule 2 to the Landlord and Tenant Act 1954, Part 2 (Notices) Regulations 2004 instead of this form.

To: (*insert name and address of tenant*)

From: (*insert name and address of landlord*)

1. This notice relates to the following property: (*insert address or description of property*)
2. I am giving you notice under section 25 of the Landlord and Tenant Act 1954 to end your tenancy on (*insert date*).
3. I am opposed to the grant of a new tenancy.
4. You may ask the court to order the grant of a new tenancy. If you do, I will oppose your application on the ground(s) mentioned in paragraph(s)* of section 30(1) of that Act. I draw your attention to the Table in the Notes below, which sets out all the grounds of opposition.
   *(*insert letter(s) of the paragraph(s) relied on*)
5. If you wish to ask the court for a new tenancy you must do so before the date in paragraph 2 unless, before that date, we agree in writing to a later date.
6. I can ask the court to order the ending of your tenancy without granting you a new tenancy. I may have to pay you compensation if I have relied only on one or more of the grounds mentioned in paragraphs (e), (f) and (g) of section 30(1). If I ask the court to end your tenancy, you can challenge my application.
7. Please send all correspondence about this notice to:

Name:

Address:

Signed: Date:

*[Landlord] *[On behalf of the landlord] *[Mortgagee] *[On behalf of the mortgagee]

(**delete if inapplicable*)

IMPORTANT NOTE FOR THE TENANT

This notice is intended to bring your tenancy to an end on the date specified in paragraph 2.

Your landlord is not prepared to offer you a new tenancy. You will not get a new tenancy unless you successfully challenge in court the grounds on which your landlord opposes the grant of a new tenancy.

If you want to continue to occupy your property you must act quickly. The notes below should help you to decide what action you now need to take. If you want to challenge your landlord's refusal to renew your tenancy, get advice immediately from a solicitor or a surveyor.

NOTES

The sections mentioned below are sections of the Landlord and Tenant Act 1954, as amended, (most recently by the Regulatory Reform (Business Tenancies) (England and Wales) Order 2003).

Ending of your tenancy

This notice is intended to bring your tenancy to an end on the date given in paragraph 2. Section 25 contains rules about the date that the landlord can put in that paragraph.

Your landlord is not prepared to offer you a new tenancy. If you want a new tenancy you will need to apply to the court for a new tenancy and successfully challenge the landlord's grounds for opposition (see the section below headed '*Landlord's opposition to new tenancy*'). If you wish to apply to the court you must do so before the date given in paragraph 2 of this notice, unless you and your landlord have agreed in writing, before that date, to extend the deadline (sections 29A and 29B).

If you apply to the court your tenancy will continue after the date given in paragraph 2 of this notice while your application is being considered (section 24). You may not apply to the court if your landlord has already done so (section 24(2A) and (2B)).

You may only stay in the property after the date given in paragraph 2 (or such later date as you and the landlord may have agreed in writing) if before that date you have asked the court to order the grant of a new tenancy or the landlord has asked the court to order the ending of your tenancy without granting you a new one.

If you are in any doubt about what action you should take, get advice immediately from a solicitor or a surveyor.

Landlord's opposition to new tenancy

If you apply to the court for a new tenancy, the landlord can only oppose your application on one or more of the grounds set out in section 30(1). If you match the letter(s) specified in paragraph 4 of this notice with those in the first column in the Table below, you can see from the second column the ground(s) on which the landlord relies.

Paragraph of section 30(1)	*Grounds*
(a)	Where under the current tenancy the tenant has any obligations as respects the repair and maintenance of the holding, that the tenant ought not to be granted a new tenancy in view of the state of repair of the holding, being a state resulting from the tenant's failure to comply with the said obligations.
(b)	That the tenant ought not to be granted a new tenancy in view of his persistent delay in paying rent which has become due.
(c)	That the tenant ought not to be granted a new tenancy in view of other substantial breaches by him of his obligations under the current tenancy, or for any other reason connected with the tenant's use or management of the holding.
(d)	That the landlord has offered and is willing to provide or secure the provision of alternative accommodation for the tenant, that the terms on which the alternative accommodation is available are reasonable having regard to the terms of the current tenancy and to all other relevant circumstances, and that the accommodation and the time at which it will be available are suitable for the tenant's requirements (including the requirement to preserve goodwill) having regard to the nature and class of his business and to the situation and extent of, and facilities afforded by, the holding.
(e)	Where the current tenancy was created by the sub-letting of part only of the property comprised in a superior tenancy and the landlord is the owner of an interest in reversion expectant on the termination of that superior tenancy, that the aggregate of the rents reasonably obtainable on separate lettings of the holding and the remainder of that property would be substantially less than the rent reasonably obtainable on a letting of that property as a whole, that on the termi-

	nation of the current tenancy the landlord requires possession of the holding for the purposes of letting or otherwise disposing of the said property as a whole, and that in view thereof the tenant ought not to be granted a new tenancy.
(f)	That on the termination of the current tenancy the landlord intends to demolish or reconstruct the premises comprised in the holding or a substantial part of those premises or to carry out substantial work of construction on the holding or part thereof and that he could not reasonably do so without obtaining possession of the holding.
(g)	On the termination of the current tenancy the landlord intends to occupy the holding for the purposes, or partly for the purposes, of a business to be carried on by him therein, or as his residence.

In this Table 'the holding' means the property that is the subject of the tenancy.

In ground (e), 'the landlord is the owner of an interest in reversion expectant on the termination of that superior tenancy' means that the landlord has an interest in the property that will entitle him or her, when your immediate landlord's tenancy comes to an end, to exercise certain rights and obligations in relation to the property that are currently exercisable by your immediate landlord.

If the landlord relies on ground (f), the court can sometimes still grant a new tenancy if certain conditions set out in section 31A are met.

If the landlord relies on ground (g), please note that 'the landlord' may have an extended meaning. Where a landlord has a controlling interest in a company then either the landlord or the company can rely on ground (g). Where the landlord is a company and a person has a controlling interest in that company then either of them can rely on ground (g) (section 30(1A) and (1B)). A person has a 'controlling interest' in a company if, had he been a company, the other company would have been its subsidiary (section 46(2)).

The landlord must normally have been the landlord for at least five years before he or she can rely on ground (g).

Compensation

If you cannot get a new tenancy solely because one or more of grounds (e), (f) and (g) applies, you may be entitled to compensation under section 37. If your landlord has opposed your application on any of the other grounds as well as (e), (f) or (g) you can only get compensation if the court's refusal to grant a new tenancy is based solely on one or more of grounds (e), (f) and (g). In other words, you cannot get compensation under section 37 if the court has refused your tenancy on *other* grounds, even if one or more of grounds (e), (f) and (g) also applies.

If your landlord is an authority possessing compulsory purchase powers (such as a local authority) you may be entitled to a disturbance payment under Part 3 of the Land Compensation Act 1973.

Validity of this notice

The landlord who has given you this notice may not be the landlord to whom you pay your rent (sections 44 and 67). This does not necessarily mean that the notice is invalid.

If you have any doubts about whether this notice is valid, get advice immediately from a solicitor or a surveyor.

Further information

An explanation of the main points to consider when renewing or ending a business tenancy, 'Renewing and Ending Business Leases: a Guide for Tenants and Landlords', can be found at **www.odpm.gov.uk**. Printed copies of the explanation, but not of this form, are available from 1st June 2004 from Free Literature, PO Box 236, Wetherby, West Yorkshire, LS23 7NB (0870 1226 236).

FORM 3 TENANT'S REQUEST FOR A NEW BUSINESS TENANCY

Section 26 of the Landlord and Tenant Act 1954

To (*insert name and address of landlord*):

From (*insert name and address of tenant*):

1. This notice relates to the following property: (*insert address or description of property*).
2. I am giving you notice under section 26 of the Landlord and Tenant Act 1954 that I request a new tenancy beginning on (*insert date*).
3. You will find my proposals for the new tenancy, which we can discuss, in the Schedule to this notice.
4. If we cannot agree on all the terms of a new tenancy, either you or I may ask the court to order the grant of a new tenancy and settle the terms on which we cannot agree.
5. If you wish to ask the court to order the grant of a new tenancy you must do so by the date in paragraph 2, unless we agree in writing to a later date and do so before the date in paragraph 2.
6. You may oppose my request for a new tenancy only on one or more of the grounds set out in section 30(1) of the Landlord and Tenant Act 1954. You must tell me what your grounds are within two months of receiving this notice. If you miss this deadline you will not be able to oppose renewal of my tenancy and you will have to grant me a new tenancy.
7. Please send all correspondence about this notice to:

Name:

Address:

Signed: Date:

*[Tenant] *[On behalf of the tenant] (*delete whichever is inapplicable*)

SCHEDULE

TENANT'S PROPOSALS FOR A NEW TENANCY

(*attach or insert proposed terms of the new tenancy*)

IMPORTANT NOTE FOR THE LANDLORD

This notice requests a new tenancy of your property or part of it. If you want to oppose this request you must act quickly.

Read the notice and all the Notes carefully. It would be wise to seek professional advice.

NOTES

The sections mentioned below are sections of the Landlord and Tenant Act 1954, as amended, (most recently by the Regulatory Reform (Business Tenancies) (England and Wales) Order 2003).

Tenant's request for a new tenancy

This request by your tenant for a new tenancy brings his or her current tenancy to an end on the day before the date mentioned in paragraph 2 of this notice. Section 26 contains rules about the date that the tenant can put in paragraph 2 of this notice.

Your tenant can apply to the court under section 24 for a new tenancy. You may apply for a new tenancy yourself, under the same section, but not if your tenant has already served an application. Once an application has been made to the court, your tenant's current tenancy will continue after the date mentioned in paragraph 2 while the application is being considered by the court. Either you or your tenant can ask the court to fix the rent which your tenant will have to pay whilst the tenancy continues (sections 24A to 24D). The court will settle any terms of a new tenancy on which you and your tenant disagree (sections 34 and 35).

Time limit for opposing your tenant's request

If you do not want to grant a new tenancy, you have two months from the making of your tenant's request in which to notify him or her that you will oppose any application made to the court for a new tenancy. You do not need a special form to do this, but the notice must be in writing and it must state on which of the grounds set out in section 30(1) you will oppose the application. If you do not use the same wording of the ground (or grounds), as set out below, your notice may be ineffective.

If there has been any delay in your seeing this notice, you may need to act very quickly. If you are in any doubt about what action you should take, get advice immediately from a solicitor or a surveyor.

Grounds for opposing tenant's application

If you wish to oppose the renewal of the tenancy, you can do so by opposing your tenant's application to the court, or by making your own application to the court for termination without renewal. However, you can only oppose your tenant's application, or apply for termination without renewal, on one or more of the grounds set out in section 30(1). These grounds are set out below. You will only be able to rely on the ground(s) of opposition that you have mentioned in your written notice to your tenant.

In this Table 'the holding' means the property that is the subject of the tenancy.

Paragraph of section 30(1)	*Grounds*
(a)	Where under the current tenancy the tenant has any obligations as respects the repair and maintenance of the holding, that the tenant ought not to be granted a new tenancy in view of the state of repair of the holding, being a state resulting from the tenant's failure to comply with the said obligations.

Paragraph of section 30(1)	*Grounds*
(b)	That the tenant ought not to be granted a new tenancy in view of his persistent delay in paying rent which has become due.
(c)	That the tenant ought not to be granted a new tenancy in view of other substantial breaches by him of his obligations under the current tenancy, or for any other reason connected with the tenant's use or management of the holding.
(d)	That the landlord has offered and is willing to provide or secure the provision of alternative accommodation for the tenant, that the terms on which the alternative accommodation is available are reasonable having regard to the terms of the current tenancy and to all other relevant circumstances, and that the accommodation and the time at which it will be available are suitable for the tenant's requirements (including the requirement to preserve goodwill) having regard to the nature and class of his business and to the situation and extent of, and facilities afforded by, the holding.
(e)	Where the current tenancy was created by the sub-letting of part only of the property comprised in a superior tenancy and the landlord is the owner of an interest in reversion expectant on the termination of that superior tenancy, that the aggregate of the rents reasonably obtainable on separate lettings of the holding and the remainder of that property would be substantially less than the rent reasonably obtainable on a letting of that property as a whole, that on the termination of the current tenancy the landlord requires possession of the holding for the purposes of letting or otherwise disposing of the said property as a whole, and that in view thereof the tenant ought not to be granted a new tenancy.
(f)	That on the termination of the current tenancy the landlord intends to demolish or reconstruct the premises comprised in the holding or a substantial part of those premises or to carry out substantial work of construction on the holding or part thereof and that he could not reasonably do so without obtaining possession of the holding.
(g)	On the termination of the current tenancy the landlord intends to occupy the holding for the purposes, or partly for the purposes, of a business to be carried on by him therein, or as his residence.

Compensation

If your tenant cannot get a new tenancy solely because one or more of grounds (e), (f) and (g) applies, he or she is entitled to compensation under section 37. If you have opposed your tenant's application on any of the other grounds mentioned in section 30(1), as well as on one or more of grounds (e), (f) and (g), your tenant can only get compensation if the court's refusal to grant a new tenancy is based solely on ground (e), (f) or (g). In other words, your tenant cannot get compensation under section 37 if the court has refused the tenancy on *other* grounds, even if one or more of grounds (e), (f) and (g) also applies.

If you are an authority possessing compulsory purchase powers (such as a local authority), your tenant may be entitled to a disturbance payment under Part 3 of the Land Compensation Act 1973.

Negotiating a new tenancy

Most tenancies are renewed by negotiation and your tenant has set out proposals for the new tenancy in paragraph 3 of this notice. You are not obliged to accept these proposals and may put forward your own. You and your tenant may agree in writing to extend the deadline for making an application to the court while negotiations continue. Your tenant may not apply to the court for a new tenancy until two months have passed from the date of the making of the request contained in this notice, unless you have already given notice opposing your tenant's request as mentioned in paragraph 6 of this notice (section 29A(3)).

If you try to agree a new tenancy with your tenant, remember:

- that one of you will need to apply to the court before the date in paragraph 2 of this notice, unless you both agree to extend the period for making an application.
- that any such agreement must be in writing and must be made before the date in paragraph 2 (sections 29A and 29B).

Validity of this notice

The tenant who has given you this notice may not be the person from whom you receive rent (sections 44 and 67). This does not necessarily mean that the notice is invalid.

If you have any doubts about whether this notice is valid, get advice immediately from a solicitor or a surveyor.

Further information

An explanation of the main points to consider when renewing or ending a business tenancy, 'Renewing and Ending Business Leases: a Guide for Tenants and Landlords', can be found at **www.odpm.gov.uk**. Printed copies of the explanation, but not of this form, are available from 1st June 2004 from Free Literature, PO Box 236, Wetherby, West Yorkshire, LS23 7NB (0870 1226 236).

FORM 4 LANDLORD'S REQUEST FOR INFORMATION ABOUT OCCUPATION AND SUB-TENANCIES

Section 40(1) of the Landlord and Tenant Act 1954

To: *(insert name and address of tenant)*

From: *(insert name and address of landlord)*

1. This notice relates to the following premises: *(insert address or description of premises)*
2. I give you notice under section 40(1) of the Landlord and Tenant Act 1954 that I require you to provide information –
   (a) by answering questions (1) to (3) in the Table below;
   (b) if you answer 'yes' to question (2), by giving me the name and address of the person or persons concerned;
   (c) if you answer 'yes' to question (3), by also answering questions (4) to (10) in the Table below;
   (d) if you answer 'no' to question (8), by giving me the name and address of the sub-tenant; and
   (e) if you answer 'yes' to question (10), by giving me details of the notice or request.

TABLE

(1)	Do you occupy the premises or any part of them wholly or partly for the purposes of a business that is carried on by you?
(2)	To the best of your knowledge and belief, does any other person own an interest in reversion in any part of the premises?
(3)	Does your tenancy have effect subject to any sub-tenancy on which your tenancy is immediately expectant?
(4)	What premises are comprised in the sub-tenancy?
(5)	For what term does it have effect or, if it is terminable by notice, by what notice can it be terminated?
(6)	What is the rent payable under it?
(7)	Who is the sub-tenant?
(8)	To the best of your knowledge and belief, is the sub-tenant in occupation of the premises or of part of the premises comprised in the sub-tenancy?
(9)	Is an agreement in force excluding, in relation to the sub-tenancy, the provisions of sections 24 to 28 of the Landlord and Tenant Act 1954?
(10)	Has a notice been given under section 25 or 26(6) of that Act, or has a request been made under section 26 of that Act, in relation to the sub-tenancy?

3. You must give the information concerned in writing and within the period of one month beginning with the date of service of this notice.
4. Please send all correspondence about this notice to:

Name:

Address:

Signed: Date:

*[Landlord] *[on behalf of the landlord] **delete whichever is inapplicable*

IMPORTANT NOTE FOR THE TENANT

This notice contains some words and phrases that you may not understand. The Notes below should help you, but it would be wise to seek professional advice, for example, from a solicitor or surveyor, before responding to this notice.

Once you have provided the information required by this notice, you must correct it if you realise that it is not, or is no longer, correct. This obligation lasts for six months from the date of service of this notice, but an exception is explained in the next paragraph. If you need to correct information already given, you must do so within one month of becoming aware that the information is incorrect.

The obligation will cease if, after transferring your tenancy, you notify the landlord of the transfer and of the name and address of the person to whom your tenancy has been transferred.

If you fail to comply with the requirements of this notice, or the obligation mentioned above, you may face civil proceedings for breach of the statutory duty that arises under section 40 of the Landlord and Tenant Act 1954. In any such proceedings a court may order you to comply with that duty and may make an award of damages.

NOTES

The sections mentioned below are sections of the Landlord and Tenant Act 1954, as amended, (most recently by the Regulatory Reform (Business Tenancies) (England and Wales) Order 2003).

Purpose of this notice

Your landlord (or, if he or she is a tenant, possibly your landlord's landlord) has sent you this notice in order to obtain information about your occupation and that of any sub-tenants. This information may be relevant to the taking of steps to end or renew your business tenancy.

Time limit for replying

You must provide the relevant information within one month of the date of service of this notice (section 40(1), (2) and (5)).

Information required

You do not have to give your answers on this form; you may use a separate sheet for this purpose. The notice requires you to provide, in writing, information in the form of answers to questions (1) to (3) in the Table above and, if you answer 'yes' to question (3), also to provide information in the form of answers to questions (4) to (10) in that Table. Depending on your answer to question (2) and, if applicable in your case, questions (8) and (10), you must also provide the information referred to in paragraph 2(b), (d) and (e) of this notice. Question (2) refers to a person who owns an interest in reversion. You should answer 'yes' to this question if you know or believe that there is a person who receives, or is entitled to receive, rent in respect of any part of the premises (other than the landlord who served this notice).

When you answer questions about sub-tenants, please bear in mind that, for these purposes, a sub-tenant includes a person retaining possession of premises by virtue of the Rent (Agriculture) Act 1976 or the Rent Act 1977 after the coming to an end of a sub-tenancy, and 'sub-tenancy' includes a right so to retain possession (section 40(8)).

You should keep a copy of your answers and of any other information provided in response to questions (2), (8) or (10) above.

If, once you have given this information, you realise that it is not, or is no longer, correct, you must give the correct information within one month of becoming aware that the previous information is incorrect. Subject to the next paragraph, your duty to correct any information that you have already given continues for six months after you receive this notice (section 40(5)). You should give the correct information to the landlord who gave you this notice unless you receive notice of the transfer of his or her interest, and of the name and address of the person to whom that interest has been transferred. In that case, the correct information must be given to that person.

If you transfer your tenancy within the period of six months referred to above, your duty to correct information already given will cease if you notify the landlord of the transfer and of the name and address of the person to whom your tenancy has been transferred.

If you do not provide the information requested, or fail to correct information that you have provided earlier, after realising that it is not, or is no longer, correct, proceedings may be taken against you and you may have to pay damages (section 40B).

If you are in any doubt about the information that you should give, get immediate advice from a solicitor or a surveyor.

Validity of this notice

The landlord who has given you this notice may not be the landlord to whom you pay your rent (sections 44 and 67). This does not necessarily mean that the notice is invalid.

If you have any doubts about whether this notice is valid, get advice immediately from a solicitor or a surveyor.

Further information

An explanation of the main points to consider when renewing or ending a business tenancy, 'Renewing and Ending Business Leases: a Guide for Tenants and Landlords', can be found at **www.odpm.gov.uk**. Printed copies of the explanation, but not of this form, are available from 1st June 2004 from Free Literature, PO Box 236, Wetherby, West Yorkshire, LS23 7NB (0870 1226 236).

FORM 5 TENANT'S REQUEST FOR INFORMATION FROM LANDLORD OR LANDLORD'S MORTGAGEE ABOUT LANDLORD'S INTEREST

Section 40(3) of the Landlord and Tenant Act 1954

To: (*insert name and address of reversioner or reversioner's mortgagee in possession [see the first note below]*)

From: (*insert name and address of tenant*)

1. This notice relates to the following premises: (*insert address or description of premises*)
2. In accordance with section 40(3) of the Landlord and Tenant Act 1954 I require you –
   (a) to state in writing whether you are the owner of the fee simple in respect of the premises or any part of them or the mortgagee in possession of such an owner,
   (b) if you answer 'no' to (a), to state in writing, to the best of your knowledge and belief –
      (i) the name and address of the person who is your or, as the case may be, your mortgagor's immediate landlord in respect of the premises or of the part in respect of which you are not, or your mortgagor is not, the owner in fee simple;
      (ii) for what term your or your mortgagor's tenancy has effect and what is the earliest date (if any) at which that tenancy is terminable by notice to quit given by the landlord; and
      (iii) whether a notice has been given under section 25 or 26(6) of the Landlord and Tenant Act 1954, or a request has been made under section 26 of that Act, in relation to the tenancy and, if so, details of the notice or request;
   (c) to state in writing, to the best of your knowledge and belief, the name and address of any other person who owns an interest in reversion in any part of the premises;
   (d) if you are a reversioner, to state in writing whether there is a mortgagee in possession of your interest in the premises; and

(e) if you answer 'yes' to (d), to state in writing, to the best of your knowledge and belief, the name and address of the mortgagee in possession.

3. You must give the information concerned within the period of one month beginning with the date of service of this notice.
4. Please send all correspondence about this notice to:

Name:

Address:

Signed: Date:

*[Tenant] *[on behalf of the tenant] (*delete whichever is inapplicable*)

IMPORTANT NOTE FOR LANDLORD OR LANDLORD'S MORTGAGEE

This notice contains some words and phrases that you may not understand. The Notes below should help you, but it would be wise to seek professional advice, for example, from a solicitor or surveyor, before responding to this notice.

Once you have provided the information required by this notice, you must correct it if you realise that it is not, or is no longer, correct. This obligation lasts for six months from the date of service of this notice, but an exception is explained in the next paragraph. If you need to correct information already given, you must do so within one month of becoming aware that the information is incorrect.

The obligation will cease if, after transferring your interest, you notify the tenant of the transfer and of the name and address of the person to whom your interest has been transferred.

If you fail to comply with the requirements of this notice, or the obligation mentioned above, you may face civil proceedings for breach of the statutory duty that arises under section 40 of the Landlord and Tenant Act 1954. In any such proceedings a court may order you to comply with that duty and may make an award of damages.

NOTES

The sections mentioned below are sections of the Landlord and Tenant Act 1954, as amended, (most recently by the Regulatory Reform (Business Tenancies) (England and Wales) Order 2003).

Terms used in this notice

The following terms, which are used in paragraph 2 of this notice, are defined in section 40(8):

'mortgagee in possession' includes a receiver appointed by the mortgagee or by the court who is in receipt of the rents and profits;

'reversioner' means any person having an interest in the premises, being an interest in reversion expectant (whether immediately or not) on the tenancy; and

'reversioner's mortgagee in possession' means any person being a mortgagee in possession in respect of such an interest.

Section 40(8) requires the reference in paragraph 2(b) of this notice to your mortgagor to be read in the light of the definition of 'mortgagee in possession'.

A mortgagee (mortgage lender) will be 'in possession' if the mortgagor (the person who owes money to the mortgage lender) has failed to comply with the terms of the mortgage. The mortgagee may then be entitled to receive rent that would normally have been paid to the mortgagor.

The term 'the owner of the fee simple' means the freehold owner.

The term 'reversioner' includes the freehold owner and any intermediate landlord as well as the immediate landlord of the tenant who served this notice.

Purpose of this notice and information required

This notice requires you to provide, in writing, the information requested in paragraph 2(a) and (c) of the notice and, if applicable in your case, in paragraph 2(b), (d) and (e). You do not need to use a special form for this purpose.

If , once you have given this information, you realise that it is not, or is no longer, correct, you must give the correct information within one month of becoming aware that the previous information is incorrect. Subject to the last paragraph in this section of these Notes, your duty to correct any information that you have already given continues for six months after you receive this notice (section 40(5)).

You should give the correct information to the tenant who gave you this notice unless you receive notice of the transfer of his or her interest, and of the name and address of the person to whom that interest has been transferred. In that case, the correct information must be given to that person.

If you do not provide the information requested, or fail to correct information that you have provided earlier, after realising that it is not, or is no longer, correct, proceedings may be taken against you and you may have to pay damages (section 40B).

If you are in any doubt as to the information that you should give, get advice immediately from a solicitor or a surveyor.

If you transfer your interest within the period of six months referred to above, your duty to correct information already given will cease if you notify the tenant of that transfer and of the name and address of the person to whom your interest has been transferred.

Time limit for replying

You must provide the relevant information within one month of the date of service of this notice (section 40(3), (4) and (5)).

Validity of this notice

The tenant who has given you this notice may not be the person from whom you receive rent (sections 44 and 67). This does not necessarily mean that the notice is invalid.

If you have any doubts about the validity of the notice, get advice immediately from a solicitor or a surveyor.

Further information

An explanation of the main points to consider when renewing or ending a business tenancy, 'Renewing and Ending Business Leases: a Guide for Tenants and Landlords', can be found at **www.odpm.gov.uk**. Printed copies of the explanation, but not of this form, are available from 1st June 2004 from Free Literature, PO Box 236, Wetherby, West Yorkshire, LS23 7NB (0870 1226 236).

FORM 6 LANDLORD'S WITHDRAWAL OF NOTICE TERMINATING TENANCY

Section 44 of, and paragraph 6 of Schedule 6 to, the Landlord and Tenant Act 1954

To: *(insert name and address of tenant)*

From: *(insert name and address of landlord)*

1. This notice is given under section 44 of, and paragraph 6 of Schedule 6 to, the Landlord and Tenant Act 1954 ('the 1954 Act').
2. It relates to the following property: *(insert address or description of property)*
3. 1 have become your landlord for the purposes of the 1954 Act.
4. I withdraw the notice given to you by *(insert name of former landlord)*, terminating your tenancy on *(insert date)*.
5. Please send any correspondence about this notice to:

Name:

Address:

Signed: Date:

*[Landlord] *[on behalf of the landlord] (**delete whichever is inapplicable*)

IMPORTANT NOTE FOR THE TENANT

If you have any doubts about the validity of this notice, get advice immediately from a solicitor or a surveyor.

NOTES

The sections and Schedule mentioned below are sections of, and a Schedule to, the Landlord and Tenant Act 1954, as amended, (most recently by the Regulatory Reform (Business Tenancies) (England and Wales) Order 2003).

Purpose of this notice

You were earlier given a notice bringing your tenancy to an end, but there has now been a change of landlord. This new notice is given to you by your new landlord and withdraws the earlier notice, which now has no effect. However, the new landlord can, if he or she wishes, give you a fresh notice with the intention of bringing your tenancy to an end (section 44 and paragraph 6 of Schedule 6).

Validity of this notice

The landlord who has given you this notice may not be the landlord to whom you pay your rent (sections 44 and 67). This does not necessarily mean that the notice is invalid.

If you have any doubts about whether this notice is valid, get advice immediately from a solicitor or a surveyor. If this notice is *not* valid, the original notice will have effect. Your tenancy will end on the date given in that notice (stated in paragraph 4 of this notice).

Further information

An explanation of the main points to consider when renewing or ending a business tenancy, 'Renewing and Ending Business Leases: a Guide for Tenants and Landlords', can be found at **www.odpm.gov.uk**. Printed copies of the explanation, but not of this form, are available from 1st June 2004 from Free Literature, PO Box 236, Wetherby, West Yorkshire, LS23 7NB (0870 1226 236).

FORM 7 LANDLORD'S NOTICE ENDING A BUSINESS TENANCY (WITH REASONS FOR REFUSING A NEW TENANCY) WHERE THE LEASEHOLD REFORM ACT 1967 MAY APPLY

Section 25 of the Landlord and Tenant Act 1954 and paragraph 10 of Schedule 3 to the Leasehold Reform Act 1967

IMPORTANT NOTE FOR THE LANDLORD: Use this form where you wish to oppose the grant of a new tenancy, and the tenant may be entitled to acquire the freehold or an extended lease. Complete this form and send it to the tenant. If you are opposed to the grant of a new tenancy, and the tenant is not entitled to acquire the freehold or an extended lease, use form 2 in Schedule 2 to the Landlord and Tenant Act 1954, Part 2 (Notices) Regulations 2004 instead of this form.

To: (*insert name and address of tenant*)

From: (*insert name and address of landlord*)

1. This notice relates to the following property: (*insert address or description of property*)
2. I am giving you notice under section 25 of the Landlord and Tenant Act 1954 to end your tenancy on (*insert date*).
3. I am opposed to the grant of a new tenancy.
4. You may ask the court to order the grant of a new tenancy. If you do, I will oppose your application on the ground(s) mentioned in paragraph(s)* of section 30(1) of that Act. I draw your attention to the Table in the Notes below, which sets out all the grounds of opposition.
   * (*insert letter(s) of the paragraph(s) relied on*)
5. If you wish to ask the court for a new tenancy you must do so by the date in paragraph 2 unless, before that date, we agree in writing to a later date.
6. I can ask the court to order the ending of your tenancy without granting you a new tenancy. I may have to pay you compensation if I have relied only on one or more of the grounds mentioned in paragraph (e), (f) and (g) of section 30(1). If I ask the court to end your tenancy, you can challenge my application.
7. If you have a right under Part 1 of the Leasehold Reform Act 1967 to acquire the freehold or an extended lease of property comprised in the tenancy, notice of your desire to have the freehold or an extended lease cannot be given more than two months after the service of this notice. If you have that right, and give notice of your desire to have the freehold or an extended lease within those two months, this notice will not operate, and I may take no further proceedings under Part 2 of the Landlord and Tenant Act 1954.

*8. If you give notice of your desire to have the freehold or an extended lease, I will be entitled to apply to the court under section 17/section 18** of the Leasehold Reform Act 1967, and propose to do so. If I am successful I may have to pay you compensation. (***delete the reference to section 17 or section 18, as the circumstances require*)

OR

*8. If you give notice of your desire to have the freehold or an extended lease, I will be entitled to apply to the court under section 17/section 18** of the Leasehold Reform Act 1967, but do not propose to do so. (***delete the reference to section 17 or section 18, as the circumstances require*)

OR

*8. If you give notice of your desire to have the freehold or an extended lease, I will not be entitled to apply to the court under section 17 or section 18 of the Leasehold Reform Act 1967.

* *DELETE TWO versions of this paragraph, as the circumstances require*

*9. I know or believe that the following persons have an interest superior to your tenancy or to be the agent concerned with the property on behalf of someone who has such an interest (*insert names and addresses*):

* *delete if inapplicable*

10. Please send all correspondence about this notice to:

Name:

Address:

Signed: Date:

*[Landlord] *[On behalf of the landlord] *[Mortgagee] *[On behalf of the mortgagee] (**delete if inapplicable*)

IMPORTANT NOTE FOR THE TENANT

This Notice is intended to bring your tenancy to an end on the date specified in paragraph 2.

Your landlord is not prepared to offer you a new tenancy. You will not get a new tenancy unless you successfully challenge in court the grounds on which your landlord opposes the grant of a new tenancy.

If you want to continue to occupy your property you must act quickly. The notes below should help you to decide what action you now need to take. If you want to challenge your landlord's refusal to renew your tenancy, get advice immediately from a solicitor or a surveyor.

NOTES

Unless otherwise stated, the sections mentioned below are sections of the Landlord and Tenant Act 1954, as amended, (most recently by the Regulatory Reform (Business Tenancies) (England and Wales) Order 2003).

Ending of your tenancy

This notice is intended to bring your tenancy to an end on the date given in paragraph 2. Section 25 contains rules about the date that the landlord can put in paragraph 2 of this notice.

Your landlord is not prepared to offer you a new tenancy. If you want a new tenancy you will need to apply to the court for a new tenancy and successfully challenge the landlord's opposition (see the section below headed '*Landlord's opposition to new tenancy*'). If you wish to apply to the court you must do so before the date given in paragraph 2 of this notice, unless you and your landlord have agreed in writing, before that date, to extend the deadline (sections 29A and 29B).

If you apply to the court your tenancy will continue after the date given in paragraph 2 of this notice while your application is being considered (section 24). You may not apply to the court if your landlord has already done so (section 24(2A) and (2B)).

You may only stay in the property after the date given in paragraph 2 (or such later date as you and the landlord may have agreed in writing) if before that date you have asked the court to order the grant of a new tenancy or the landlord has asked the court to order the ending of your tenancy without granting you a new one.

If you are in any doubt about what action you should take, get advice immediately from a solicitor or a surveyor.

Landlord's opposition to new tenancy

If you apply to the court for a new tenancy, the landlord can only oppose your application on one or more of the grounds set out in section 30(1). If you match the letter(s) specified in paragraph 4 of the notice with those in the first column in the Table below, you can see from the second column the ground(s) on which the landlord relies.

Paragraph of section 30(1)	*Grounds*
(a)	Where under the current tenancy the tenant has any obligations as respects the repair and maintenance of the holding, that the tenant ought not to be granted a new tenancy in view of the state of repair of the holding, being a state resulting from the tenant's failure to comply with the said obligations.
(b)	That the tenant ought not to be granted a new tenancy in view of his persistent delay in paying rent which has become due.
(c)	That the tenant ought not to be granted a new tenancy in view of other substantial breaches by him of his obligations under the current tenancy, or for any other reason connected with the tenant's use or management of the holding.
(d)	That the landlord has offered and is willing to provide or secure the provision of alternative accommodation for the tenant, that the terms on which the alternative accommodation is available are reasonable having regard to the terms of the current tenancy and to all other relevant circumstances, and that the accommodation and the time at which it will be available are suitable for the tenant's requirements (including the requirement to preserve goodwill) having regard to the nature and class of his business and to the situation and extent of, and facilities afforded by, the holding.

(e)	Where the current tenancy was created by the sub-letting of part only of the property comprised in a superior tenancy and the landlord is the owner of an interest in reversion expectant on the termination of that superior tenancy, that the aggregate of the rents reasonably obtainable on separate lettings of the holding and the remainder of that property would be substantially less than the rent reasonably obtainable on a letting of that property as a whole, that on the termination of the current tenancy the landlord requires possession of the holding for the purposes of letting or otherwise disposing of the said property as a whole, and that in view thereof the tenant ought not to be granted a new tenancy.
(f)	That on the termination of the current tenancy the landlord intends to demolish or reconstruct the premises comprised in the holding or a substantial part of those premises or to carry out substantial work of construction on the holding or part thereof and that he could not reasonably do so without obtaining possession of the holding.
(g)	On the termination of the current tenancy the landlord intends to occupy the holding for the purposes, or partly for the purposes, of a business to be carried on by him therein, or as his residence.

In this Table 'the holding' means the property that is the subject of the tenancy.

In ground (e), 'the landlord is the owner of an interest in reversion expectant on the termination of that superior tenancy' means that the landlord has an interest in the property that will entitle him or her, when your immediate landlord's tenancy comes to an end, to exercise certain rights and obligations in relation to the property that are currently exercisable by your immediate landlord.

If the landlord relies on ground (f), the court can sometimes still grant a new tenancy if certain conditions set out in section 31A are met.

If the landlord relies on ground (g), please note that 'the landlord' may have an extended meaning. Where a landlord has a controlling interest in a company then either the landlord or the company can rely on ground (g). Where the landlord is a company and a person has a controlling interest in that company then either of them can rely on ground (g) (section 30(1A) and (1B)). A person has a 'controlling interest' in a company if, had he been a company, the other company would have been its subsidiary (section 46(2)).

The landlord must normally have been the landlord for at least five years before he or she can rely on ground (g).

Rights under the Leasehold Reform Act 1967

If the property comprised in your tenancy is a house, as defined in section 2 of the Leasehold Reform Act 1967 ('the 1967 Act'), you may have the right to buy the freehold of the property or an extended lease. If the house is for the time being let under two or more tenancies, you will not have that right if your tenancy is subject to a sub-tenancy and the sub-tenant is himself or herself entitled to that right.

You will have that right if all the following conditions are met:

(i) your lease was originally granted for a term of more than 35 years, or was preceded by such a lease which was granted or assigned to you; and

(ii) your lease is of the whole house; and

(iii) your lease is at a low rent. If your tenancy was entered into before 1 April 1990 (or later if you contracted before that date to enter into the tenancy) 'low rent' means that your present annual rent is less than two-thirds of the rateable value of your house as assessed either on 23 March 1965, or on the first day of the term in the case of a lease granted to commence after 23 March 1965; and the property had a rateable value other than nil when the tenancy began or at any time before 1 April 1990. If your tenancy was granted on or after 1 April 1990, 'low rent' means that the present annual rent is not more than £1,000 in London or £250 elsewhere; and

(iv) you have been occupying the house (or any part of it) as your only or main residence (whether or not it has been occupied for other purposes) either for the whole of the last two years, or for a total of two years in the last ten years; and

(v) the rateable value of your house was at one time within certain limits.

Claiming your rights under the 1967 Act

If you have a right to buy the freehold or an extended lease and wish to exercise it you must serve the appropriate notice on the landlord. A special form is prescribed for this purpose; it is Form 1 as set out in the Schedule to the Leasehold Reform (Notices) (Amendment) (England) Regulations 2002 (S.I. 2002/1715) or, if the property is in Wales, the Leasehold Reform (Notices) (Amendment) (Wales) Regulations 2002 (S.I. 2002/3187) (W.303). Subject to the two exceptions mentioned below, you must serve the notice claiming to buy the freehold or an extended lease within two months after the date of service of this notice. The first exception is where, within that two-month period, you apply to the court to order the grant of a new tenancy. In that case your claim to buy the freehold or an extended lease must be made when you make the application to the court. The second exception is where the landlord agrees in writing to your claim being made after the date on which it should have been made.

There are special rules about the service of notices. If there has been any delay in your seeing this notice, you may need to act very quickly.

If you are in any doubt about your rights under the 1967 Act or what action you should take, get advice immediately from a solicitor or a surveyor.

Landlord's opposition to claims under the 1967 Act

If your landlord acquired his or her interest in the house not later than 18 February 1966 he or she can object to your claim to buy the freehold or an extended lease on the grounds that he or she needs to occupy the house or that the house is needed for occupation by a member of his or her family. This objection will be under section 18 of the 1967 Act.

If you claim an extended lease, your landlord can object under section 17 of the 1967 Act on the grounds that he or she wishes to redevelop the property.

You will be able to tell from paragraph 8 of this notice whether your landlord intends to apply to the court and, if so, whether for the purposes of occupation or redevelopment of the house.

Compensation

If you cannot get a new tenancy solely because one or more of grounds (e), (f) and (g) in section 30(1) applies, you may be entitled to compensation under section 37. If your landlord has opposed your application on any of the other grounds as well as (e), (f) or (g) you can only get compensation if the court's refusal to grant a new tenancy is based solely on one or more of grounds (e), (f) and (g). In other words, you cannot get compensation under section 37 if the court has refused your tenancy on other grounds, even if one or more of grounds (e), (f) and (g) also applies.

If your landlord is an authority possessing compulsory purchase powers (such as a local authority) you may be entitled to a disturbance payment under Part 3 of the Land Compensation Act 1973.

If you have a right under the 1967 Act to buy the freehold or an extended lease but the landlord is able to obtain possession of the premises, compensation is payable under section 17(2) or section 18(4) of the 1967 Act. Your solicitor or surveyor will be able to advise you about this.

Negotiations with your landlord

If you try to buy the property by agreement or negotiate an extended lease with the landlord, remember:

- that your present tenancy will not be extended under the 1954 Act after the date in paragraph 2 of this notice unless you agree in writing to extend the deadline for applying to the court under the 1954 Act or you (or the landlord) has applied to the court before that date (sections 29, 29A and 29B), and
- that you may lose your right to serve a notice claiming to buy the freehold or an extended lease under the 1967 Act if you do not observe the two-month time limit referred to in the note headed *Claiming your rights under the 1967 Act.*

Validity of this notice

The landlord who has given you this notice may not be the landlord to whom you pay your rent (sections 44 and 67). This does not necessarily mean that the notice is invalid.

If you have any doubts about whether this notice is valid, get advice immediately from a solicitor or a surveyor.

Further information

An explanation of the main points to consider when renewing or ending a business tenancy, 'Renewing and Ending Business Leases: a Guide for Tenants and Landlords', can be found at **www.odpm.gov.uk**. Printed copies of the explanation, but not of this form, are available from 1st June 2004 from Free Literature, PO Box 236, Wetherby, West Yorkshire, LS23 7NB (0870 1226 236).

FORM 8 NOTICE ENDING A BUSINESS TENANCY ON PUBLIC INTEREST GROUNDS

Sections 25 and 57 of the Landlord and Tenant Act 1954

IMPORTANT NOTE FOR THE LANDLORD: Use this form if you have a section 57 certificate, but where the tenant may be entitled to acquire the freehold or an extended lease, use form 13 in Schedule 2 to the Landlord and Tenant Act 1954, Part 2 (Notices) Regulations 2004 instead of this form.

To: (*insert name and address of tenant*)

From: (*insert name and address of landlord*)

1. This notice relates to the following property: (*insert address or description of property*)

2. I am giving you notice under section 25 of the Landlord and Tenant Act 1954 ('the 1954 Act') to end your tenancy on (*insert date*).
3. A certificate has been given by (*state the title of the Secretary of State on whose authority the certificate was issued or, if the certificate was issued by the National Assembly for Wales, insert* 'the National Assembly for Wales') under section 57 of the 1954 Act that the use or occupation of all or part of the property should be changed by (*insert date*). A copy of the certificate appears in the Schedule to this notice.
4. Please send all correspondence about this notice to:

Name:

Address:

Signed: Date:

[Landlord][On behalf of the landlord] *[Mortgagee] *[On behalf of the mortgagee]

(*delete if inapplicable*)

SCHEDULE

CERTIFICATE UNDER SECTION 57

(*attach or insert a copy of the section 57 certificate*)

IMPORTANT NOTE FOR THE TENANT

This notice is intended to bring your tenancy to an end on the date specified in paragraph 2.
The landlord is not prepared to offer you a new tenancy because it has been certified that the occupation or use of the premises should be changed no later than the date specified in paragraph 2. The date by which the change must have taken place is specified in paragraph 3.

NOTES

The sections mentioned below are sections of the Landlord and Tenant Act 1954, as amended, (most recently by the Regulatory Reform (Business Tenancies) (England and Wales) Order 2003).

Ending of your tenancy

This notice is intended to bring your tenancy to an end on the date stated in paragraph 2 of the notice.

Your landlord is both giving you notice that your current tenancy will end on the date stated in paragraph 2 of this notice and drawing attention to a certificate under section 57 that would prevent you from applying to the court for a new tenancy.

Usually, tenants who have tenancies under Part 2 of the Landlord and Tenant Act 1954 can apply to the court for a new tenancy. However, the effect of the section 57 certificate that it is requisite that the use or occupation of all or part of the property should be changed by a certain date, is to prevent the tenant from making an application to the court for a new tenancy.

Compensation

Because the court cannot order the grant of a new tenancy, you may be entitled to compensation when you leave the property (section 59). If your landlord is an authority possessing compulsory purchase powers (such as a local authority) you may also be entitled to a disturbance payment under Part 3 of the Land Compensation Act 1973.

Validity of this notice

The landlord who has given you this notice may not be the landlord to whom you pay your rent (sections 44 and 67). This does not necessarily mean that the notice is invalid.

If you have any doubts about whether this notice is valid, get advice immediately from a solicitor or a surveyor.

Further information

An explanation of the main points to consider when renewing or ending a business tenancy, 'Renewing and Ending Business Leases: a Guide for Tenants and Landlords', can be found at **www.odpm.gov.uk**. Printed copies of the explanation, but not of this form, are available from 1st June from Free Literature, PO Box 236, Wetherby, West Yorkshire, LS23 7NB (0870 1226 236).

FORM 9 NOTICE ENDING A BUSINESS TENANCY WHERE A CHANGE IS REQUIRED AT A FUTURE DATE AND THE LANDLORD OPPOSES A NEW TENANCY

Sections 25 and 57 of the Landlord and Tenant Act 1954

IMPORTANT NOTE FOR THE LANDLORD: Use this form if you have a section 57 certificate and you wish to oppose the grant of a new tenancy, for the period between the end of the current tenancy and the date given in the section 57 certificate, on any of the grounds in section 30(1) of the Landlord and Tenant Act 1954.

If you are willing to grant a new tenancy for that period, use form 10 in Schedule 2 to the Landlord and Tenant Act 1954, Part 2 (Notices) Regulations 2004 instead of this form.

If the tenant may be entitled to acquire the freehold or an extended lease, use form 14 in that Schedule, instead of this form or form 10.

To: (*insert name and address of tenant*)

From: (*insert name and address of landlord*)

1. This notice relates to the following property: (*insert address or description of property*)
2. I am giving you notice under section 25 of the Landlord and Tenant Act 1954 ('the 1954 Act') to end your tenancy on (*insert date*).
3. A certificate has been given by (*state the title of the Secretary of State on whose authority the certificate was issued or, if the certificate was issued by the National Assembly for Wales,*

insert 'the National Assembly for Wales') under section 57 of the 1954 that the use or occupation of all or part of the property should be changed by (*insert date*). A copy of the certificate appears in the Schedule to this notice.

4. I do not intend to grant you a new tenancy between the end of your current tenancy and the date specified in the section 57 certificate.
5. You may ask the court to order the grant of a new tenancy for a term ending not later than the date specified in the section 57 certificate. If you do, I will oppose your application on the ground(s) mentioned in paragraph(s)* of section 30(1) of the Act. I draw your attention to the Table in the Notes below, which sets out all the grounds of opposition.
   * (*insert letter(s) of the paragraph(s) relied on*)
6. If you wish to ask the court for a new tenancy you must do so by the date in paragraph 2 unless, before that date, we agree in writing to a later date.
7. I can ask the court to order the ending of your tenancy without granting you a new tenancy. If I do, you can challenge my application.
8. Please send all correspondence about this notice to:

Name:

Address:

Signed: Date:

[Landlord][On behalf of the landlord] *[Mortgagee] *[On behalf of the mortgagee]

(**delete if inapplicable*)

IMPORTANT NOTE FOR THE TENANT

This Notice is intended to bring your tenancy to an end on the date specified in paragraph 2.

A certificate has been given that it is requisite that occupation or use of the premises should be changed by the date specified in paragraph 3 of this notice.

Your landlord has indicated that he will oppose your application for a new tenancy (if you decide to make one). You will not get a new tenancy unless you successfully challenge in court the grounds on which your landlord opposes the grant of a new tenancy.

If you want to continue to occupy your property you must act quickly. The notes below should help you to decide what action you now need to take. If you want to challenge your landlord's refusal to renew your tenancy, get advice immediately from a solicitor or a surveyor.

NOTES

The sections mentioned below are sections of the Landlord and Tenant Act 1954, as amended, (most recently by the Regulatory Reform (Business Tenancies) (England and Wales) Order 2003).

Ending of your tenancy

This notice is intended to bring your tenancy to an end on the date specified in paragraph 2 of the notice.

Claiming a new tenancy

Your landlord is not prepared to offer you a new tenancy for a limited period pending the effect of the section 57 certificate (see the section below headed '*Effect of section 57 certificate*'). If you want a new tenancy for this period you will need to apply to the court for a new tenancy and successfully challenge the landlord's opposition (see the section below headed '*Landlord's opposition to new tenancy*').

If you wish to apply to the court you must do so before the date specified in paragraph 2 of this notice, unless you and your landlord have agreed in writing, before that date, to extend the deadline (sections 29A and 29B). However, before you take that step, read carefully the section below headed '*Effect of section 57 certificate*'.

If you apply to the court your tenancy will continue after the date specified in paragraph 2 of this notice while your application is being considered (section 24).

If you are in any doubt about what action you should take, get advice immediately from a solicitor or a surveyor.

Landlord's opposition to new tenancy

If you apply to the court for a new tenancy, the landlord can only oppose your application on one or more of the grounds set out in section 30(1). If you match the letter(s) specified in paragraph 5 of the notice with those in the first column in the Table below, you can see from the second column the ground(s) on which the landlord relies.

Paragraph of section 30(1)	*Grounds*
(a)	Where under the current tenancy the tenant has any obligations as respects the repair and maintenance of the holding, that the tenant ought not to be granted a new tenancy in view of the state of repair of the holding, being a state resulting from the tenant's failure to comply with the said obligations.
(b)	That the tenant ought not to be granted a new tenancy in view of his persistent delay in paying rent which has become due.
(c)	That the tenant ought not to be granted a new tenancy in view of other substantial breaches by him of his obligations under the current tenancy, or for any other reason connected with the tenant's use or management of the holding.
(d)	That the landlord has offered and is willing to provide or secure the provision of alternative accommodation for the tenant, that the terms on which the alternative accommodation is available are reasonable having regard to the terms of the current tenancy and to all other relevant circumstances, and that the accommodation and the time at which it will be available are suitable for the tenant's requirements (including the requirement to preserve goodwill) having regard to the nature and class of his business and to the situation and extent of, and facilities afforded by, the holding.
(e)	Where the current tenancy was created by the sub-letting of part only of the property comprised in a superior tenancy and the landlord is the owner of an interest in reversion expectant on the termination of that superior tenancy, that the aggregate of the rents reasonably obtainable on separate lettings of the holding and the remainder of

Paragraph of section 30(1)	*Grounds*
	that property would be substantially less than the rent reasonably obtainable on a letting of that property as a whole, that on the termination of the current tenancy the landlord requires possession of the holding for the purposes of letting or otherwise disposing of the said property as a whole, and that in view thereof the tenant ought not to be granted a new tenancy.
(f)	That on the termination of the current tenancy the landlord intends to demolish or reconstruct the premises comprised in the holding or a substantial part of those premises or to carry out substantial work of construction on the holding or part thereof and that he could not reasonably do so without obtaining possession of the holding.
(g)	On the termination of the current tenancy the landlord intends to occupy the holding for the purposes, or partly for the purposes, of a business to be carried on by him therein, or as his residence.

In this Table 'the holding' means the property that is the subject of the tenancy.

In ground (e), 'the landlord is the owner of an interest in reversion expectant on the termination of that superior tenancy' means that the landlord has an interest in the property that will entitle him, when your immediate landlord's tenancy comes to an end, to exercise certain rights and obligations in relation to the property that are currently exercisable by your immediate landlord.

If the landlord relies on ground (f), the court can sometimes still grant a new tenancy if certain conditions set out in section 31A are met.

If the landlord relies on ground (g), please note that 'the landlord' may have an extended meaning. Where a landlord has a controlling interest in a company then either the landlord or the company can rely on ground (g). Where the landlord is a company and a person has a controlling interest in that company then either of them can rely on ground (g) (section 30(1A) and (1B)). A person has a 'controlling interest' in a company if, had he been a company, the other company would have been its subsidiary (section 46(2)).

The landlord must normally have been the landlord for at least five years before he or she can rely on ground (g).

Effect of section 57 certificate

A copy of a certificate issued under section 57 appears in the Schedule to this notice. The effect of the certificate is that, even if you are successful in challenging your landlord's opposition to the grant of a new tenancy, and the court orders the grant of a new tenancy, the new tenancy must end not later than the date specified in the certificate (section 57(3)(b)). Any new tenancy will not be a tenancy to which Part 2 of the 1954 Act applies (section 57(3)(b)).

Compensation

If you cannot get a new tenancy solely because one or more of grounds (e), (f) and (g) applies, you may be entitled to compensation under section 37. If your landlord has opposed your application on any of the other grounds as well as (e), (f) or (g) you can only get compensation if the court's refusal to grant a new tenancy is based solely on one or more of grounds (e), (f) and (g). In other words, you cannot get compensation under section 37 if the court has refused your tenancy on other grounds, even if one or more of grounds (e), (f) and (g) also applies.

If the court orders the grant of a new tenancy, you may be entitled to compensation under section 59 when you leave the property (on or before the date specified in the section 57 certificate).

If your landlord is an authority possessing compulsory purchase powers (such as a local authority) you may be entitled to a disturbance payment under Part 3 of the Land Compensation Act 1973.

Validity of this notice

The landlord who has given you this notice may not be the landlord to whom you pay your rent (sections 44 and 67). This does not necessarily mean that the notice is invalid.

If you have any doubts about whether this notice is valid, get advice immediately from a solicitor or a surveyor.

Further information

An explanation of the main points to consider when renewing or ending a business tenancy, 'Renewing and Ending Business Leases: a Guide for Tenants and Landlords', can be found at **www.odpm.gov.uk**. Printed copies of the explanation, but not of this form, are available from 1st June 2004 from Free Literature, PO Box 236, Wetherby, West Yorkshire, LS23 7NB (0870 1226 236).

FORM 10 NOTICE ENDING A BUSINESS TENANCY WHERE A CHANGE IS REQUIRED AT A FUTURE DATE AND THE LANDLORD DOES NOT OPPOSE A NEW TENANCY

Sections 25 and 57 of the Landlord and Tenant Act 1954

IMPORTANT NOTE FOR THE LANDLORD: Use this form if you have a section 57 certificate and you are willing to grant a new tenancy for the period between the end of the current tenancy and the date given in the section 57 certificate.

If you wish to oppose the grant of a new tenancy for that period on any of the grounds in section 30(1) of the Landlord and Tenant Act 1954, use form 9 in Schedule 2 to the Landlord and Tenant Act 1954, Part 2 (Notices) Regulations 2004 instead of this form.

If the tenant may be entitled to acquire the freehold or an extended lease, use form 14 in that Schedule, instead of this form or form 9.

To: (*insert name and address of tenant*)

From: (*insert name and address of landlord*)

1. This notice relates to the following property: (*insert address or description of property*)
2. I am giving you notice under section 25 of the Landlord and Tenant Act 1954 ('the 1954 Act') to end your tenancy on (*insert date*).
3. A certificate has been given by (*state the title of the Secretary of State, Minister or Board on whose authority the certificate was issued or, if the certificate was issued by the National Assembly for Wales, insert* 'the National Assembly for Wales') under section

57 of the 1954 Act that the use or occupation of all or part of the property should be changed by (*insert date*). A copy of the certificate appears in Schedule 1 to this notice.

4. If you apply to the court under Part 2 of the 1954 Act for the grant of a new tenancy, I will not oppose your application. However, the court can only order the grant of a new tenancy for a term ending not later than the date in paragraph 3.
5. You will find my proposals for the new tenancy, which we can discuss, in Schedule 2 to this notice.
6. If we cannot agree on all the terms of a new tenancy, either you or I may ask the court to order the grant of a new tenancy and settle the terms on which we cannot agree.
7. Please send all correspondence about this notice to:

Name:

Address:

Signed: Date:

[Landlord][On behalf of the landlord] *[Mortgagee] *[On behalf of the mortgagee]

(**delete if inapplicable*)

SCHEDULE 1

CERTIFICATE UNDER SECTION 57

(*attach or insert a copy of the section 57 certificate*)

SCHEDULE 2

LANDLORD'S PROPOSALS FOR A NEW TENANCY

(*attach or insert proposed terms of the new tenancy*)

IMPORTANT NOTE FOR THE TENANT

This notice is intended to bring your tenancy to an end on the date specified in paragraph 2.

A certificate has been issued that it is requisite that occupation or use of the premises should be changed by the date specified in paragraph 3.

However, the landlord is prepared to offer you a new tenancy for the whole or part of the period between the dates in paragraphs 2 and 3 of the notice. You will find his or her proposed terms in Schedule 2 to this notice. You are not bound to accept these terms. They are merely suggestions as a basis for negotiation. In the event of disagreement, ultimately the court would settle the terms of the new tenancy.

It would be wise to seek professional advice before agreeing to accept the landlord's terms or putting forward your own proposals.

If you want to continue to occupy your property you must act quickly. The notes below should help you to decide what action you now need to take.

NOTES

The sections mentioned below are sections of the Landlord and Tenant Act 1954, as amended, (most recently by the Regulatory Reform (Business Tenancies) (England and Wales) Order 2003).

Ending of your tenancy

This notice is intended to bring your tenancy to an end on the date specified in paragraph 2 of the notice.

A certificate has been given under section 57 and a copy appears in Schedule 1 to this notice. The certificate states that it is requisite that occupation or use of the premises should be changed by the date specified in paragraph 3 of the notice.

However, your landlord is prepared to offer you a new tenancy, for the whole or part of the period between the dates specified in paragraphs 2 and 3 of the notice. You will find his or her proposals in Schedule 2 to this notice. You are not obliged to accept these proposals and may put forward your own.

Claiming a new tenancy

If you and your landlord are unable to agree terms, you may apply to the court (unless the landlord has already made his or her own application to the court (section 24(2A)). However, before you take that step, read carefully the section below headed '*Effect of section 57 certificate*'.

An application to the court must be made by the date set out in paragraph 2, unless you and your landlord have agreed in writing, before that date, to extend the deadline (sections 29A and 29B). Otherwise, you will lose the right to renew the tenancy.

If you apply to the court, your tenancy will continue after the date shown in paragraph 2 of this notice while your application is being considered (section 24). Either you or your landlord can ask the court to fix the rent that you will have to pay while the tenancy continues (section 24A and B). The terms of any new tenancy not agreed between you and the landlord will be settled by the court (section 25).

If you are in any doubt about the action that you should take, get advice immediately from a solicitor or a surveyor.

Effect of section 57 certificate

The effect of the section 57 certificate is that, if the court orders the grant of a new tenancy, the new tenancy must end not later than the date specified in the certificate (section 57(3)(b)).

Any new tenancy will not be a tenancy to which Part 2 of the 1954 Act applies (section 57(3)(b)).

Compensation

You may be entitled to compensation under section 59 when you leave the property (on or before the date specified in the section 57 certificate).

If your landlord is an authority possessing compulsory purchase powers (such as a local authority) you may be entitled to a disturbance payment under Part 3 of the Land Compensation Act 1973.

Validity of this notice

The landlord who has given you this notice may not be the landlord to whom you pay your rent (sections 44 and 67). This does not necessarily mean that the notice is invalid.

If you have any doubts about whether this notice is valid, get advice immediately from a solicitor or a surveyor.

Further information

An explanation of the main points to consider when renewing or ending a business tenancy, 'Renewing and Ending Business Leases: a Guide for Tenants and Landlords', can be found at **www.odpm.gov.uk**. Printed copies of the explanation, but not of this form, are available from 1st June 2004 from Free Literature, PO Box 236, Wetherby, West Yorkshire, LS23 7NB (0870 1226 236).

FORM 11 NOTICE ENDING A BUSINESS TENANCY ON GROUNDS OF NATIONAL SECURITY AND WITHOUT THE OPTION TO RENEW

Sections 25 and 58 of the Landlord and Tenant Act 1954

To: (*insert name and address of tenant*)

From: (*insert name and address of landlord*)

1. This notice relates to the following property: (*insert address or description of property*)
2. I am giving you notice under section 25 of the Landlord and Tenant Act 1954 to end your tenancy on (*insert date*).
3. A certificate has been given by (*state the title of the Secretary of State, Minister or Board on whose authority the certificate was issued or, if the certificate was issued by the National Assembly for Wales, insert* 'the National Assembly for Wales') under section 58 of the 1954 Act that it is necessary for reasons of national security that the use or occupation of the property should be discontinued or changed. A copy of the certificate appears in the Schedule to this notice.
4. The certificate prevents me from granting you a new tenancy. It also means that you will not be able to make an application to the court under section 24(1) of the Landlord and Tenant Act 1954 for the grant of a new tenancy.
5. Please send all correspondence about this notice to:

Name:

Address:

Signed: Date:

[Landlord][On behalf of the landlord]*[Mortgagee]*[On behalf of the mortgagee]

(**delete if inapplicable*)

SCHEDULE

CERTIFICATE UNDER SECTION 58

(attach or insert a copy of the section 58 certificate)

IMPORTANT NOTE FOR THE TENANT

This notice is intended to bring your tenancy to an end on the date specified in paragraph 2.

The national security certificate referred to in paragraph 3 of this notice means that the landlord cannot grant you a new tenancy, and the court cannot order the grant of a new tenancy.

You may be entitled to compensation. You may wish to seek professional advice in connection with this notice.

NOTES

The sections mentioned below are sections of the Landlord and Tenant Act 1954, as amended, (most recently by the Regulatory Reform (Business Tenancies) (England and Wales) Order 2003).

Ending of your tenancy

This notice is intended to bring your tenancy to an end on the date shown in paragraph 2 of the notice. Section 25 contains rules about the date that the landlord can put in that paragraph.

Tenants under tenancies to which Part 2 of the Landlord and Tenant Act 1954 applies can normally apply to the court for the grant of a new tenancy. However, a certificate has been given that it is necessary for reasons of national security that the use or occupation of the property should be discontinued or changed (section 58). The combined effect of this notice and the certificate is that you will be unable to apply to the court for the grant of a new tenancy.

Compensation

You may be entitled to compensation under section 59 when you leave the property (on or before the date specified in the section 58 certificate).

You may also be entitled to a disturbance payment under Part 3 of the Land Compensation Act 1973.

Validity of notice

The landlord who has given you this notice may not be the landlord to whom you pay your rent (sections 44 and 67). This does not necessarily mean that the notice is invalid.

If you have any doubts about whether this notice is valid, get advice immediately from a solicitor or a surveyor.

Further information

An explanation of the main points to consider when renewing or ending a business tenancy, 'Renewing and Ending Business Leases: a Guide for Tenants and Landlords', can be found at **www.odpm.gov.uk**. Printed copies of the explanation, but not of this form, are available from 1st June 2004 from Free Literature, PO Box 236, Wetherby, West Yorkshire, LS23 7NB (0870 1226 236).

FORM 12 NOTICE ENDING A BUSINESS TENANCY WHERE THE PROPERTY IS REQUIRED FOR REGENERATION

Sections 25, 58 and 60 of the Landlord and Tenant Act 1954

IMPORTANT NOTE FOR THE LANDLORD: Use this form if you have a certificate under section 58 (as applied by section 60), but if the tenant may be entitled to acquire the freehold or an extended lease, use form 15 in Schedule 2 to the Landlord and Tenant Act 1954, Part 2 (Notices) Regulations 2004 instead of this form.

To: (*insert name and address of tenant*)

From: (*insert name and address of landlord*)

1. This notice relates to the following property, which is situated in an area for the time being specified as a development area or intermediate area by an order made, or having effect as if made, under section 1 of the Industrial Development Act 1982: (*insert address or description of property*)
2. I am giving you notice under section 25 of the Landlord and Tenant Act 1954 ('the 1954 Act') to end your tenancy on (*insert date*).
3. A certificate has been given by (*state the title of the Secretary of State, Minister or Board on whose authority the certificate was issued*) that it is necessary or expedient for the purpose mentioned in section 2(1) of the Local Employment Act 1972 that the use or occupation of the property should be changed. A copy of the certificate appears in the Schedule to this notice.
4. The certificate prevents me from granting you a new tenancy. It also means that you will not be able to make an application to the court under section 24(1) of the 1954 Act for the grant of a new tenancy.
5. Please send all correspondence about this notice to:

Name:

Address:

Signed: Date:

*[Landlord] *[On behalf of the landlord]

(**delete if inapplicable*)

SCHEDULE

CERTIFICATE UNDER SECTION 58

(attach or insert a copy of the section 58 certificate)

IMPORTANT NOTE FOR THE TENANT

This Notice is intended to bring your tenancy to an end on the date specified in paragraph 2.

The certificate referred to in paragraph 3 of this notice means that the landlord cannot grant you a new tenancy, and the court cannot order the grant of a new tenancy.

You may wish to seek professional advice in connection with this notice.

NOTES

The sections mentioned below are sections of the Landlord and Tenant Act 1954, as amended, (most recently by the Regulatory Reform (Business Tenancies) (England and Wales) Order 2003).

Ending of your tenancy

This notice is intended to bring your tenancy to an end. Section 25 contains rules about the date that the landlord can put in paragraph 2 of this notice.

Your landlord is both giving you notice that your current tenancy will end on the date stated in paragraph 2 of this notice and drawing attention to a certificate under section 58 (as applied by section 60) that would prevent you from applying to the court for a new tenancy.

Usually, tenants who have tenancies under Part 2 of the Landlord and Tenant Act 1954 can apply to the court for a new tenancy. However, where a Government Minister has certified that it is necessary or expedient for the purpose mentioned in section 2(1) of the Local Employment Act 1972 that the use or occupation of the property should be changed, the landlord may prevent the tenant from making an application to the court for a new tenancy.

Validity of this notice

The landlord who has given you this notice may not be the landlord to whom you pay your rent (sections 44 and 67). This does not necessarily mean that the notice is invalid.

If you have any doubts about whether this notice is valid, get advice immediately from a solicitor or a surveyor.

Further information

An explanation of the main points to consider when renewing or ending a business tenancy, 'Renewing and Ending Business Leases: a Guide for Tenants and Landlords', can be found at **www.odpm.gov.uk**. Printed copies of the explanation, but not of this form, are available from 1st June 2004 from Free Literature, PO Box 236, Wetherby, West Yorkshire, LS23 7NB (0870 1226 236).

FORM 13 NOTICE ENDING A BUSINESS TENANCY ON PUBLIC INTEREST GROUNDS WHERE THE LEASEHOLD REFORM ACT 1967 MAY APPLY

Sections 25 and 57 of the Landlord and Tenant Act 1954

Paragraph 10 of Schedule 3 to the Leasehold Reform Act 1967

IMPORTANT NOTE FOR THE LANDLORD

This form *must* be used (instead of Form 8 in Schedule 2 to the Landlord and Tenant Act 1954, Part 2 (Notices) Regulations 2004) if –

(a) no previous notice terminating the tenancy has been given under section 4 or 25 of the Landlord and Tenant Act 1954 Act or under paragraph 4(1) of Schedule 10 to the Local Government and Housing Act 1989; and
(b) the tenancy is of a house as defined for the purposes of Part 1 of the Leasehold Reform Act 1967 ('the 1967 Act'); and
(c) the tenancy is a long tenancy at a low rent within the meaning of the 1967 Act; and
(d) the tenant is not a company or other artificial person.

To: (*insert name and address of tenant*)

From: (*insert name and address of landlord*)

1. This notice relates to the following property: (*insert address or description of property*)
2. I am giving you notice under sections 25 of the Landlord and Tenant Act 1954 ('the 1954 Act') to end your tenancy on (*insert date*).
3. A certificate has been given by (*state the title of the Secretary of State, Minister or Board on whose authority the certificate was issued or, if the certificate was issued by the National Assembly for Wales, insert* 'the National Assembly for Wales') under section 57 of the 1954 Act that the use or occupation of all or part of the property should be changed by (*insert date*). A copy of the certificate appears in the Schedule to this notice.
4. If you have a right under Part 1 of the Leasehold Reform Act 1967 to acquire the freehold or an extended lease of property comprised in the tenancy, notice of your desire to have the freehold or an extended lease cannot be given more than two months after the service of this notice. If you have that right, and give notice of your desire to have the freehold or an extended lease within those two months, this notice will not operate, and I may take no further proceedings under Part 2 of the 1954 Act.

*5. If you give notice of your desire to have the freehold or an extended lease, I will be entitled to apply to the court under section 17 of the Leasehold Reform Act 1967, and propose to do so. If I am successful I may have to pay you compensation.

OR

*5. If you give notice of your desire to have the freehold or an extended lease, I will be entitled to apply to the court under section 17 of the Leasehold Reform Act 1967, but do not propose to do so.

OR

*5. If you give notice of your desire to have the freehold or an extended lease, I will not be entitled to apply to the court under section 17 of the Leasehold Reform Act 1967.

* *DELETE TWO versions of this paragraph, as the circumstances require*

*6. I know or believe that the following persons have an interest superior to your tenancy or to be the agent concerned with the property on behalf of someone who has such an interest (*insert names and addresses*):

**delete if inapplicable*

7. Please send all correspondence about this notice to:

Name:

Address:

Signed: Date:

[Landlord][On behalf of the landlord] *[Mortgagee] *[On behalf of the mortgagee]

(**delete if inapplicable*)

SCHEDULE

CERTIFICATE UNDER SECTION 57

(attach or insert a copy of the section 57 certificate)

IMPORTANT NOTE FOR THE TENANT

This Notice is intended to bring your tenancy to an end on the date specified in paragraph 2.

The landlord is not prepared to offer you a new lease because it has been certified that it is requisite that occupation or use of the premises should be changed.

NOTES

Unless otherwise stated, the sections mentioned below are sections of the Landlord and Tenant Act 1954, as amended, (most recently by the Regulatory Reform (Business Tenancies) (England and Wales) Order 2003).

Ending of your tenancy

This notice is intended to bring your tenancy to an end on the date stated in paragraph 2 of the notice.

Your landlord is both giving you notice that your current tenancy will end on the date stated in paragraph 2 of this notice and drawing attention to a certificate under section 57 that would prevent you from applying to the court for a new tenancy.

Usually, tenants who have tenancies under Part 2 of the Landlord and Tenant Act 1954 can apply to the court for a new tenancy. However, it has been certified that it is requisite that the use or occupation of all or part of the property should be changed by a certain date, the landlord may prevent the tenant from making an application to the court for a new tenancy.

Rights under the Leasehold Reform Act 1967

If the property comprised in your tenancy is a house, as defined in section 2 of the Leasehold Reform Act 1967 ('the 1967 Act'), you may have the right to buy the freehold of the property or to get an extended lease. If the house is for the time being let under two or more tenancies, you will not have that right if your tenancy is subject to a sub-tenancy and the sub-tenant is himself or herself entitled to that right.

You will have that right if all the following conditions are met:

(i) your lease was originally granted for a term of more than 35 years, or was preceded by such a lease which was granted or assigned to you; and
(ii) your lease is of the whole house; and
(iii) your lease is at a low rent. If your tenancy was entered into before 1 April 1990 (or later if you contracted before that date to enter into the tenancy) 'low rent' means that your present annual rent is less than two-thirds of the rateable value of your house as assessed either on 23 March 1965, or on the first day of the term in the case of a lease granted to commence after 23 March 1965; and the property had a rateable value other than nil when the tenancy began or at any time before 1 April 1990. If your tenancy was granted on or after 1 April 1990, 'low rent' means that the present annual rent is not more than £1,000 in London or £250 elsewhere; and
(iv) you have been occupying the house (or any part of it) as your only or main residence (whether or not it has been occupied for other purposes) either for the whole of the last two years, or for a total of two years in the last ten years; and
(v) the rateable value of your house was at one time within certain limits.

However, if you have a right to buy the freehold or to get an extended lease, you will not be able to exercise it in this case because of the certificate that has been given under section 57. That is the effect of section 28 of the 1967 Act.

Compensation

Because the court cannot order the grant of a new tenancy, you are entitled to compensation when you leave the property (section 59).

If you have a right under the 1967 Act to buy the freehold or to get an extended lease but you cannot exercise that right because of the section 57 certificate, compensation will be payable under section 17(2) of the 1967 Act.

You cannot, however, get compensation under both the 1954 Act and the 1967 Act. The compensation payable under the 1967 Act is likely to be greater than that payable under the 1954 Act. In order to be able to claim compensation under the 1967 Act you must serve the appropriate notice on the landlord. A special form is prescribed for this purpose; it is Form 1 as set out in the Schedule to the Leasehold Reform (Notices) (Amendment) (England) Regulations 2002 (S.I. 2002/1715), or if the property is in Wales, the Leasehold Reform (Notices) (Amendment) (Wales) Regulations 2002 (S.I. 2002/3187) (W.303). Subject to the exception mentioned below, you must serve the notice claiming to buy the freehold or to get an extended lease within two months after the date of service of this notice. The exception is where the landlord agrees in writing to your claim being made after the date on which it should have been made.

If there has been any delay in your seeing this notice you may need to act very quickly. If you are in any doubt about the action that you should take, get advice immediately from a solicitor or a surveyor.

If your landlord is an authority possessing compulsory purchase powers (such as a local authority) you may also be entitled to a disturbance payment under Part 3 of the Land Compensation Act 1973.

Validity of this notice

The landlord who has given you this notice may not be the landlord to whom you pay your rent (sections 44 and 67). This does not necessarily mean that the notice is invalid.

If you have any doubts about whether this notice is valid, get advice immediately from a solicitor or a surveyor.

Further information

An explanation of the main points to consider when renewing or ending a business tenancy, 'Renewing and Ending Business Leases: a Guide for Tenants and Landlords', can be found at **www.odpm.gov.uk**. Printed copies of the explanation, but not of this form, are available from 1st June 2004 from Free Literature, PO Box 236, Wetherby, West Yorkshire, LS23 7NB (0870 1226 236).

An explanation of the rights of leaseholders to buy the freehold or to have an extended lease, 'Residential Long Leaseholders – A Guide to Your Rights and Responsibilities', can be found at **www.odpm.gov.uk**. Printed copies of the explanation, but not of this form, are available from 1st June 2004 from Free Literature, PO Box 236, Wetherby, West Yorkshire, LS23 7NB (0870 1226 236).

FORM 14 NOTICE ENDING A BUSINESS TENANCY ON PUBLIC INTEREST GROUNDS WHERE A CHANGE IS REQUIRED AT A FUTURE DATE AND WHERE THE LEASEHOLD REFORM ACT 1967 MAY APPLY

Sections 25 and 57 of the Landlord and Tenant Act 1954

Paragraph 10 of Schedule 3 to the Leasehold Reform Act 1967

IMPORTANT NOTE FOR THE LANDLORD

This form *must* be used (instead of Form 9 or 10 in Schedule 2 to the Landlord and Tenant Act 1954, Part 2 (Notices) Regulations 2004) if –

(a) no previous notice terminating the tenancy has been given under section 4 or 25 of the Landlord and Tenant Act 1954 or under paragraph 4(1) of Schedule 10 to the Local Government and Housing Act 1989; and
(b) the tenancy is of a house as defined for the purposes of Part 1 of the Leasehold Reform Act 1967 ('the 1967 Act'); and
(c) the tenancy is a long tenancy at a low rent within the meaning of the 1967 Act; and
(d) the tenant is not a company or other artificial person.

To: *(insert name and address of tenant)*

From: *(insert name and address of landlord)*

1. This notice relates to the following property: (*insert address or description of property*)
2. I am giving you notice under sections 25 of the Landlord and Tenant Act 1954 ('the 1954 Act') to end your tenancy on (*insert date*).

*3. If you apply to the court under Part 2 of the 1954 Act for the grant of a new tenancy, I will not oppose your application.

OR* *DELETE ONE version of this paragraph, as the circumstances require.*

3. If you apply to the court under Part 2 of the 1954 Act for the grant of a new tenancy, I will oppose your application on the ground(s) mentioned in paragraph(s) of section 30(1) of the 1954 Act. I draw your attention to the Table in the Notes below, which sets out all the grounds of opposition.
   * *(insert letter(s) of the paragraph(s) relied on)*

4. A certificate has been given by *(state the title of the Secretary of State, Minister or Board on whose authority the certificate was issued or, if the certificate was issued by the National Assembly for Wales, insert* 'the National Assembly for Wales') under section 57 of the 1954 Act that the use or occupation of all or part of the property should be changed by *(insert date)*. A copy of the certificate appears in the Schedule to this notice.

5. If you have a right under Part 1 of the Leasehold Reform Act 1967 to acquire the freehold or an extended lease of property comprised in the tenancy, notice of your desire to have the freehold or an extended lease cannot be given more than two months after the service of this notice. If you have that right, and give notice of your desire to have the freehold or an extended lease within those two months, this notice will not operate, and I may take no further proceedings under Part 2 of the Landlord and Tenant Act 1954.

**6. If you give notice of your desire to have the freehold or an extended lease, I will be entitled to apply to the court under section 17 of the Leasehold Reform Act 1967, and propose to do so. If I am successful I may have to pay you compensation.

OR

**6. If you give notice of your desire to have the freehold or an extended lease, I will be entitled to apply to the court under section 17 of the Leasehold Reform Act 1967, but do not propose to do so.

OR

**6. If you give notice of your desire to have the freehold or an extended lease, I will not be entitled to apply to the court under section 17 of the Leasehold Reform Act 1967.

** *DELETE TWO versions of this paragraph, as the circumstances require*

*7. I know or believe that the following persons have an interest superior to your tenancy or to be the agent concerned with the property on behalf of someone who has such an interest *(insert names and addresses)*:

*(*delete if inapplicable*)

8. Please send all correspondence about this notice to:

Name:

Address:

Signed: Date:

[Landlord][On behalf of the landlord] *[Mortgagee] *[On behalf of the mortgagee]

(**delete if inapplicable*)

SCHEDULE

CERTIFICATE UNDER SECTION 57

(attach or insert a copy of the section 57 certificate)

IMPORTANT NOTE FOR THE TENANT

This Notice is intended to bring your tenancy to an end on the date specified in paragraph 2.

Your landlord may have indicated in paragraph 3 that he will oppose your application for a new tenancy (if you decide to make one). You will not get a new tenancy unless you successfully challenge in court the grounds indicated in paragraph 3 on which your landlord opposes the grant of a new tenancy.

It has been certified that it is requisite that occupation or use of the premises should be changed by the date specified in paragraph 4.

If you want to continue to occupy your property you must act quickly. The notes below should help you to decide what action you now need to take. If you are unsure about what you should do, get advice immediately from a solicitor or a surveyor.

NOTES

Unless otherwise stated, the sections mentioned below are sections of the Landlord and Tenant Act 1954, as amended, (most recently by the Regulatory Reform (Business Tenancies) (England and Wales) Order 2003).

Ending of your tenancy

This notice is intended to bring your tenancy to an end on the date stated in paragraph 2 of the notice.

Claiming a new tenancy

If you wish to apply to the court for a new tenancy you must do so by the date set out in paragraph 2 of this notice, unless you and your landlord have agreed in writing, before that date, to extend the deadline (sections 29A and 29B). However, before you take that step, read carefully the section below headed '*Effect of section 57 certificate*'.

If you apply to the court, your tenancy will continue after the date shown in paragraph 2 of this notice while your application is being considered (section 24).

If you are in any doubt about what action you should take, get advice immediately from a solicitor or a surveyor.

Landlord's opposition to claim for a new tenancy

If paragraph 3 of this notice indicates that your landlord is opposed to the grant of a new tenancy, you will not get a new tenancy unless you apply to the court and successfully challenge the ground(s) of your landlord's opposition.

If you apply to the court for a new tenancy, the landlord can only oppose your application on one or more of the grounds set out in section 30(1). If you match the letter(s) specified in paragraph 3 of this notice with those in the first column in the Table below, you can see from the second column the ground(s) on which the landlord relies.

Paragraph of section 30(1)	*Grounds*
(a)	Where under the current tenancy the tenant has any obligations as respects the repair and maintenance of the holding, that the tenant ought not to be granted a new tenancy in view of the state of repair of the holding, being a state resulting from the tenant's failure to comply with the said obligations.
(b)	That the tenant ought not to be granted a new tenancy in view of his persistent delay in paying rent which has become due.
(c)	That the tenant ought not to be granted a new tenancy in view of other substantial breaches by him of his obligations under the current tenancy, or for any other reason connected with the tenant's use or management of the holding.
(d)	That the landlord has offered and is willing to provide or secure the provision of alternative accommodation for the tenant, that the terms on which the alternative accommodation is available are reasonable having regard to the terms of the current tenancy and to all other relevant circumstances, and that the accommodation and the time at which it will be available are suitable for the tenant's requirements (including the requirement to preserve goodwill) having regard to the nature and class of his business and to the situation and extent of, and facilities afforded by, the holding.
(e)	Where the current tenancy was created by the sub-letting of part only of the property comprised in a superior tenancy and the landlord is the owner of an interest in reversion expectant on the termination of that superior tenancy, that the aggregate of the rents reasonably obtainable on separate lettings of the holding and the remainder of that property would be substantially less than the rent reasonably obtainable on a letting of that property as a whole, that on the termination of the current tenancy the landlord requires possession of the holding for the purposes of letting or otherwise disposing of the said property as a whole, and that in view thereof the tenant ought not to be granted a new tenancy.
(f)	That on the termination of the current tenancy the landlord intends to demolish or reconstruct the premises comprised in the holding or a substantial part of those premises or to carry out substantial work of construction on the holding or part thereof and that he could not reasonably do so without obtaining possession of the holding.
(g)	On the termination of the current tenancy the landlord intends to occupy the holding for the purposes, or partly for the purposes, of a business to be carried on by him therein, or as his residence.

In the Table 'the holding' means the property that is the subject of the tenancy.

In ground (e), 'the landlord is the owner of an interest in reversion expectant on the termination of that superior tenancy' means that the landlord has an interest in the property that will entitle him, when your immediate landlord's tenancy comes to an end, to exercise certain rights and obligations in relation to the property that are currently exercisable by your immediate landlord.

If ground (f) is specified, the court can sometimes still grant a new tenancy if certain conditions set out in section 31A of the 1954 Act can be met.

If ground (g) is specified, please note that 'the landlord' may have an extended meaning. Where a landlord has a controlling interest in a company then either the landlord or the company can rely on ground (g). Where the landlord is a company and a person has a controlling interest in that company then either of them can rely on ground (g) (section 30(1A) and (1B)). A person has a 'controlling interest' in a company if, had he been a company, the other company would have been its subsidiary (section 46(2)).

The landlord must normally have been the landlord for at least five years before he or she can use ground (g).

Effect of section 57 certificate

A copy of a certificate issued under section 57 appears in the Schedule to this notice. The effect of the certificate is that, even if you are successful in challenging your landlord's opposition to the grant of a new tenancy, and the court orders the grant of a new tenancy, the new tenancy must end not later than the date specified in the certificate (section 57(3)(b)).

Any new tenancy will not be a tenancy to which Part 2 of the 1954 Act applies (section 57(3)(b)).

Rights under the Leasehold Reform Act 1967

If the property comprised in your tenancy is a house, as defined in section 2 of the Leasehold Reform Act 1967 ('the 1967 Act'), you may have the right to buy the freehold of the property or to get an extended lease. If the house is for the time being let under two or more tenancies, you will not have that right if your tenancy is subject to a sub-tenancy and the sub-tenant is himself or herself entitled to that right.

You will have that right if *all* the following conditions are met:

(i) your lease was originally granted for a term of more than 35 years, or was preceded by such a lease which was granted or assigned to you; and

(ii) your lease is of the whole house; and

(iii) your lease is at a low rent. If your tenancy was entered into before 1 April 1990 (or later if you contracted before that date to enter into the tenancy) 'low rent' means that your present annual rent is less than two-thirds of the rateable value of your house as assessed either on 23 March 1965, or on the first day of the term in the case of a lease granted to commence after 23 March 1965; and the property had a rateable value other than nil when the tenancy began or at any time before 1 April 1990. If your tenancy was granted on or after 1 April 1990, 'low rent' means that the present annual rent is not more than £1,000 in London or £250 elsewhere; and

(iv) you have been occupying the house (or any part of it) as your only or main residence (whether or not it has been occupied for other purposes) either for the whole of the last two years, or for a total of two years in the last ten years; and

(v) the rateable value of your house was at one time within certain limits.

However, if you have a right to buy the freehold or to get an extended lease, you will not be able to exercise it in this case because of the certificate that has been given under section 57. That is the effect of section 28 of the 1967 Act.

Compensation

If you cannot get a new tenancy solely because one or more of grounds (e), (f) and (g) applies, you may be entitled to compensation under section 37. If your landlord has opposed your application on any of the other grounds as well as (e), (f) or (g) you can only get compensation if the court's refusal to grant a new tenancy is based solely on one or more of grounds (e), (f) and (g). In other words, you cannot get compensation under section 37 if the court has refused your tenancy on *other* grounds, even if one or more of grounds (e), (f) and (g) also applies.

If the court orders the grant of a new tenancy, you may be entitled to compensation under section 59.

If you have a right under the 1967 Act to buy the freehold or to get an extended lease but you cannot exercise that right because of the section 57 certificate, compensation will be payable under that Act.

You cannot, however, get compensation under both the 1954 Act and the 1967 Act. The compensation payable under the 1967 Act is likely to be greater than that payable under the 1954 Act. In order to be able to claim compensation under the 1967 Act you must serve the appropriate notice on the landlord. A special form is prescribed for this purpose; it is Form 1 as set out in the Schedule to the Leasehold Reform (Notices) (Amendment) (England) Regulations 2002 (S.I. 2002/1715), or if the property is in Wales, the Leasehold Reform (Notices) (Amendment) (Wales) Regulations 2002 (S.I. 2002/3187) (W.303). Subject to the exception mentioned below, you must serve the notice claiming to buy the freehold or to get an extended lease within two months after the date of service of this notice. The exception is where the landlord agrees in writing to your claim being made after the date on which it should have been made.

If there has been any delay in your seeing this notice you may need to act very quickly. If you are in any doubt about what action you should take, get advice immediately from a solicitor or a surveyor.

If your landlord is an authority possessing compulsory purchase powers (such as a local authority) you may be entitled to a disturbance payment under Part 3 of the Land Compensation Act 1973.

Validity of this notice

The landlord who has given you this notice may not be the landlord to whom you pay your rent (sections 44 and 67). This does not necessarily mean that the notice is invalid.

If you have any doubts about whether this notice is valid, get advice immediately from a solicitor or a surveyor.

Further information

An explanation of the main points to consider when renewing or ending a business tenancy, 'Renewing and Ending Business Leases: a Guide for Tenants and Landlords', can be found at **www.odpm.gov.uk**. Printed copies of the explanation, but not of this form, are available from 1st June 2004 from Free Literature, PO Box 236, Wetherby, West Yorkshire, LS23 7NB (0870 1226 236).

An explanation of the rights of leaseholders to buy the freehold or to have an extended lease, 'Residential Long Leaseholders – A Guide to Your Rights and Responsibilities', can be found at **www.odpm.gov.uk**. Printed copies of the explanation, but not of this form, are available from 1st June 2004 from Free Literature, PO Box 236, Wetherby, West Yorkshire, LS23 7NB (0870 1226 236).

FORM 15 NOTICE ENDING A BUSINESS TENANCY WHERE THE PROPERTY IS REQUIRED FOR REGENERATION AND THE LEASEHOLD REFORM ACT 1967 MAY APPLY

Sections 25, 58 and 60 of the Landlord and Tenant Act 1954

Paragraph 10 of Schedule 3 to the Leasehold Reform Act 1967

IMPORTANT NOTE FOR THE LANDLORD

This form *must* be used (instead of Form 12 in Schedule 2 to the Landlord and Tenant Act 1954, Part 2 (Notices) Regulations 2004) if –

(a) no previous notice terminating the tenancy has been given under section 4 or 25 of the Landlord and Tenant Act 1954 or under paragraph 4(1) of Schedule 10 to the Local Government and Housing Act 1989; and
(b) the tenancy is of a house as defined for the purposes of Part 1 of the Leasehold Reform Act 1967 ('the 1967 Act'); and
(c) the tenancy is a long tenancy at a low rent within the meaning of the 1967 Act; and
(d) the tenant is not a company or other artificial person.

To: (*insert name and address of tenant*)

From: (*insert name and address of landlord*)

1. This notice relates to the following property, which is situated in an area for the time being specified as a development area or intermediate area by an order made, or having effect as if made, under section 1 of the Industrial Development Act 1982: (*insert address or description of property*)
2. I am giving you notice under section 25 of the Landlord and Tenant Act 1954 ('the 1954 Act') to end your tenancy on (*insert date*).
3. A certificate has been given by (*state the title of the Secretary of State, Minister or Board on whose authority the certificate was issued*) under section 58 of the 1954 Act (as applied by section 60 of that Act) that it is necessary or expedient for the purpose mentioned in section 2(1) of the Local Employment Act 1972 that the use or occupation of the property should be changed. A copy of the certificate appears in the Schedule to this notice.
4. The certificate prevents me from granting you a new tenancy. It also means that you will not be able to make an application to the court under section 24(1) of the 1954 Act for the grant of a new tenancy.
5. If you have a right under Part 1 of the Leasehold Reform Act 1967 to acquire the freehold or an extended lease of property comprised in the tenancy, notice of your desire to have the freehold or an extended lease cannot be given more than two months after the service of this notice. If you have that right, and give notice of your desire to have the freehold or an extended lease within those two months, this notice will not operate, and I may take no further proceedings under Part 2 of the 1954 Act.

*6. If you give notice of your desire to have the freehold or an extended lease, I will be entitled to apply to the court under section 17 of the Leasehold Reform Act 1967, and propose to do so. If I am successful I may have to pay you compensation.

OR

*6. If you give notice of your desire to have the freehold or an extended lease, I will be entitled to apply to the court under section 17 of the Leasehold Reform Act 1967, but do not propose to do so.

OR

*6. If you give notice of your desire to have the freehold or an extended lease, I will not be entitled to apply to the court under section 17 of the Leasehold Reform Act 1967.

* *DELETE TWO versions of this paragraph, as the circumstances require*

**7. I know or believe that the following persons have an interest superior to your tenancy or to be the agent concerned with the property on behalf of someone who has such an interest (*insert names and addresses*):

**(*delete if inapplicable*)

8. Please send all correspondence about this notice to:

Name:

Address:

Signed: Date:

[Landlord][On behalf of the landlord] (**delete if inapplicable*)

SCHEDULE

CERTIFICATE UNDER SECTION 58

(attach or insert a copy of the section 58 certificate)

IMPORTANT NOTE FOR THE TENANT

This notice is intended to bring your tenancy to an end on the date specified in paragraph 2.

A Government Minister has decided that it is necessary or expedient that occupation or use of the premises should be changed.

It would be wise to seek professional advice.

NOTES

Unless otherwise stated, the sections mentioned below are sections of the Landlord and Tenant Act 1954, as amended, (most recently by the Regulatory Reform (Business Tenancies) (England and Wales) Order 2003).

Ending of your tenancy

This notice is intended to bring your tenancy to an end on the date stated in paragraph 2 of the notice.

Your landlord is both giving you notice that your current tenancy will end on the date stated in paragraph 2 of this notice and drawing attention to a certificate under section

58 (as applied by section 60) that would prevent you from applying to the court for a new tenancy.

Usually, tenants who have tenancies under Part 2 of the Landlord and Tenant Act 1954 can apply to the court for a new tenancy. However, where a Government Minister has certified that it is necessary or expedient for the purpose mentioned in section 2(1) of the Local Employment Act 1972 that the use or occupation of the property should be changed, the landlord may prevent the tenant from making an application to the court for a new tenancy.

Rights under the Leasehold Reform Act 1967

If the property comprised in your tenancy is a house, as defined in section 2 of the Leasehold Reform Act 1967 ('the 1967 Act'), you may have the right to buy the freehold of the property or to get an extended lease. If the house is for the time being let under two or more tenancies, you will not have that right if your tenancy is subject to a sub-tenancy and the sub-tenant is himself or herself entitled to that right.

You will have that right if *all* the following conditions are met:

(i) your lease was originally granted for a term of more than 35 years, or was preceded by such a lease which was granted or assigned to you; *and*

(ii) your lease is of the whole house; *and*

(iii) your lease is at a low rent. If your tenancy was entered into before 1 April 1990 (or later if you contracted before that date to enter into the tenancy) 'low rent' means that your present annual rent is less than two-thirds of the rateable value of your house as assessed either on 23 March 1965, or on the first day of the term in the case of a lease granted to commence after 23 March 1965; and the property had a rateable value other than nil when the tenancy began or at any time before 1 April 1990. If your tenancy was granted on or after 1 April 1990, 'low rent' means that the present annual rent is not more than £1,000 in London or £250 elsewhere; *and*

(iv) you have been occupying the house (or any part of it) as your only or main residence (whether or not it has been occupied for other purposes) either for the whole of the last two years, or for a total of two years in the last ten years; *and*

(v) the rateable value of your house was at one time within certain limits.

However, if you have a right to buy the freehold or to get an extended lease, you will not be able to exercise it in this case because of the certificate that has been given. That is the effect of section 28 of the 1967 Act.

Compensation

If you have a right under the 1967 Act to buy the freehold or to get an extended lease but you cannot exercise that right because of the certificate, compensation will be payable under that Act.

In order to be able to claim compensation under the 1967 Act you must serve the appropriate notice on the landlord. A special form is prescribed for this purpose; it is Form 1 as set out in the Schedule to the Leasehold Reform (Notices) (Amendment) (England) Regulations 2002 (S.I. 2002/1715). Subject to the exception mentioned below, you must serve the notice claiming to buy the freehold or to get an extended lease within two months after the date of service of this notice. The exception is where the landlord agrees in writing to your claim being made after the date on which it should have been made.

If there has been any delay in your seeing this notice you may need to act very quickly. If you are in any doubt about what steps you should take, get advice immediately from a solicitor or a surveyor.

Validity of this notice

The landlord who has given you this notice may not be the landlord to whom you pay your rent (sections 44 and 67). This does not necessarily mean that the notice is invalid.

If you have any doubts about whether this notice is valid, get advice immediately from a solicitor or a surveyor.

Further information

An explanation of the main points to consider when renewing or ending a business tenancy, 'Renewing and Ending Business Leases: a Guide for Tenants and Landlords', can be found at **www.odpm.gov.uk**. Printed copies of the explanation, but not of this form, are available from 1st June 2004 from Free Literature, PO Box 236, Wetherby, West Yorkshire, LS23 7NB (0870 1226 236).

An explanation of the rights of leaseholders to buy the freehold or to have an extended lease, 'Residential Long Leaseholders – A Guide to Your Rights and Responsibilities', can be found at **www.odpm.gov.uk**. Printed copies of the explanation, but not of this form, are available from 1st June 2004 from Free Literature, PO Box 236, Wetherby, West Yorkshire, LS23 7NB (0870 1226 236).

FORM 16 NOTICE ENDING A BUSINESS TENANCY OF WELSH DEVELOPMENT AGENCY PREMISES WHERE THE PROPERTY IS REQUIRED FOR EMPLOYMENT PURPOSES

Sections 25, 58 and 60A of the Landlord and Tenant Act 1954

IMPORTANT NOTE

This form must *not* be used if –

(a) no previous notice terminating the tenancy has been given under section 4 or 25 of the Landlord and Tenant Act 1954, or under paragraph 4(1) of Schedule 10 to the Local Government and Housing Act 1989, and
(b) the tenancy is of a house as defined for the purposes of Part 1 of the Leasehold Reform Act 1967, and
(c) the tenancy is a long tenancy at a low rent within the meaning of that Act, and
(d) the tenant is not a company or other artificial person.

If (a) to (d) apply, use form 17 in Schedule 2 to the Landlord and Tenant Act 1954, Part 2 (Notices) Regulations 2004 instead of this form.

To: (*insert name and address of tenant*)

From: (*insert name and address of landlord*)

1. This notice relates to the following property, of which you are the tenant: (*insert address or description of property*)
2. We give you notice under section 25 of the Landlord and Tenant Act 1954 ('the 1954 Act') to end your tenancy on: (*insert date*)
3. A certificate has been given by the National Assembly for Wales under section 58 of the 1954 Act (as applied by section 60A of that Act) that it is necessary or expedient, for the purposes of providing employment appropriate to the needs of the area in

which the premises are situated, that the use or occupation of the property should be changed. A copy of the certificate appears in the Schedule to this notice.

4. The certificate prevents us from granting you a new tenancy. It also means that you will not be able to make an application to the court under section 24(1) of the 1954 Act for the grant of a new tenancy. However, you may be entitled to compensation.
5. Please send all correspondence about this notice to:

Name:

Address:

Signed: Date:

*[Landlord] *[On behalf of the landlord]

(**delete if inapplicable*)

SCHEDULE

CERTFICATE UNDER SECTION 58

(attach or insert a copy of the section 58 certificate)

IMPORTANT NOTE FOR THE TENANT

This notice is intended to bring your tenancy to an end on the date specified in paragraph 2 above.

The certificate referred to in paragraph 3 above means that the landlord cannot grant you a new tenancy, and the court cannot order the grant of a new tenancy. However, you may be entitled to compensation.

It would be wise to seek professional advice immediately in connection with this notice.

NOTES

Unless otherwise stated, the sections mentioned below are sections of the Landlord and Tenant Act 1954, as amended, (most recently by the Regulatory Reform (Business Tenancies) (England and Wales) Order 2003 S.I. 2003/3096)).

Ending of your tenancy

1. This notice is intended to bring your tenancy to an end on the date specified in paragraph 2 of this notice. Section 25 contains rules about the date that the landlord can put in that paragraph.
2. Your landlord is both giving you notice that your tenancy will end on the date specified in paragraph 2 of this notice and drawing attention, in paragraph 3 of this notice, to a certificate given by the National Assembly for Wales under section 58 (as applied by section 60A) that would prevent you from applying to the court for a new tenancy under Part 2 of the Landlord and Tenant Act 1954.
3. Usually, tenants who have tenancies under Part 2 of the Landlord and Tenant Act 1954 can apply to the court for a new tenancy. However, where the National Assembly for

Wales has certified that it is necessary or expedient, for the purposes of providing employment appropriate to the needs of the area in which the premises are situated, that the use or occupation of the property should be changed, the landlord may prevent the tenant from making an application to the court for a new tenancy.

Compensation

4. You will be entitled to compensation under section 59 when you leave the property UNLESS:
   (a) the premises vested in the Welsh Development Agency under section 7 or 8 of the Welsh Development Agency Act 1975; *or*
   (b) you were not the tenant of the premises when the Welsh Development Agency acquired the interest by virtue of which the certificate referred to in paragraph 3 of this notice was given.
5. You may also be entitled to a disturbance payment under Part 3 of the Land Compensation Act 1973.

Validity of this notice

6. The landlord who has given you this notice may not be the landlord to whom you pay your rent (sections 44 and 67). This does not necessarily mean that the notice is invalid.
7. If you have any doubts about whether this notice is valid, get advice immediately from a solicitor or a surveyor.

Further information

8. An explanation of the main points to consider when renewing or ending a business tenancy, 'Renewing and Ending Business Leases: a Guide for Tenants and Landlords', can be found at **www.odpm.gov.uk**. Printed copies of the explanation, but not of this form, are available from 1st June 2004 from Free Literature, PO Box 236, Wetherby, West Yorkshire, LS23 7NB (0870 1226 236).

FORM 17 NOTICE ENDING A BUSINESS TENANCY OF WELSH DEVELOPMENT AGENCY PREMISES WHERE THE PROPERTY IS REQUIRED FOR EMPLOYMENT PURPOSES AND THE LEASEHOLD REFORM ACT 1967 MAY APPLY

Sections 25, 58 and 60A of the Landlord and Tenant Act 1954

Paragraph 10 of Schedule 3 to the Leasehold Reform Act 1967

IMPORTANT NOTE

This form *must* be used (instead of Form 16 in Schedule 2 to the Landlord and Tenant Act 1954, Part 2 (Notices) Regulations 2004) if –

(a) no previous notice terminating the tenancy has been given under section 4 or 25 of the Landlord and Tenant Act 1954 Act or under paragraph 4(1) of Schedule 10 to the Local Government and Housing Act 1989; and
(b) the tenancy is of a house as defined for the purposes of Part 1 of the Leasehold Reform Act 1967; and

(c) the tenancy is a long tenancy at a low rent within the meaning of the 1967 Act; and
(d) the tenant is not a company or other artificial person.

To: *(insert name and address of tenant)*

From: *(insert name and address of landlord)*

1. This notice relates to the following property, of which you are the tenant: *(insert address or description of property)*
2. We give you notice under section 25 of the Landlord and Tenant Act 1954 ('the 1954 Act') to end your tenancy on: *(insert date)*
3. A certificate has been given by the National Assembly for Wales under section 58 of the 1954 Act (as applied by section 60A of that Act) that it is necessary or expedient, for the purposes of providing employment appropriate to the needs of the area in which the premises are situated, that the use or occupation of the property should be changed. A copy of the certificate appears in the Schedule to this notice.
4. The certificate prevents us from granting you a new tenancy. It also means that you will not be able to make an application to the court under section 24(1) of the 1954 Act for the grant of a new tenancy. However, you may be entitled to compensation.
5. If you have a right under Part 1 of the Leasehold Reform Act 1967 ('the 1967 Act') to acquire the freehold or to get an extended lease of property comprised in the tenancy, notice of your desire to have the freehold or an extended lease cannot be given more than two months after the service of this notice. If you have that right, and give notice of your desire to have the freehold or an extended lease within those two months, this notice will not operate, and we may take no further proceedings under Part 2 of the 1954 Act.

*6. If you give notice of your desire to have the freehold or an extended lease, we will be entitled to apply to the court under section 17 of the 1967 Act, and propose to do so. If we are successful we may have to pay you compensation.

OR

*6. If you give notice of your desire to have the freehold or an extended lease, we will be entitled to apply to the court under section 17 of the 1967 Act, but do not propose to do so.

OR

*6. If you give notice of your desire to have the freehold or an extended lease, we will not be entitled to apply to the court under section 17 of the 1967 Act.

**(DELETE TWO versions of paragraph 6, as the circumstances require)*

**7. We know or believe that the following persons have an interest superior to your tenancy or to be the agent concerned with the property on behalf of someone who has such an interest *(insert names and addresses)*:

***(delete if inapplicable)*

8. Please send all correspondence about this notice to:

Name:

Address:

Signed: Date:

*[Landlord] *[On behalf of the landlord]

(delete if inapplicable)*

SCHEDULE

CERTFICATE UNDER SECTION 58

(attach or insert a copy of the section 58 certificate)

IMPORTANT NOTE FOR THE TENANT

This notice is intended to bring your tenancy to an end on the date specified in paragraph 2 above.

The National Assembly for Wales has certified that it is necessary or expedient that occupation or use of the premises should be changed.

It would be wise to seek professional advice immediately in connection with this notice.

NOTES

Unless otherwise stated, the sections mentioned below are sections of the Landlord and Tenant Act 1954, as amended, (most recently by the Regulatory Reform (Business Tenancies) (England and Wales) Order 2003 (S.I. 2003/3096)).

Ending of your tenancy

1. This notice is intended to bring your tenancy to an end on the date specified in paragraph 2 of this notice. Section 25 contains rules about the date that the landlord can put in that paragraph.
2. Your landlord is both giving you notice that your tenancy will end on the date specified in paragraph 2 of this notice and drawing attention, in paragraph 3 of this notice, to a certificate given by the National Assembly for Wales under section 58 (as applied by section 60A) that would prevent you from applying to the court for a new tenancy under Part 2 of the Landlord and Tenant Act 1954.
3. Usually, tenants who have tenancies under Part 2 of the Landlord and Tenant Act 1954 can apply to the court for a new tenancy. However, where the National Assembly for Wales has certified that it is necessary or expedient, for the purposes of providing employment appropriate to the needs of the area in which the premises are situated, that the use or occupation of the property should be changed, the landlord may prevent the tenant from making an application to the court for a new tenancy under that Part 2.
4. However, the Leasehold Reform Act 1967 ('the 1967 Act') may also apply in your case. If it does, you may be able to buy the freehold of the property or get an extended lease under that Act (see *Rights under the 1967 Act*: notes 5 to 7 below and *Claiming your rights under the 1967 Act*: notes 8 and 9 below). If you claim an extended lease your landlord may still be able to get possession of the property (see *Landlord's opposition to claims under the 1967 Act*: note 10 below). If he does, you may be able to get compensation (see *Compensation*: notes 11 to 14 below). The amount of any compensation will depend on the steps you have taken and under which Act (it is likely to be greater under the 1967 Act). If you have any doubt about what you should do, get professional advice immediately.

Rights under the 1967 Act

5. If the property comprised in your tenancy is a house, as defined in section 2 of the 1967 Act, you may have the right to buy the freehold of the property or to get an extended lease.
6. If the house is for the time being let under two or more tenancies, you will not have that right if your tenancy is subject to a sub-tenancy and the sub-tenant is himself or herself entitled to that right.
7. You will have that right if *all* the following conditions (i) – (v) are met:
   (i) your lease was originally granted for a term of more than 35 years, or was preceded by such a lease which was granted or assigned to you; *and*
   (ii) your lease is of the whole house; *and*
   (iii) (where applicable) your lease is at a low rent. If your tenancy was entered into before 1 April 1990 (or later if you contracted before that date to enter into the tenancy) 'low rent' means that your present annual rent is less than two-thirds of the rateable value of your house as assessed either on 23 March 1965, or on the first day of the term in the case of a lease granted to commence after 23 March 1965, and the property had a rateable value other than nil when the tenancy began or any time before 1 April 1990. If your tenancy was granted on or after 1 April 1990, 'low rent' means that the present annual rent is not more than £250; *and*
   (iv) you have been occupying the house (or any part of it) as your only or main residence (whether or not it has been occupied for other purposes) either for the whole of the last two years, or for a total of two years in the last ten years; *and*
   (v) the rateable value of your house was at one time within certain limits.

Claiming your rights under the 1967 Act

8. If you have the right to buy the freehold or to get an extended lease and wish to exercise it, you must serve the appropriate notice on the landlord. A special form is prescribed for this purpose; it is Form 1 as set out in the Schedule to the Leasehold Reform (Notices) (Amendment) (Wales) Regulations 2002 (S.I. 2002/3187)(W.303). Subject to the exception mentioned below, you must serve the notice claiming to buy the freehold or to get an extended lease within two months after the date of service of this notice. The exception is where the landlord agrees in writing to your claim being made after the date on which it should have been made.
9. There are special rules about the service of notices. If there has been any delay in your seeing this notice you may need to act very quickly. If you are in any doubt about what you should do, get advice immediately from a solicitor or a surveyor.

Landlord's opposition to claims under the 1967 Act

10. If you claim a right under the 1967 Act, your landlord can object under section 17 of the 1967 Act on the grounds that he wishes to redevelop the property. Paragraph 6 of the notice will tell you whether the landlord believes he has the right to apply to the court under section 17 and whether or not he proposes to do so.

Compensation

11. Because the court cannot order the grant of a new tenancy under the 1954 Act in your case, you may be entitled to compensation under the 1954 Act when you leave the property. You will not be entitled to such compensation if either:
    (a) the premises were vested in the Welsh Development Agency under section 7 or 8 of the Welsh Development Agency Act 1975; or

(b) you were not the tenant of the premises when the Agency acquired the interest by virtue of which the certificate referred to in paragraph 3 of this notice was given.

12. You may be entitled to a disturbance payment under Part 3 of the Land Compensation Act 1973.
13. If you have a right under the 1967 Act to buy the freehold or to get an extended lease of your premises but the landlord is able to obtain possession of the premises (see *Landlord's opposition to claims under the 1967 Act*: note 10 above), compensation under the 1967 Act is payable. This is normally higher than compensation under the 1954 Act. Your professional adviser will be able to advise you on this.
14. In order to be able to claim compensation under the 1967 Act you must serve the appropriate notice on the landlord within the stated time limit (see *Claiming your Rights under the 1967 Act*: notes 8 and 9 above).

Validity of this notice

15. The landlord who has given you this notice may not be the landlord to whom you pay your rent (sections 44 and 67). This does not necessarily mean that the notice is invalid.
16. If you have any doubts about whether this notice is valid, get advice immediately from a solicitor or a surveyor.

Further information

17. An explanation of the main points to consider when renewing or ending a business tenancy, 'Renewing and Ending Business Leases: a Guide for Tenants and Landlords', can be found at **www.odpm.gov.uk**. Printed copies of the explanation, but not of this form, are available from 1st June 2004 from Free Literature, PO Box 236, Wetherby, West Yorkshire, LS23 7NB (0870 1226 236).
18. An explanation of the rights of leaseholders to buy the freehold or to have an extended lease, 'Residential Long Leaseholders – A Guide to Your Rights and Responsibilities', can be found at **www.odpm.gov.uk**. Printed copies of the explanation, but not of this form, are available from Free Literature, PO Box 236, Wetherby, West Yorkshire, LS23 7NB (0870 1226 236).

INDEX

Agreements to surrender xii, 26, 27, 39–40
Assured shorthold tenancies 28–9

Break clause notice 3
Business Tenancies: A Periodic Review of the Landlord and Tenant Act 1954, Part II xi

Civil Procedure Rules
acknowledgement of service form 51, 52, 58, 59, 62
commencing the claim 55
all cases 56
landlord's claim for renewal 57
landlord's termination proceedings 58
tenant's claim for renewal 56–7
evidence, filing of 52
generally 50–3
interim rent 51–2, 63–4
landlord's termination proceedings 58, 61–2, 63
management of claim
opposed claims 63
unopposed claims 62
priority of claims 53–4
responding to claim
opposed claims where claimant is landlord 61–2
opposed claims where claimant is tenant 60–1
unopposed claims where claimant is landlord 59–60
unopposed claims where claimant is tenant 58–9
stay of proceedings 51
tenant's renewal proceedings 58–9, 60–1
type of procedural claim 54–5
Companies 41–3
Compensation
calculation of 46
distinction between whole and part 47–8
generally 46
misrepresentation, for 48–9
reversion is split, where 48
when payable 46–7
Consequential amendments 44–5
Consultation paper xi
Contracting-out provisions
agreements to surrender xii, 26, 27, 39–40
transition 40
alternation of negotiated terms of intended tenancy 37–8
debate over 26–7
the declaration 30
notice given 14 days before entry 30–2
notice given less than 14 days before entry 33–4
generally xi, xii, 27–8
instrument creating the tenancy 34, 35
options to renew 38
research on 26–7
schedule 1 notice 28–9
assured shorthold tenancies regime compared 28–9
declaration process 30–4
drafting 29
'health warning' 28, 32
persons giving and receiving 35–7
service of 29, 34–7
transition 38–9
Court applications
generally 13–14
landlord's tenancy termination proceedings 13, 17–19

Court applications (*cont.*)
tenancy renewal proceedings
extension agreements 6, 15–16
landlord's renewal proceedings 13, 16–17
tenant's renewal proceedings 13, 14, 17, 58–9, 60–1
time limits 13, 14–16

Fixed-term tenancy
interim rent 21
termination of xii
vacating property before expiry of 1–3

Information-gathering *see* Section 40 notice
Interim rent
application for 20–1, 51–2
Civil Procedure Rules 51–2, 63–4
concept of 20
date from which payable 21–2
fixed-term tenancy 21
generally xii, 20–1
new right 21
'relevant tenancy' 21
section 25 notice, and 20–5 *passim*
section 26 request, and 20–5 *passim*
landlord's counternotice 22, 24
time limit for claim 21
valuation 20–1, 22
new tenancy for whole property granted and no opposition from landlord (section 24C) 22–5
rent payable under sub-tenancy, effect of 25
section 24D, under 25

Landlord's claim for renewal 13, 16–17, 57, 59–60
Landlord's counternotice 8–9, 18, 55
interim rent, and 22, 24
Landlord's termination proceedings 13, 17–19
Civil Procedure Rules 58, 61–2, 63
grounds of opposition 18, 58
Law Commission's recommendations xi

Misrepresentation, compensation for 48–9

Options to renew 38

Post-Action Protocol for Business Tenancy Renewal cases 52–3

Regulatory reform orders xi, xii

Schedule 1 notice *see* Contracting-out provisions
Section 25 notice xiii, 2, 3–6, 13, 18, 55
contents of 4, 5, 29
extension agreements 6, 15–16
grounds of 'possession' 3
'health warning' 5
interim rent, and 20–5 *passim*
new notices 4–6
proposals in 5–6
service of 3, 4, 5, 6, 29
tenant's counternotice xii, 6–8, 9
time limits 5–6
Section 26 request xiii, 8, 13
interim rent, and 20–5 *passim*
landlord's counternotice 8–9, 18, 22, 24, 55
Section 27 notice 1–3
Section 40 notice 9–12
forms 12
sanctions for failure to comply with duties 9, 12
served by landlord on tenant 10
served by tenant on landlord 10–11
transfer by giver or recipient of 11–12
transition 12
Security of tenure
agreements to exclude *see* Contracting-out provisions
termination of xi, xii
Severed reversions 43–4
compensation, and 48
Surrender-back clauses 39–40
see also Agreements to surrender

Tenancy renewal proceedings
extension agreements 6, 15–16
landlord's claim for renewal 13, 16–17
commencing 57
responding to claim 59–60
tenant's claim for renewal 13, 14, 17
commencing 56–7
responding to claim 58–9, 60–1
time limits 13, 14–16
Tenant's counternotice xii, 6–8, 9
Termination proceedings *see* Landlord's termination proceedings
Terms of new tenancy 41